Though the Mountains Tremble

Though the Mountains Tremble

Biblical Reflections on Contemporary Society

GENE L. DAVENPORT

WIPF & STOCK · Eugene, Oregon

THOUGH THE MOUNTAINS TREMBLE
Biblical Reflections on Contemporary Society

Copyright © 2009 Gene L. Davenport. All rights reserved. Except for brief quotations in critical publications or reviews, no part of this book may be reproduced in any manner without prior written permission from the publisher. Write: Permissions, Wipf and Stock Publishers, 199 W. 8th Ave., Suite 3, Eugene, OR 97401.

Wipf & Stock
A Division of Wipf and Stock Publishers
199 W. 8th Ave., Suite 3
Eugene, OR 97401
www.wipfandstock.com

ISBN 13: 978-1-55635-562-2

Manufactured in the U.S.A.

The radio commentaries in this volume were delivered in their original form on the radio program *A Closer Look* over WTJS, Jackson, Tennessee and are the property of the author. The newspaper columns were printed in their original form in the Jackson *Sun*, Jackson, Tennessee, and are printed here, many in edited form, with the permission of the *Sun*. Unless otherwise noted, all biblical quotations are from the 1952 edition of the Revised Standard Version, published by Thomas Nelson and Sons, copyright by the Division of Christian Education of the National Council of Churches of Christ in the United States of America.

For Will D. Campbell—mentor, friend, and brother in Christ
and
For Ken Carder—friend and brother in Christ.

Both, faithful witnesses of the Word.

God is our refuge and strength,
a very present help in trouble.
Therefore we will not fear
though the earth should change,
though the mountains shake in the heart of the sea;
though its waters roar and foam,
though the mountains tremble with its tumult.

Psalm 46:1–3

Contents

Preface ix

PART ONE COLUMNS AND COMMENTARIES 1

1 Religion and Politics 3

2 Violence and Terror 38

3 Economics 48

4 Liturgical Seasons 57

5 The Church 69

6 The Bible 90

7 Human Identity 96

8 Children 114

9 Theology and Ethics 118

10 Islam 142

11 The Environment 147

PART TWO SERMONS, PRESENTATIONS, AND BOOK REVIEWS 155

12 Sermons 157

13 Addresses and Presentations 173

14 Book Reviews 195

Preface

IN THE EARLY SPRING of 2004, WTJS-AM, the oldest radio station in Jackson, Tennessee, was expanding its programming. Along with two sister FM stations, it recently had been purchased by Clear Channel, the corporate media system that seemed at the time bent on establishing a media empire. WTJS offered each college and university in the area thirty minutes of free air time each week for programming. Since all the colleges and universities in the area are church related institutions, this offer was part of a plan to make the station's Sunday morning schedule consist exclusively of religious programs until noon.

When I was invited to do the program for Lambuth University's half-hour, I decided to host a conversation program that would sometimes deal with a topic of a religious nature, sometimes a secular topic, and close each program I would do a brief commentary. Sometimes the commentary would be on the topic of the program for the day, but not necessarily always or even usually. The University was pleased, the station was pleased, and I was pleased.

The program was called *A Closer Look*, and after just over a year, it was expanded into a one-hour program. The guests were both local persons and persons from outside the area. I was fortunate to have by phone guests of national note such as Phyllis Tickle, widely known author and social critic; John L. Allen Jr., senior correspondent for the National Catholic Reporter; Will Campbell, well-known Southern author; and Richard Land, prominent official in the Southern Baptist Convention. A diverse group, to say the least.

At first, the weekly commentaries were one and one-half minutes in length, but when the program expanded to one hour, the commentaries became two and one-half to three minutes in length. They were what I referred to as my chance to get my two cents worth in.

In the commentaries I attempted to look at the world and some of its problems and issues from a theological, usually a biblical, perspective.

I was a concerned to educate at least as much as to advocate, but I was especially concerned to show that looking at and understanding the world through biblical eyes is different from attempting to apply biblical principles to a problem or issue. John Calvin remarked somewhere that the Bible is the spectacles (eye-glasses) through which we see the world as it really is. I believe that to the extent we are able to see the world from that perspective, we will sometimes appear conservative, sometimes appear liberal, and sometimes have a view different from either of these.

In the fall of 2007 I was invited to write a weekly column for the Jackson *Sun*, a Gannett newspaper that is accused by many readers of being completely liberal, but that backed John McCain for President in the fall of 2008. I wish to thank the *Sun* for permission to rework and use those columns.

My radio program was over a station that daily broadcasts Rush Limbaugh, Sean Hannity, and Bill O'Reilly and the morning show of which is hosted by a young man who is right at home with those three. Needless to say, my program was a bit different. I ended the program in the fall of 2007 because my cardiologist was not pleased that I was averaging only five hours of sleep at night.

When I began selecting commentaries and columns for this collection, I realized that over the years I also had written many things of various types that easily could fit into the book. Consequently, I have included a few sermons, addresses, and book reviews. I have edited and modified most of the pieces. Some have been edited only slightly, matters of grammar or expression. Others have been heavily edited to include new comments for which there was not time on the radio or space in the newspaper. In writing both commentaries and columns I usually write in a stream of consciousness manner and then begin the hard work of editing and rewriting. The original drafts for most commentaries would have taken five or six minutes to read aloud. Original drafts of the columns usually contain as many as 1,800 words, which must then be trimmed down to 650 to 750 words. Obviously, much that might be said usually isn't, and for purposes of this collection I have taken the liberty of enlarging many of the finished products. Now and then, a newspaper column will be a total rewrite of an idea originally used for a commentary. In those cases, I usually have merged the two into a single piece.

Because of the nature of the book, you will find from place to place a certain amount of repetition—some might say redundancy. The reason is quite simple. Anyone who attempts to view the world from a biblical perspective likely will find that certain ideas gradually dominate his or her perception. As you will see if you read the entire book, the dominant ideas that inform my perception are a deep belief in

- the fallen condition of the Creation,
- the active presence of transcendent Powers in the Creation, created by God but now at work, under their own initiative, to frustrate and hinder the work of God,
- the institutions of the world as the primary embodiments of the Powers,
- God's work in Jesus Christ as the means by which God begins to reassert sovereign reign over the Creation,
- God's use of nations and individuals in judging and redeeming the world and, ultimately, the Creation,
- the fractured, but nevertheless continuing responsibility of humankind, as the corporate image of God (that is, as God's representatives) to care for God's world,
- the history of the Creation as divided into two eras, the Old Aeon (Age) and the New Aeon,
- the church as God's primary, though not only, institution in the renewal of the world and the Creation as God brings in the New Aeon,
- baptism and the Lord's Supper as God's means of building up, strengthening, and transforming the life of the church,
- the responsibility of the church to remind the institutions (the Powers) of their responsibility under God to establish and maintain a just order in the world,
- the unity of all Christians with all other human beings, by virtue of their baptism into the death of Christ, which was for the entire Creation.

I would like to express my appreciation to several people who have read many of the radio commentaries in their original forms and urged me to seek a publisher for a collection of them, especially Phyllis Tickle, Ken Carder, Will Campbell, Doug Meeks, David Waters, and Susan Kupisch. Their urging was not necessarily because they always agreed, but because they thought the ideas worth putting forth. I trust their urging was not misplaced.

Twenty-sixth week after Pentecost, 2008

PART ONE

Columns and Commentaries

1

Religion and Politics

RELIGION AND THE PRESIDENCY

RELIGION HAS BEEN A major element in the current presidential campaign more than in any campaign since 1960, when John F. Kennedy addressed the Greater Houston Ministerial Association of Texas. Mike Huckabee unabashedly asserts his belief in Jesus Christ, and some fear his Evangelical Christian background. Mr. Huckabee asked whether Mormons believe that Jesus and Satan are brothers, and Mr. Romney made a lengthy statement denying that the Mormon Church would influence his decisions.

Since the Constitution prohibits a religious test as a qualification for any public office, some contend that questions about religious belief should not be out of bounds. But a law or a party policy prohibiting someone from being a candidate because of his or her religion would be one thing; the role a candidate's religion might play in influencing government policy is quite another. For example, asking whether a candidate's religion or denomination's opposition to abortion would lead the candidate to seek the overturning of the Supreme Court's Jane Doe decision would be entirely appropriate. Asking whether a candidate's membership in a peace church such as the Quakers would cause the candidate to be unwilling ever to ask Congress to declare war also would be appropriate, as would asking a candidate's position on capital punishment if the candidate were affiliated with a church or other religious body that officially opposes capital punishment.

It is sadly revealing that people who are suspicious of Evangelical Christians and Mormons seem not to be suspicious of other Christians. For example, why are Methodist, Baptist, and Presbyterian candidates not asked whether their foreign policy will be influenced by Jesus' instructions on mercy, loving the enemy, and turning the other cheek? The simple answer is that most people assume that most self-avowed Christians are adept at rationalizing away the harder teachings of Jesus.

Robert Kaplan recognizes the potential threat of Christian teachings and therefore rejects them as a basis for national and international conduct. In his book *Warrior Politics*, Kaplan contends that the stability of the world depends upon leaders who reject Christian teachings such as meekness and embrace what he calls "the pagan virtue of enlightened self-interest."[1] The Christian teaching of meekness, says Kaplan, would allow the wicked to dominate the world. Self-interest works, he contends, because it meets other nations at the point of their own self-interest, and the result is a detente. Such was the kind of diplomacy advocated by Machiavelli, practiced most notably in the modern world by Henry Kissinger, and advocated in economics by Adam Smith, in philosophy by Ayn Rand, and in theology by Reinhold Niebuhr.

Since the scriptures and leading teachers of all major world religions—including Jesus and the Apostle Paul—have viewed self interest as basic to human nature, Kaplan can make a strong case for his position. But those religions and their major interpreters have not on that basis recommended the use of self-interest as a tool, but have viewed it as something against which we are to struggle. All teach, as a basic principle, treating others as you wish to be treated, or—in its negative formulation—not treating others in a manner in which you would not want to be treated. Jesus, for example, warned his followers that he was sending them into the world as sheep among wolves, and he warned them that though they must be as wise as serpents, they must be as innocent as doves.

The institutions of and individuals in Christianity, Judaism, and Islam can rest content with a world driven by self-interest only by denying their respective faiths. Each is called to live by a different ethos—to bear witness to a different ordering of life, a life possible here and now and also promised as the future condition of the entire world.

Though many United States leaders—both political and religious—have embodied what Kaplan advocates, their self-interest usually has not been truly enlightened, but mere self-interest. Consequently, the nation sometimes has become involved in wars that backfired—with many

---

1. Robert Kaplan, *Warrior Politics: Why Leadership demands A Pagan Ethos* (New York: Random House, 2002).

Christians waving the national flag in support—and leaving in their wake more grief and sorrow than triumph.

Given the corrupted condition of human nature, any nation probably must to some degree adopt Kaplan's approach. The scriptures of the world's religions do not teach that nations are to be forced to live by those scriptures' teachings. But each nation would be wise to consider that the inevitable outcome of self-interest as the driving motivation is cannibalism.

January 14, 2008

THE UNITED STATES AND RELIGION—BACKGROUNDS AND INFLUENCES

The debate over religion and politics seems to have no end, and one of the major issues in the debate is whether the United States is (or was intended to be) a Christian nation. The position of many on this question seems to depend on their point of reference in the nation's history. Those who insist on its Christian identity tend to emphasize the colonial period. Those who reject that identity tend to emphasize the Constitution and the intentions of the Founding Fathers.

The early English settlements on this continent must be viewed against the background of two important historical elements, one of which is seldom discussed in narratives of the nation's beginnings. The first element was the reason why there were English settlements in the first place. In the sixteenth century, the kings of England claimed for themselves the entire North American coastal area from what is now Florida to Canada. They called it Virginia. Seeing the new world as a source of gold, silver, and furs, the kings granted charters to various entrepreneurial companies to establish settlements as bases for exploration and conquest. The trade companies, in turn, either established their own settlements or granted patents to other groups for those purposes.

In 1606, James I granted a charter to the Virginia Company, a group of London entrepreneurs, to establish a satellite English settlement in North America for the purposes of establishing a settlement, finding gold, and—still pursuing Columbus's dream—find a water way to the East. On May 14, 1607, one hundred and four "gentlemen", artisans, craftsmen, and laborers, representing the Virginia Company, landed on Jamestown Island and founded the Jamestown colony, essentially intended as a base of operations for a wider range of activities, none of which was specifically religious.

The second important background element was the Protestant Reformation. Shortly after the followers of Martin Luther and John Calvin had established their own churches apart from the Catholic Church over theological issues, Henry VIII (the King of England) declared the English church independent of the Catholic Church over more personal and political issues and declared himself the head of the Church of England. Originally, Henry had opposed the Protestant efforts at reformation, and after the break with the Catholic Church, he seems to have done little to move away from Catholic practices and tradition.

The initial efforts at serious reform came after Henry's death and were undertaken by people influenced by the Lutheran wing of the Reformation. Luther had not seen fit to eliminate as many traditional elements of the church as Calvin wished to eliminate, and this meant that the reform elements in the Church of England did not go as far as some members had hoped in eliminating medieval practices. When the Calvinists gained influence, however, even they did not go as far in eliminating medieval elements as some desired.

Some members of the church, believing that the church would never carry out more thorough reforms, broke completely with the church. In 1609, one such congregation moved to Holland, where they soon began to fear they would completely lose their English identity. They persuaded the Virginia (trading) Company, therefore, to grant them a patent for a colony in North America. In 1620, they arrived in North America on the Mayflower and established the Plymouth colony, the second permanent English settlement in the new world. Today those settlers are remembered as "the Pilgrims". The Plymouth colony, then, used a patent intended for trade and exploration to establish a colony for their own purposes of religion.

The third group of colonists, remembered as the Puritans, did not come as a single group, but came in several waves, beginning in the early 1630's. They, too, wanted to see Calvin's reforms enacted in the Church of England, but chose to work from within. Receiving a patent as a trading colony, they intended to build a biblically based society as a model for later colonists and for the Church of England itself.

It should be noted, however, that the Puritans would not have made the distinction we make today between religion and politics. Many, though not all of them, desired some degree or other of a theocracy. All but two of the colonies eventually had at least semi-established churches.

Whatever their various purposes for coming, all the early settlers shared a European value system, a system influenced primarily by Christianity, but actually by a blending of biblical, Greek philosophical, and "pagan" elements. For example, major Christian holy days such as Christmas and All Saints' Day still are celebrated in ways that combine both biblical and pagan folk elements.

The earliest European settlements on this continent, then, were built on a European base under the influence of Protestant Christianity. But the question is: When the colonies became a nation, how did their British and their colonial experiences affect their vision?

Stay tuned.

July 15, 2008

THE INTOLERANCE OF THE COLONIAL CHURCHES

The English colonial period of this nation (1607–1783) holds clear examples of the difficulties faced in any attempt to establish a political structure identified with a specific religion, in this case the Christian religion. Among those difficulties are 1) defining the word *Christian*, 2) deciding who makes the laws, which logically should be expected to reflect Christian morality, and 3) deciding the relation between the nation as a Christian body and the religion of individuals in the nation. For example, is a citizen of a Christian nation automatically a Christian by virtue of that citizenship? Are people who are not Christian to be permitted to live in the nation and are they to be permitted to hold office or to vote?

All these questions, in one form or another, were faced by the early English colonies, and the answers in most of the colonies left a lot to be desired. It is commonly pointed out that the earliest settlers—the Pilgrims and the Puritans—did not come to this continent for religious liberty in general, but for their own religious liberty. They had no intention of granting religious liberty to anyone whose views and practices were incompatible with theirs. Though they had come under the provisions of commercial charters, and therefore as commercial ventures of the chartering companies, they actually had come for the explicit purpose of establishing churches based on a New Testament model, and to establish Christian settlements centered in those churches. In this respect, those early settlers had assumed, as was common in those days, that the church is the glue that holds the society together.

The establishment of such a community, however, requires a discipline affirmed and embraced by all the members of the community. How is it possible to have a disciplined community when an increasing majority of the community does not share the religious beliefs and views upon which the community is established? How far is it possible for the leaders to enforce law in the name of promoting discipline? Obviously, the rapid influx of settlers who had come for purposes other than religion—and even those who came for purposes of religion but whose views were not the same as the founders of a community—were a threat. Even the Mayflower Compact had not been signed by all the eligible passengers. In most colonies there was a back-and-forth pendulum swing between an emphasis on order and faithfulness and an attitude of toleration.

By the mid-1600s most of the colonies had established churches. Although there was some toleration in the Middle colonies, the Christianity of the colonies, more often than not, was an intolerant one. Church laws were colonial laws and usually were enforced by the civil courts. In most of the colonies religious minorities were not allowed to hold their own worship services and Jews and Roman Catholics were not allowed to vote.

Although most of the established churches were disestablished between 1776 and 1781, there were official churches in Virginia until 1786, in Georgia until 1789, in New Hampshire and South Carolina until 1790, and in Connecticut until 1818. Also, even where there was no established church, intolerance continued. In New Hampshire, until the mid-1800's only Protestants were permitted to hold public office, from 1780 until 1833 Massachusetts required every adult male to belong to a church, and until 1836 North Carolina permitted only Christians to hold public office.

The Massachusetts Constitution (1780) required anyone elected to the office of Governor, Lieutenant Governor, or Legislator to take an oath of office that began, "I,___, do declare that I believe in the Christian religion"; the Maryland Constitution (1776) required that all elected state officials show proof of faith in Christ; and the Delaware Constitution (1776) required faith in the three Persons of the Trinity and in the Old and New Testaments as divinely inspired.

Although most of the religious restrictions and requirements of State Constitutions were removed by the mid 1800s, it was not until the early 1940s that the U.S. Supreme Court ruled that the First Amendment applied to states as well as to the federal government. In fact, the First Amendment sometimes had been used to argue that Congress could not pass a law prohibiting a state from having an established religion.

Those who use the colonial period as a point of reference, then, have some support in claiming that this nation began as a Christian nation. But do those who hold this view want to return to the political conditions of the colonial period? What still must be explored is the changing make-up of the U.S. population and the establishment of the nation under the Constitution and the Bill of Rights.

July 28, 2008

THE FIRST AMENDMENT AND RELIGIOUS DIVERSITY

When the Bill of Rights to the U.S. Constitution became law, on December 15, 1791, most of the states had official churches. Even those that did not have official churches provided support of one kind or another to churches within their borders. The religion supported by the states was Protestant Christianity, and though providing for freedom of religion in general, several states excluded Roman Catholics, Jews, and Muslims from public office. A few required specific belief in Jesus Christ as part of the oath of office.

Although some suppose that in those days the word "religion" was not understood in terms of the various world religions of which we are aware today, documents from the period indicate otherwise. A speaker in one state's legislature, for example, contended that without a religious test for holding office, "pagans, deists, and Mohametans (the term commonly used in those days for Muslims)" might be elected[2]. Benjamin Franklin said that a building he had helped provide for preaching was such that even someone preaching Mohammedanism (another common term for Islam at the time) would find a pulpit at his service.[3] Thomas Jefferson spread the net even wider. The Virginia Statute for Religious Freedom, he said, meant to "comprehend, within the mantle of its protection, the Jew

---

2. Albert Bushnell Hall, *New American History* (New York: American Book Co., 1917) 188.

3. From Franklin's autobiography.

and the Gentile, the Christian and Mahometan, the Hindoo, and infidel of every denomination."[4]

Much of the support among eighteenth century political officials even for discriminatory religion was because of the wide-spread view that religion helps preserve the social order. Alexis de Tocqueville frequently is quoted as to the widespread presence of religion in the United States in the 1830's, but he also said that he did not know how sincere the people were in their religion. He was certain, however, that people of all ranks in the nation considered religion indispensable to the "preservation of republican institutions."[5] Local churches usually were places for community social gatherings. Church attendance, therefore, did not necessarily mean piety.

Although it is estimated that from 1700 to 1740 75—80% of the populace of the colonies attended church, Franklin Littell, in *From State Church to Pluralism*, says that in 1776 only about 5% of the people of the colonies claimed church membership; and in 1800, only about 6.9%. The percentage did not exceed 50% until 1926.[6]

Debate continues over interpretation of the First Amendment with regard to the relationship between church and state. There also were differences of opinion, however, among the colonies, the states and the Founding Fathers themselves. Washington, Adams, Jefferson, and Madison differed over whether the President should declare national days of religious observance, whether financial aid should be given to church schools, whether there should be salaried chaplains in Congress and in the military, and how to interpret the phrase "establishment of religion."

Whereas today, many Christians who call themselves Evangelicals decry Jefferson's expression of a "wall between church and state" (which Madison adopted), in Jefferson and Madison's day, because of the Evangelicals' belief that our relationship with God is an inner one over which no state should have authority, Evangelicals were the two men's staunchest supporters.

To raise again the question with which this series began, Is the United States in any sense a Christian nation? From the standpoint of the

---

4. From Jefferson's autobiography.

5. Alexis de Tocqueville, *Democracy in America*, Tr Arthur Goldhammer (New York: Library of America, 2004) 337–38.

6. Franklin H. Littell, *From State Church to Pluralism* (New York: Doubleday and Company, 1962).

nation's history, the answer seems to be that although some of the earliest settlers wanted to establish a nation centered in the church, those settlers were outnumbered by people who did not share to such a vision. Thus, it became impossible.

Is the U.S., then, a religious nation? It seems more accurate to say that the U.S. is a nation with a population widely divergent in its religious beliefs and practices—so much so that the only peaceable arrangement is one that accepts any and all religious expressions that do not destroy the social fabric. I say "accepts", not "tolerates", for toleration implies a correct position that permits incorrect positions to be held. The First Amendment—whatever else it does or does not do—makes it impossible for Congress to declare the United States a Christian nation, to treat Christianity as the nation's primary religion, or to make laws giving the Christian religion privileges over any other religion—Hinduism, Judaism, Islam, or even Wicca. Some of the colonists and some of the Founding Fathers would have approved; others would have objected strenuously. The debate is as old as the nation, and I, for one, do not expect it to end in the near future.

July 28, 2008

BIBLICAL ARGUMENTS AGAINST THE U.S. BEING A CHRISTIAN NATION

The previous three columns on whether the United States is a Christian nation considered the question from the standpoint of history. It is essential, however, also to consider the question from a New Testament perspective.

It seems impossible to say from a New Testament perspective that any nation either is or can be a Christian nation. For one thing, Jesus taught and lived a way of life that his disciples were to follow throughout history. To be a Christian nation, a nation's laws and customs would have to reflect those teachings and that way of life. At the heart of Jesus' teachings and basic to his life and death were 1) rejection of secular power and 2) self-sacrifice for the well-being of others. Disciples were to love even their enemies. The Apostle Paul instructed his readers to give food and drink to the hungry and thirsty enemy (Rom 12:20-21).

In the wilderness Satan tempted Jesus with secular power (Matt 4:9). Jesus rejected it, and in his teachings he instructed his disciples that they too were to reject secular power and authority (Matt 10:42–44). On the cross he refused to save his life at the expense of others—even at the expense of his enemies—and in his teachings he instructed disciples to follow his example.

The United States, on the other hand, was born from the colonies' determination to wrest power from England and to claim it for themselves. Taking this power was accomplished by a conflict that could never meet the tests of the just war theory. Although I consider the just war theory to be in conflict with the New Testament, the dominant view of most churches since the time of Augustine has been that it is legitimate and that it is to be used to decide when the church can support a war. Among its criteria are that, a just war is be for the purpose of restoring justice and that fighting must be the last alternative, after all other means have failed. It can be argued that injustice in the colonies was not nearly as bad as colonial propaganda insisted, and it certainly can be shown that diplomacy had not been exhausted.

The United States today has no intention of basing either its domestic or its foreign policy either on the Sermon on the Mount or on any of Jesus' parables. The United States continues to exercise power through economic pressure, overt military conflict, and covert schemes of subversion. No nation, the United States included, will ever give up its life for the enemy. But Jesus himself asked why people called him Lord, but did not do what he told them to do. To say that any nation is a Christian nation requires a definition of Christian that either rejects Jesus' teachings and ministry as having no bearing on the definition, denies history, or both.

Another reason why the United States cannot, from the standpoint of the New Testament, be accurately called a Christian nation is that the New Testament—like the Old—views all secular nations as components of a fallen world, hostile to God. All secular nations are viewed as hostile to God and determined to make their own way in the world, a way different from God's way.

The New Testament sees the church itself as a nation set apart (1 Pet 2:9), called, as a part of biblical Israel, to be God's instrument for the blessing of the secular nations. Unfortunately, across the centuries, the church has become as corrupt, as power and money hungry, and as violent as any secular nation. The institutional church today is itself one of the greatest stumbling blocks to people who otherwise might have taken seriously the message of the New Testament. It fell into this trap at least as far back as the fourth century, when it embraced Constantine's favor in the Roman Empire. It is precisely that corrupted nature of the church that enables many of its members to contend that the United States, a corrupted nation, is a Christian nation.

August 19, 2008

THE IDOLATRY OF GOVERNMENT IDEOLOGY

There has been much talk in this country in recent years about spreading democracy to other parts of the world. One of the more recently established criteria the administration has declared as the basis for leaving Iraq is sufficient headway toward a democratic form of government there. Of course, there has been occasional acknowledgment that if a democratic form of government is established in Iraq or in any other Middle Eastern country, it will not be a carbon copy of western democracy, but will be a form rooted in the needs and perspectives of the country in which it is formed.

Actually, the U.S. Constitution never uses the word *democracy*, but speaks of the *republic*—a fact often overlooked by people who, finding their personal desires thwarted, complain, "But I thought we lived in a democracy."

It is interesting that so many Christians who have grown up in what they consider a democracy assume a closer tie between democratic government and the Christian gospel than between the gospel and other forms of government. From a biblical perspective, all particular forms of government are human creations and thus partake of the same sinful, corrupted, broken condition of the Creation that frustrates all other human institutions. A late minister friend of mine once remarked that the ideal form of government would be a beneficent monarchy.

Deciding what is the best form of government for humankind requires first considering the purpose of humankind. According to the Creation narratives in Genesis, human beings were created to serve as God's representatives in caring for the earth and its creatures; for Christians, the New Testament connects loving God with loving both the neighbor and the enemy. From this perspective, then, the question put to any form of government should be not the degree of self-satisfaction it permits me, but the degree to which it either enables or inhibits my living responsibly with regard to the earth and its creatures and the degree to which it either permits or inhibits my ability to love my neighbor and my enemy as I love myself. Any human form of government is capable of permitting these, but also is inclined to make them impossible. The effort, then, of any nation to impose upon another a particular form of government on the assumption that the form itself is closer to the will of God is simply another form of idolatry.

February 18, 2007

GOD AND GOVERNMENT: THE DEBATE CONTINUES

The people of Iraq are now debating an issue that was debated a few months ago in Europe and is perennially debated in this country—the question of whether religion should have an official role in government. In Iraq the question is whether Islam is to be one of the bases of law in the new government. In Europe the question was whether the Constitution of a United Europe should acknowledge Christianity as a formative element in European history.

In the United States the question is whether the authors of the Constitution intended an absolute separation of church and state. Actually, the so-called wall of separation has never been absolute. Churches are tax exempt, the Senate and House have salaried chaplains, both bodies open their sessions with prayer, and the Supreme Court begins its sessions by invoking the blessing of God. And on the list could go.

In Europe and Iraq the question involves *specific* religions— Christianity and Islam—while in the United States the question revolves, for the most part, around religion in general. The primary arena of conflict in this country is public education, and the conflict is fueled by bothersome misunderstandings of court decisions. Contrary to the impression left by a few over-reacting public officials here and there, it is not unconstitutional for students to pray or read the Bible in school—*provided* these activities do not interfere with class room activity or infringe upon the privacy of other students.

Why do some Christians, of all people, want required religious activities in the public schools. The public schools are branches of secular government. Consequently, public school activities such as classroom assemblies, baccalaureate services, and school-wide assembly programs are, by virtue of being sponsored by the schools, government sponsored activities, subject to government rules and regulations. Persons who are willing for secular government to decide for their children what prayers and scriptures are permitted, are, in effect, offering to hand over to secular government decisions about the faith of their children, an act contrary not only to one of the basic reasons this nation was founded, but to the biblical tradition itself.

September 4, 2005

THE PROBLEM WITH FAITH-BASED INITIATIVES

In a recent op-ed piece in the New York *Times*, David Kuo and John Dilulio—former Deputy Director and Director, respectively, of the White House Office of Faith-Based and Community Initiatives—complained that President Bush's faith-based initiative has not done what the President originally promised. Faith-based grants are funds granted to religious groups for social service programs.

Mr. Kuo and Mr. Dilulio charge that the program has failed in two areas: 1) Not as many people as anticipated are being served, and 2) grants have been shifted away from local "armies of compassion" toward large, national organizations with religious affiliations.

The op-ed piece was written in the wake of President Bush's State of the Union Address, in which the President promised to continue to support faith-based and community groups that "bring hope to harsh places" and also proposed a three year plan involving pastors, among others, to help organizations keep young people out of gangs.

President Bush is not alone in his determination. Every major contender for the office of President supports the program. To show the urgency of the program, the op-ed piece quotes the contenders at the time, reporting their heart-wrenching examples of homeless men and women, of drug addicted children, of children in severe poverty, and of other dismal conditions.

People of faith should be as committed to aiding people in desperate conditions as are any other humane persons. But that does not automatically mean that churches and other religious groups should enter into partnership with government at any level to provide that aid. When a supposed faith-based group requests funds from the government, the government must decide whether the group actually is a faith-based unit, and in order to do that the government must define faith. The government always will make such a decision on purely pragmatic grounds—that is, on the basis of what is in the best interest of the programs at issue. Let a

Wiccan group request a grant and see how quickly some Christian groups will challenge the group's identity as a community of faith. The definition of faith, however, is not a legitimate matter for political speculation, political convenience, or political whim.

No religious group and no member of a religious group—not just Christian, Jew, or Muslim—should participate in the faith-based initiative program. To do so is to assume that the church should evaluate its actions by what secular law permits; the People of God (a biblical designation of Israel and of the church) must not look to what can be called figuratively "the government of Caesar" for verification of their identity.

Actually, such a do-si-do between religious groups and the government is neither new nor surprising. Churches and other religious groups have long looked to secular government not only to affirm their identity, but also to do much of their work for them. Many Christians want laws that enforce their moral beliefs so they won't have the discomfort or the difficulty of teaching their children that to be Christian may lead to being unpopular.

To avoid the separation of church and state issue while engaging in social programs, some churches set up legally separate organizations, pretending that they have not entered into contract with Caesar. Such churches use government money to feed the hungry, clothe the naked, and provide shelter for the homeless rather than sacrifice some of their accommodations (church buildings and upper middle class parsonages and manses) or call on their members to modify their middle or upper middle class style of living.

To pretend that an agency spawned by the church is not really an arm of the church, however, is to tell the government that in order to do what it wants to do, the church will quit being the church in one area of its life, thus making Caesar the master of that part.

A passage from the New Testament gives clear warning with regard to such self-delusions. Jesus warned that no one can serve two masters. Whoever attempts to do so, he said, will end up loving one and hating the other or hating one and loving the other. My guess is that most of us will think we are truly serving both and will never realize how much we have come to love the one with whom we thought we could make an accommodation and to hate the one we thought we loved.

February 15, 2008

WHO DETERMINES WHO IS OF FAITH?

A movement is underway to persuade those whom leaders of the movement call "people of faith" to urge U.S. Senators to outlaw the filibuster in the nomination process for federal judges. The Senate judiciary committee has been unable to secure the sixty percent vote necessary to nominate a few conservative judges for the federal courts. The new movement has called the holding back of these nominations an attack upon people of faith and has urged "people of faith" to become lobbyists against the filibuster.

The word *filibuster* originally was related to the word *freebooter* and meant anyone—especially pirates—who lived by plundering others. Making long, irrelevant speeches as a means of impeding Senate action on an issue is never mentioned in the Constitution, but is a tactic that originated in the nineteenth century and quickly received its present name.

Whether the filibuster is appropriate as a legislative tool is a legitimate matter for debate. What is not a legitimate matter for political debate is the definition of "people of faith." Are conservative Christians the only people of faith? What about liberal and moderate Christians? What about Jews and Muslims of various political persuasions? Those guiding the movement seem to assume that anyone supporting the filibuster is not a person of faith.

From a biblical perspective, the people of God have not only the right, but the responsibility, to remind governments of their responsibility before God to maintain a just order in a fallen world.[7] Inevitably, there will be differences of opinion among the people of God themselves on ways to achieve and preserve a just order. The filibuster is a political tactic that can be used by liberals and conservatives alike—by people of faith and by people of no faith. But to equate political opinion in such matters with authentic faith reveals at least a misguided understanding of faith itself.

May 1, 2005

THE PRIDE OF NATIONS

Nations and leaders of nations, once they achieve power, find it difficult—if not impossible—to resist the temptation to make the world over in their own image. Alexander, Prince of Macedon, had been a student

---

7. For a good discussion of this position see John Howard Yoder, *The Christian Witness to the State*, (Scottdale: Herald Press, 2002).

of the famous philosopher Aristotle, and from Aristotle he developed a great love for Greek philosophy and Greek culture. When he succeeded his father as king, Alexander set out to conquer the world and to impose Greek culture upon it. Nations whose culture was other than Greek were called "barbarians". In brief, Alexander considered himself to be civilizing the rest of the world. And if civilizing the world required the use of force, so be it.

Alexander, of course, became Alexander the Great, and he was by no means the last person to attempt to "civilize" other nations. The Old Testament book of Daniel, which is presented as a series of stories about four young Judean men in the sixth century BCE, actually is a disguised account of how Greek rulers in the second century BCE resumed Alexander's efforts. The author of Daniel takes a dim view of this effort and warns that all human empires are flawed and will ultimately crumble before the coming reign of Israel's God.

The United States is no more immune than any other nation to the temptation to "civilize" others. Of course, the United States has sometimes been extraordinarily generous to other nations, even those it has defeated in war. The Marshall Plan after World War II is an obvious example. But the United States has an ambiguous past, and its good deeds must not blind us to the human misery caused by its frequent "civilizing" efforts. Much of the nation's land was acquired through broken treaties, warfare, and acts of attempted genocide against the Native Americans in the guise of "manifest destiny". Native American children were forced into religious schools in which their own languages were prohibited and in which their own cultures were to be eradicated. The Greeks called their subjects "barbarians"; the U.S. called its subjects "savages". Today, the eradication of a people's culture is included in a general definition of genocide.

Most Christian missionaries and their denominations in the western world now acknowledge that in the colonial period in Africa and Asia, they erroneously identified the Christian gospel with western culture. A glaring example of this error was reflected in a conversation I had in the 1960s with a missionary who had been in the Congo for almost forty years. I asked whether the Methodist Church in Africa had set liturgy to native music as had been done with some of the Roman Catholic liturgy. She responded that the Africans had no music. "They just beat on drums," she said; "they had no real music."

Unfortunately, the churches' acknowledgment today that there was a problem back then has done little to overcome skepticism, suspicion, and hostility from the children and grandchildren of many of those former colonial subjects.

When President Bush and his colleagues use the motive of spreading democracy as one explanation for the invasion of Iraq, they reveal how much the United States continues to be like all other conquerors. They hold the conceit that democratic government is God's favorite form of government and that they have a responsibility to spread that form throughout the world. From a biblical perspective, the best form of government is the one that enables those under it to act responsibly as God's representatives in caring for the earth and everything on it. There are various forms of government that—when operating properly—can provide that ability. But no form of government, democratic or other, is immune to the corruption that can prevent that provision.

Despite its flaws, I prefer the form of government under which I now live because it is the one with which I am familiar. I am used to it. But the conceit that says that it is the only legitimate form of government will always lead to the horrors that we have seen in other countries into whose lives the United States has intervened—sometimes overtly by the military, sometimes covertly by the CIA—and that we now see in Iraq. Just as in ancient Greek literature, so in the Jewish and Christian scriptures, pride is the most persistent attitude through which the gods or God bring nations and empires crumbling to the ground.

September 25, 2007

PRIDE OF EMPIRE

The specific name the Old Testament prophets used for the God of Israel was *Yahweh*, a word usually translated *the LORD*. Those prophets viewed history in terms of Yahweh using various nations for the specific purpose of accomplishing his purposes in the world. Yahweh was able to do this because of his power as the creator and ruler of the universe.

The Old Testament prophets said that the reason the Assyrians were able to conquer the northern kingdom of Israel and the reason the Babylonians were able to conquer the Assyrians and take the remaining portion of Israel into exile was that both the Assyrians and the Babylonians were being used by Yahweh as instruments of his judgment.

Later, the author of the book of Daniel viewed the power of the Greeks over the southern remnant of ancient Israel as the will of Yahweh, and later still, the Gospel of Luke portrays Jesus saying that Jerusalem "will be trampled down until the end of the time of the Gentiles" (Luke 21:24).

So from a biblical perspective, the idea that God uses various nations as instruments of his will is not strange at all. But what the prophets never say is that God's use of a nation means that God is on that nation's side. In fact, the only time that God is ever viewed as taking sides is when God sides with the poor and downtrodden against the rich and powerful. And even then, God's judgment on the rich and powerful is an attempt to push them toward their own redemption.

The primary reason the Bible gives for the eventual fall of the very nations God has used as his instruments of judgment on others is pride, which motivated their conquest from the very beginning. Isaiah, for example, portrays the King of Assyria as saying that his victories are by his own power and that he is free to do as he will with the nations he has conquered (Isa 10:12–19). Classical Greek writers saw pride as the basic flaw in human nature. Their word for it was *hubris*. And a closer look at the wars of our own time suggests that were the Old Testament prophets or the ancient Greek writers around today, their view of both the conquered and the conquerors might be that very little has changed.

August 20, 2006

BY THEIR FRUITS YOU SHALL KNOW THEM

One of this nation's most touted virtues has been its insistence that in a court of law a person is to be considered innocent until proven guilty. Now, Congress has passed, and, at the time of this comment, the President is preparing to sign a bill denying to prisoners in the war on terrorism and to their lawyers the right to see all the evidence. The bill also denies prisoners the right to confront their accusers. The prisoners are, in effect, considered guilty until proven innocent and are denied reasonable means of proving themselves innocent. Actually, the bill is not anticipated to affect the situation of most of the prisoners, because they are considered combatants who, consequently, have no right to a trial.

Because of intense secrecy, the situation and condition of the prisoners are as unknown to their families as if they were missing in action in the normal sense of that term. Moreover, since the war on terrorism is expected to be of indeterminable duration, prisoners of that war could remain in prison until they die of old age, with their families never knowing what happened to them.

From a biblical perspective, any nation has the authority, in a fallen world, to protect itself. But also from a biblical perspective, a nation's actions must not contradict its own proclaimed standards of justice. God does hold nations accountable when they ignore justice and perpetrate injustice.

Apparently, the Congress and the President have been guided by the old adage that "the ends justify the means." But ends and means cannot be separated. Any accomplished goal embodies the actions taken in its accomplishment. If I steal a loaf of bread to feed my starving family, I become, by stealing, a thief. If the United States assumes that ends justify means and in the war on terrorism considers prisoners innocent until proven guilty, by that very assumption it will have transformed its own character and taken on a new identity.

Jesus said, "A good tree cannot bear bad fruit, and a bad tree cannot bear good fruit. By their fruits," he said, "you shall know them" (Matthew 7:16–18). Jesus' words apply to institutions and nations just as surely as to individuals. If the fruit of a tree is evil—or even questionable—then the tree must be judged by that fruit. Perhaps President Bush overlooked that verse from the Sermon on the Mount when he was reading the words of the person he said was the political philosopher who had had the greatest impact on his life.

October 15, 2006

A CALL THE PRESIDENT AND THE VICE-PRESIDENT DID NOT SIGN

The Council of Bishops of the United Methodist Church and the U.S. Conference of Catholic Bishops recently issued independent statements calling for a time table for withdrawing United States troops from Iraq.

A few days after the Methodist Bishops' statement, a group within the Council issued a *Call for Repentance and Peace with Justice*. In that Call, the group repented its own complicity in what it considered an unjust and immoral invasion and occupation of Iraq by remaining silent while the U.S. Administration rushed to military action based on misleading information.

Actually, some of those Methodist Bishops had spoken against the buildup for war, and the Catholic Bishops had repeatedly expressed moral concerns about the preparation for a preventive war. The Catholic Bishops consider the removal of a dictator and the holding of elections to be achievements, but they also mourn the deaths of thousands of U.S. military and tens of thousands of Iraqis, as well as the injury and maiming of countless numbers of persons. Both statements and the Call to Repentance speak of the lives lost on both sides.

It should be noted that neither the Roman Catholic nor the United Methodist Church rejects war under all circumstances. Both officially oppose war as such, but both either explicitly or implicitly support the just war theory. Among the requirements of that theory are that war be a last resort; that the goals be clearly spelled out before the war begins and not shift as the war progresses; that the force used must be proportional to the stated goals; and that conditions in the outcome of the war must be calculated to be better than before the war.

The Catholic Bishops' statement, while never calling the war in Iraq an unjust war, speaks of it as having been waged preemptively without a clear projection of the outcome, and it refers pointedly to the requirement that the amount of force used must be in direct proportion to the stated purpose of the war and that civilians not be targeted.

The United Methodist Bishops never say explicitly which, if any, of the criteria for a just war have been violated, but they suggest that the war was waged too quickly, without exhausting all other possible alternatives, and that the suffering of the people now is worse than under Sadam Hussein.

The Methodist Bishops' statement and Call for Repentance were issued in November, 2005. The Call was signed by ninety-six of the Council's 107 active and retired Bishops, and as of the second day of March, 6,650 other persons have signed the Call. And for purposes of self-disclosure, I will say that I too signed it.

An interesting element in all this is that President Bush and Vice-President Cheney both are members of the United Methodist Church. Needless to say, neither the President nor the Vice-President has signed the Call.

March 12, 2006

LIES, DISTORTIONS OF LANGUAGE, AND POLITICAL CAMPAIGNS

In political campaigns, accuracy frequently is treated as an inconvenience. Recent postings at FactCheck.org—the Annenberg Public Policy Center's website that keeps track of errors, distortions, and outright lies in public life—show how both the Obama and the McCain campaigns continue to put their own spins on facts. Taking a sentence out of context, leaving words out of a sentence, twisting the meaning of a word, a sentence, or a phrase—all are weapons in a war waged with words.

The McCain camp misrepresents Obama's position on sex education for pre-school children, and the Obama camp misrepresents McCain's position on spending for education in general. Words are taken out of context to make it appear that Obama was belittling Sarah Palin, and a pro-Obama blog lists one hundred books that Palin is falsely accused of having wanted banned from the Wasilla library. Long after the facts are reported, Palin continues to repeat her distorted claim about her opposition to the "bridge to nowhere" and her false claim to have sold the state of Alaska's jet for a profit on e-bay.

Some psychological studies indicate that under certain conditions, false assertions will be believed even if they have no basis in fact and even when clear proof of the falsity of the assertions is produced. In other words, tell a lie long enough and many people will believe it. This explains why candidates sometimes continue to assert things that clearly have been shown to be false. Both sides, as have opponents in previous campaigns, borrow techniques straight from Joseph Goebbels.

Twisting freedom of speech into a distorted caricature, each side bends the truth to its own liking, and soon, the more careful listener either struggles to know whom to believe or, more likely, decides that neither side is to be believed. Why should a person willing to sacrifice the truth to gain office be trusted not to sacrifice it to remain in office? Perhaps a good rule of thumb would be to vote for the candidate who seems least to have perverted language by the misuse of words.

Human language is a gift of God, given, among other reasons, to facilitate human caring for God's world and to aid in the maintenance of human relationships. We, however, turn language into a weapon for attack. It is a habit as old as the human race. In the wake of their disobedience Adam used words to accuse Eve and Eve used words to accuse the serpent.

In a fallen world, in fact, lying is an ordinary mode of daily discourse. Contemporary society depends on lies for much of its dynamism. Where, for example, where would businesses and corporations be without the calculated duplicity we call advertising? All governments decide when to lie to their own people—in the name of national security, safety, or simple expediency—and all in the name of the people's own welfare. In wartime, governments lie about mediocre achievements or about outright defeats by skewing statistics or by creation of false ones in order to nurture optimism.

But woe to any nation when its people finally realize that their government, the commerce upon which the nation depends, and even the religious structures to which they have looked for spiritual guidance are riddled with duplicity. That nation then will succumb to suspicion, cynicism, pessimism, and the assumption that no one and no thing can any longer be trusted. It will have become a habitation of the demonic, for whether one takes the statement figuratively or literally, according to the New Testament the father of all lies is the devil.

As George Orwell showed in the novel *1984*, distortion of language leads to the dehumanization of society. Language becomes simply another technology by which to promote self-interest. Truth is trivialized. Not only in warfare, but in ordinary, everyday life as well, truth is the first victim. And when truth goes, so goes our humanity.

September 16, 2008

THE DISTASTEFUL UNDERBELLY OF POWER

In the Old Testament book 1 Samuel the Israelites asked the prophet Samuel to appoint for them a king. Until that time they had been governed by judges—military figures upon whom the power of God had come to enable them to rule on God's behalf. But for some time, the judges had been corrupt, and the Israelites wanted a different kind of leader. "Give us a king like those of the nations around us!" they demanded.[8]

Surprisingly, God condescended and told Samuel to appoint a king. But first, Samuel warned the people of what they were in for when their government became like other governments. In essence, he told them that once they had a king like those of the nations around them, the king would rule like those kings. He would use his power for his own selfish

---

8. The passage to which these comments refer is 1 Sam 8:1–18.

interests. "He will take your sons and your daughters, your servants and your livestock, and even your land and the yield of its crops and use them for his own purposes."

Samuel's words are a biblical perspective on how all human leaders eventually exercise power.

- In a monarchy the monarch looks out for his or her own interests first.
- In a democracy the majority asserts is own self-interest over against the minority. In a republic the representatives and the majority each seek their own well-being at the expense of the population.
- Even the best elected official makes decisions with at least one eye on the next election.

In those rare instances where this is not the case, the exception is because God, out of sheer mercy, continues occasionally to intervene. The secular version of this nature of government and of those in power is expressed in Lord Acton's familiar adage that power corrupts and absolute power corrupts absolutely.

Biblically oriented people should not be surprised, therefore, when elected officials use their offices for personal privilege or financial gain, to twist facts in order to bend public opinion to their own goals and schemes, and even to trick nations into going to war for purposes that have no relation to the national interest. As for those of us who are stunned that political leaders would twist facts to justify military action or outright war, the prophet Samuel—could he be summoned from the dead as Saul summoned him in the latter days of his reign—probably would be surprised that we are surprised.

January 8, 2006

A HEALTHY SKEPTICISM

Both the Old and the New Testaments have a healthy skepticism with regard to human governments. The New Testament views all human governments as time-and-space embodiments of transcendent, heavenly Powers that God created to maintain order and justice in the world. Unfortunately, these Powers—like the human beings they are supposed to protect—are engulfed in self-interest. Consequently, human governments, as embodiments of the Powers, operate according to the same motives.

The book of Revelation is strongest in this view, portraying the government of Rome as a seven-headed beast that has become the instrument of Satan. But other books reflect a similar perspective. The Apostle Paul, living in a time when the Roman Empire still was relatively gentle in its response to the Christian movement, knew that the state would put up with citizens and subjects only as long as they did not openly disagree with government policy. Paul instructed his readers to be subject to the Powers—not obey, just be subject to (Rom 13:1). In other words, violate the law if it contradicts the will of God, but then accept the punishment.

In the Old Testament the prophet Samuel warned that human governments eventually base their existence on policies that undermine the well-being of those for whom they are supposed to be the guardians (1 Sam 8:11–17). And the history of Israel, once Israel had a king, bore out Samuel's warning.

Even the little book of Ecclesiastes warns that when you are in the presence of the king, you would be wise not to be disrespectful, for, says Ecclesiastes, the king does whatever pleases him (Eccl 8:2–3).

It is clear from the full sweep of the biblical writers' views of government that they were speaking not only of kings and emperors, but of all human governments. And the prophetic tradition in both the Old and the New Testaments indicates that the People of God have an irrevocable responsibility to remind all human governments that they are to govern justly and equitably—not catering to the rich and the powerful and not enacting policies and programs for the primary purpose of accumulating power or of remaining in office.

That is precisely the reason that the church and individual Christians must be wary when any government or any branch of government begins to expand its power, even in the name of national security.

February 5, 2006

SLEEPING WITH ONE EYE OPEN

Now that Samuel Allito has been sworn in as a member of the United States Supreme Court, the question is what kind of Justice he will be. Will he support the further accumulation of power by the current Administration or will he, like Hugo Black, Earl Warren, and a few others before him, become something quite different from what his prior record suggests? Of course, it should be noted that some of the President's sharpest Democrat critics have, by their timidity on several crucial votes, contributed to his accumulation of power.

Biblical faith affirms that ultimately history is in the hands of neither the United States Senate nor the United States Supreme Court, but in the hands of God. This does not mean, however, that the Church or Christians either should or may ignore significant issues such as the election and appointment of public officials. The church and individual Christians have the responsibility to remind the state of its responsibility under God to govern justly and equitably, providing for the well-being of all its citizens and not for the wealthy and the powerful alone. Christians may honestly disagree over the best person for a particular office and over the best way to achieve justice, equity, and the well-being of all citizens. But when any head of government suggests that his or her succession to that office and the spreading of a specific form of government throughout the world are due to the will of God—while cloaking the work of his or her own administration behind a veil of secrecy and pursuing policies for the benefit the wealthy and to the detriment of the poor—then there are ample biblical grounds for questioning whether that head is governing justly and equitably.

No doubt, God will use both the best of us and the worst of us to accomplish his purposes in this world. At times, God probably will use some of our worst decisions because that is all he has with which to work. But that God ultimately will bring good out of evil will make the evil no less terrible and the pain of the sufferers no less traumatic in the meantime. Nevertheless, in such times, Christians would be well advised, while living with confidence in the ultimate triumph of God and of his Christ, to take as our motto the title of a country song recorded by Lester Flatt and Earl Scruggs over half a century ago: "I'm Gonna Sleep with One Eye Open."

February 19, 2006

THE HORSEMEN OF WAR

In the book of Revelation 6:1–8, at the beckon of a voice from some imprecise location, four horses and their riders go forth, one by one, to spread warfare, plague, and death upon the earth. The rider of the first horse, a white horse, is armed with a longbow and goes forth "conquering and to conquer." The other three horses are a red one, whose rider carries the sword of warfare; a black one, whose rider carries a measuring balance symbolizing the agricultural devastation wrought by warfare; and a pale one, whose rider is Death.

There is much difference of opinion as to the correct understanding of these figures. I am among those who consider them symbols of the perennial character of human history—an inevitable series of wars and devastations among nations and empires. The book speaks, then, to every nation and to every empire in every era of history, including our own.

Since toward the end of the book of Revelation (Rev 19:11–16), Christ is symbolized by a rider on a white horse, it would seem that the rider on the white horse among the four horsemen is an imitator of Christ. And if the horsemen represent the world's ongoing condition of warfare, then the earlier rider on a white horse indicates that in the minds of the war-makers, wars always are waged on behalf of some form of truth. In the long sweep of history, whether they are waged in the name of liberating others, of purifying the nation (as in the case of genocides), or simply of asserting some natural right of the rule of the powerful, wars always are undergirded by the assumption that either the gods, nature, or history itself is on the side of the war-maker. Every manifesto of revolution—including the Communist Manifesto and the U.S. Declaration of Independence—has claimed transcendent blessing upon its adherents.

There is now much speculation over whether the United States will launch an attack upon Iran. If it does, the rationale will be no different from that given for any other war, just as it was no different in the U.S. attack upon Iraq and is no different in the warfare waged by Osama bin Laden and his imitators. The question is what, in the case of an attack upon Iran, followers of Jesus Christ will do—seek to be peacemakers, as we are called to be, or side with the horses and their riders, led by an imitation Christ.

April 30, 2006

AUGUSTINE, FREUD, AND THE NUCLEAR POWERS

President Bush and the leaders of several European countries met this week to try to reach some agreement on certain matters in world affairs. They were not successful with regard to Iraq, but they did agree that Iran must not develop nuclear weapons. The nuclear powers of the world have said to the rest of the world, "We have nuclear weapons, but we will not allow you to have any." It seems clear that the nuclear powers of the world see themselves as responsible world citizens and the other nations—especially the nations of the Middle East—as irresponsible.

Perhaps the nuclear powers should take heed of a basic insight of Sigmund Freud and of one from the fourth century theologian Augustine. Augustine's insight was that the human race is born under the power of original sin—that is, that even our best intentions are flawed by self-interest. Not everything we do is rooted in self-interest, but no matter how good our motives and intentions, self-interest always lurks in the background, keeping them from being completely pure. Freud's insight was that we are never completely aware of our motives. Within us are at work drives of which we are completely unaware.

The same may be said of nations. When the nuclear powers say to other nations, "We forbid you to have nuclear weapons," they may really believe they are acting to keep the world safe from nuclear war. But the simple fact is that no nation is immune to self-interest. In fact, political theorists unashamedly say that it would be irresponsible for a nation to ignore self-interest. And when it comes to nuclear weapons, the nations also should hear the words of the Lord of all nations, Jesus Christ: "All who take up the sword will perish by the sword" (Matt 26:52).⁹

February 27, 2005

THE A380, THE INAUGURAL BALL, AND THE POOR

Within one week we have seen the unveiling of the largest airplane ever built and have learned that the inaugural festivities in Washington cost well over forty million dollars. The double-decker airplane will have spas, beds, and perhaps a casino. The prototype is said to have cost thirteen billion dollars. By some calculations, the money spent on inaugural events might have purchased two hundred Humvees with the best of armor or provided vaccinations and other preventive health care for twenty-two million children.

The A380 airbus is this generation's Titanic, an expression of pride as much as an instrument of utility. French President Jacques Chirac called the plane a sign of Europe's capacity to beat the rest of the world in industry.

---

9. My own translation.

The inaugural festivities reflected the same pride. In response to suggestions that because of the war in Iraq the festivities should be cancelled, we were told that they are a ceremony of our history—a ritual of our government. They are good, we were told, for Washington's economy. Others have pointed out that in 1944, President Franklin Roosevelt cancelled all activities other than the inauguration itself because of the war in Europe.

The lavishness and extravagance of these two record breaking expenditures do not sit well beside Jesus' words in the Gospel of Luke, "Blessed are you poor, for yours is the Kingdom of God," and "Woe to you who are rich, for you already have received your reward" (Luke 6:20, 24).

No poor person will ever fly in the A380. This Thursday, there were no champagne and no dancing by the men and women in Iraq. Only the sound of more bombs and gunfire interrupted the silence over the graves of the dead.

No wonder Jesus said, "It is easier for a camel to go through the eye of a needle than for a rich man to enter the kingdom."

January 23, 2005

THE SUPREME COURT, RELIGION, AND SOPHISTICATED JINGOISM

In the recent and present processes for selecting persons for seats on the U.S. Supreme Court, much has been said about the nominees' religion and the matter of whether a nominee can set aside his or her religious views when considering cases brought before the Court.

There is a great irony here. Week after week, worshippers in this country are urged, either explicitly or implicitly, not to be one-day-a-week Christians, Muslims, or Jews. We are told that a true Christian's or a devout Muslim or Jew's faith should underlie and be a guide for everything we do. Actually, genuine religion, or genuine religious faith, does influence us at every level. It forms the way we perceive the world around us. It forms and nurtures our presuppositions, what social psychology calls our frame of reference. If religion is genuine, it is not simply a sometime thing with which we can dispense when called upon to do so.

Persons with genuine religious convictions will differ over whether the Constitution should be interpreted in terms of the authors' intentions or in terms of changing conditions in society, just as they will differ over whether the Bible should be interpreted in terms of the intentions of the writers or in terms of the modern world. What is at stake in the selection of a Supreme Court Justice is not whether a person can put aside his or her religion, but whether a person can satisfactorily interpret the words of the Constitution—whether in terms of the founders' intentions or in terms of contemporary considerations—when the implications of those words lead to moral positions different from those to which the interpreters' religious sensitivities have led.

It was this dilemma that led the Anabaptists of the sixteenth century to refuse to participate in secular government at any level. They believed that baptism into Christ was a total immersion of one's whole self. No part of one's life or being was outside the realm of Christ's Lordship. Thus, they refused to accept secular government office, refused to serve on juries, and refused to participate in the military. For following their convictions they were executed in large numbers by Catholics, Lutherans, and Calvinists alike. One may agree or disagree with the Anabaptists in their position, but on one thing they got it exactly right: there is no place in genuine faith for a sort of sophisticated jingoism.

November 6, 2005

MR. GONZALEZ, THE GOVERNMENT, AND THE POWERS

John Calvin somewhere wrote that the Scriptures are eye-glasses through which we get a correct vision of the world. I think Calvin was right. I long ago came to the conclusion that the people best able to keep a proper perspective and to keep their wits about them in the midst of national or international turmoil are those who view history through biblical eyes. I don't mean those who view specific events as fulfillment of certain biblical passages, as though the writers of those passages were pointing directly to our day. I mean people whose outlook and perspective have been so shaped by their digestion of the biblical perspective that this perspective provides their frame of reference for understanding past and contemporary history.

For example, take the Old Testament (or Hebrew Bible) book of Daniel, the New Testament book of Revelation, and the letters of the Apostle Paul. The author of the book of Daniel views all human governments as beastly creatures born of chaos and ruling by violence and intimidation. Only when the Kingdom of God comes will there be true order and genuine peace (Dan 7). The author of the book of Revelation portrays the Roman Empire as a beast with seven heads and ten horns—an embodiment of chaos, violence, and death—and gives us a new metaphor by which to understand all human governments—Babylon the Great, a city characterized by violence, corruption, and internal dissent and demanding absolute obedience to the government (Rev 13, 17–18). The Apostle Paul viewed human governments as institutions God has established for the sake of relative order and justice in the midst of a fallen world, but he also understood that sooner or later, all human governments become Babylon.

Both liberal and conservative Christians think that the way to solve the problems of the world is to elect the right leaders to public office. Both either miss or simply reject the insight of the biblical writers. And the Administrations most quickly vulnerable to this entrapment are those that assume that God has called them into office to influence the world. Very quickly, the assumption of influence gives way to the assumption of rule.

It is interesting to reflect on the current turmoil in the U.S. Department of Justice against this background. The Powers rule best when they can create confusion and distrust within—which suggests that at the moment the Powers must be having a field day.

May 20, 2007

IMPERIALISM

Imperialism assumes various guises. In its more obvious form it is supported by the iron fist of military power; but in its more subtle form, by the velvet glove of economic alliances. Imperialism can arise from a lust for power, land, or raw materials; or it can be born of a misguided, and consequently demonic, desire for human well-being.

Alexander the Great, leading his armies in his drive to impose Greek culture on the world, viewed this imposition as civilizing the world and thought he was doing the world a favor. The European settlers of this continent, at least those who were not bent on genocide, thought they were doing the original inhabitants (whom they called savages) a favor. Today, of course, there is much talk, in both political parties, of spreading democracy to the countries of the Middle East as a favor to the inhabitants of those countries.

The New Testament portrays God's relationship to the world in terms of God's kingdom, or God's empire, and sets that empire over against all earthly empires. In both the Old and the New Testaments, all human nations and empires are judged as being to some degree demonic and destined for the trash heap of history.

The New Testament views the church as having the responsibility of letting the world know that God's empire is now overcoming the entire Creation—that regardless of whether it seems to be true, Jesus Christ is the true Ruler of the Universe. The church, therefore, is not to align itself with any earthly empire, whether that empire be despotic or humane. The church and individual Christians should remember this any time the nation in which they reside calls for uncompromising support in imposing what it considers a better way of life on nations it considers unenlightened.

August 15, 2004

ON REPENTANCE AND BEING SORRY

A line from the 1970 movie *Love Story* said that love means never having to say you're sorry. Six years later, Merle Haggard recorded a song the title of which, though not written in response to the movie, was a good answer to that line: "It's All in the Movies."

The last few years have seen various groups and nations engaged in apologizing to some other group or nation that it has harmed in some way—sometimes recently, sometimes a century or more ago. *Rosh ha-Shanah* and *Yom Kippur*—the days in the Jewish calendar when the community is called to repentance and renewal—remind us that there are times when all nations, individuals, institutions, organizations, and movements should stop, reflect on what they have become, consider the need to apologize, and set a different course.

In the Bible *repentance* means simply to turn around, to make a new start. Though intense, subjective remorse may precede, accompany, or follow turning around, such remorse is not essential to repentance itself. That is, repentance does not require agonizing over what we have done, what we have not done, or what we have been. Turning around is the essential element. But I doubt that deciding a change is desirable would ever be without some regret and sorrow over past actions and attitudes.

What would happen in presidential campaigns if the candidates were to say to each other, "I'm sorry—I know I twisted your words and your records in order to score points in the campaign and make you look bad"?

What would happen if tobacco companies, when sued because of cigarette-caused cancer and death, were to say, "We're sorry—we know that we spent millions of dollars on advertising to manipulate you into thinking that cigarettes are not harmful to your health"?

What would happen if nations and movements were honestly to say to each other that they were sorry for past offenses or atrocities and were honestly to try to turn around for the future?

Repentance in the area of nuclear weapons would be the repenting nation eliminating its arsenals and dismantling the equipment for making the weapons without regard to whether any other nation did so. It is unthinkable that in a baptism service for several people in which, in response to the question "do you truly repent of your sins," each person pointed to the others and said, "I will if they will." Yet this is what nations do in every area of national and international life.

Unfortunately, children are robbed of their parents, are crippled, or die; old people are uprooted, assaulted, and murdered; and millions of people live on the economic fringes of life in cities both large and small, because nations, institutions, movements, and individuals think that simply being human means never having to say, "I'm sorry."

But Hag had it right—it's all in the movies.

September 19, 2004

FREEDOM, BONDAGE, AND THE IMPOSITION OF POWER

Human history is replete with efforts to maintain freedom by the imposition of power. This is why the opening chapters of the book of Genesis are such a profound commentary on human history. God, we are told, created the world by bringing order out of chaos. The struggle to maintain a just order in the face of chaos then became the struggle between good and evil. As long as the first human beings depended on God to determine good and evil and to hold back the chaos, they were free.

The trouble began when the human beings decided they wanted to determine good and evil for themselves—to impose their own order, rather than accept the order God had established. They ate from the tree of the knowledge of good and evil, and this cost them their freedom. From that point on, they would have to battle the soil for their food and struggle with the other animals. There also would be a struggle for power between the man and the woman themselves.

We see that struggle today when one person, one group, or one nation seeks to establish or maintain its own view of order by imposing its power on another—parents who push their children to succeed in areas in which the parents failed or were less successful than they had hoped, the replacement of military colonialism by economic colonialism, congressional struggles over judgeships, the shift from a desire to make the world safe for democracy to a determination to fill the whole world with democracies—and on the list could go.

Ironically, the assertion of power usually is rooted in the conviction by those asserting it that they are enforcing good and restricting evil. Often, they are under the illusion that their efforts are expressions of love for those over whom the power is asserted. Early European settlers on this continent assumed they were liberating Native Americans from savagery. Colonialists in Africa assumed the same thing with regard to native Africans. Christian missionaries on both continents assumed they were helping the people of those continents by converting them to European culture. Self-assumed sanctimony destroyed lives and cultures in the delusion of bringing salvation. Even the Holocaust was the result of the Nazis' desire to restore, in their love of their nation, what they were deluded into believing had been a pure German nation.

May 15, 2005

A TERRIBLE CONFIDENCE IN GOD

Anyone familiar with the biblical narratives of ancient Israel and Judah shouldn't be surprised by the state of today's political life. We have long lived on sanitized versions of figures such as Saul, David, and Solomon, but a closer look at the biblical narratives themselves reveals that these kings not only were capable of, but actually were guilty of, immense acts of wickedness.

- King Saul attempted to murder David.
- David's adultery with Bathsheba was not a matter of simple seduction, but was an act in which he used his royal status to impose himself in what can only be called an incident of rape.

- Achieving Uriah's death required also the deaths of several of Uriah's comrades.
- David then had Bathsheba's husband Uriah killed and took Bathsheba for his wife.
- Later, David's son Solomon enslaved many of his own subjects to accomplish his public works program.

But the main character in these narratives is neither Saul nor David nor Solomon. The main character is God. In the stories, God works through both the best and the worst of human actions for the eventual blessing of the entire world. So the biblical narrators do not flinch from the warts on the characters in their stories, for they are confident that no matter how ugly events might be, God is at work, using those events for God's own purposes—sometimes for mercy, sometimes for judgment. But before the blessing can be accomplished there frequently must come the crucible of judgment.

As the authoritative testimony to the word of God, the biblical narrative urges us to see our own history as one in which the God of Israel still is at work both for mercy and for judgment. I believe that God is at work, even in the most distasteful of current events, but that does not mean that I expect God to grant a future of ease, comfort, and cultural renewal without a prior day of judgment. When God used the deeds of Saul, David, and Solomon, the immediate purpose was judgment and destruction. It is not out of the question that God might be using the events of our own day to bring upon us, and upon all of western society, a judgment too harsh to imagine. Ultimately, God will reign as the one who has brought redemption to the entire Creation. But the suffering that we may have to go through before that completion is frightening indeed.

November 19, 2006

DENYING THE HOLOCAUST

The recent assertion by the President of Iran that the Holocaust never occurred was more than mere bravado by an enemy of the Jews. It was, rather, part of a carefully calculated scheme to deny the right of existence for the state of Israel. The President of Iran, along with others, claims that belief in the Holocaust was the reason that in 1947 the western world supported the creation of the State of Israel. Therefore, undermine belief in the Holocaust and you eliminate justification for the existence of the State of Israel.

In fact, the idea of a state of Israel blossomed in the middle of the nineteenth century. Ever since the fall of the Roman Empire, Jews had trickled into Palestine, and in the 1800's new impetus to that immigration came from the Zionist movement, whose goal was the establishment of a Jewish state. So many Jews then moved into Palestine from various parts of the world that shortly after World War I, the British, who were in charge of Palestine at the end of that war, came to believe that it would be necessary to divide Palestine into two states—one for the Jews and one for the Arabs. So the Holocaust simply gave dramatic support to an idea half a century old.

How are we to understand the Holocaust from a theological perspective? Centuries ago, according to the book of Genesis, God created Israel to be the instrument by which God would bless the entire world. The New Testament, however, speaks of transcendent beings that God also created, even before the events reported in the book of Genesis—transcendent Powers and Principalities who constantly seek to undermine God's work on behalf of the world.

The existence of the transcendent Powers is not open to objective demonstration, however, and what some would call the work of the Powers others can account for in other terms. But if we accept the New Testament witness, the Holocaust easily can be seen as a moment in which the transcendent Powers were arrayed in all their might to undermine the hope of the world by destroying at least one of the instruments of that hope—the Jewish wing of the People of God.

So when individuals or groups deny that that the Holocaust even took place, when they reduce it to just one of history's inevitable tragedies, or when they find some excuse to ignore it, then to that extent the transcendent Powers have won. And that, to borrow words from NPR's Scott Simon, is why we still need to remember.

January 22, 2007

2

Violence and Terror

THE WAR ON TERROR AND THE GOLDEN RULE

It frequently is observed that Jesus' words commonly called the Golden Rule—"Do unto others as you would have them do unto you"—have parallels in several other religions and cultures. The parallels in the teachings of Confucius, the Talmud, Hinduism, and Buddhism—in contrast to Jesus' words—are negative in wording, calling upon the hearer to exercise restraint. "What you would not want someone to do to you," the parallels go, "do not do to them."

The closest parallel to the positive form of Jesus' words is found in the *Hadith* of Islam. "No man is a true believer," says the *Hadith*, "unless he desires for his brother that which he desires for himself."

When Jesus counseled his followers to do unto others as they wished others to do unto them, he was speaking not about restraint, but about reaching out to others, doing for others, quite apart from what others do to or for you.

Perhaps there has never been a time when certain authorities needed more to consider the various forms of the Golden Rule than our own time with what is now commonly called the war on terrorism. President Bush seems to want—and some in Congress seem willing to grant—a rewriting of certain treaties, policies, and laws in order to make legal things already being done illegally. The President says that Article Three of the Geneva Conventions is so ambiguous that it must be interpreted, and he wants to interpret it in a way that will allow whatever action he considers necessary in the interrogation of prisoners.

Senators Graham, McCain, and Warner have insisted that the United States must be careful in its treatment of prisoners because the way we treat them will have an effect on how other nations treat U.S. prisoners. These senators, whether intentionally or not, are echoing what to most cultures has seemed plain common sense.

Since all nations are embodiments of the fallen, transcendent Powers and Principalities, it is impossible for any nation to behave in a truly Christian manner. It may be impossible for a nation even to be guided by Jesus' form of the Golden Rule. But being guided by the negative version of that rule is better than falling into barbarism, chaos, and eventual oblivion. And disciples of Jesus Christ have a special responsibility to warn both nations and persons in power in those nations that God will not forever abide unchecked brutality.

October 1, 2006

THROUGH THE CONGRESSIONAL LOOKING GLASS

In Lewis Carroll's *Through the Looking Glass* Humpty Dumpty boasts, "When I use a word, it means just what I choose it to mean, neither more nor less." This seems to be the Bush administration's approach to the question of torture. With the President persisting in his assertion that the United States does not torture, his nominee for Attorney General, Michael Mukasey, has refused to label waterboarding as torture, despite others having defined it as such on numerous occasions.

There are two types of waterboarding. In one, water is pumped directly into the stomach. In the other, water is forced into the mouth and throat, giving the sensation of drowning. Banned in most of Europe in the nineteenth century, waterboarding made a comeback in the twentieth century when it was used by several nations, including the United States.

Even as waterboarding made a comeback, it was widely regarded as illegal. A U.S. Army major was suspended from command and fined for using it during the Spanish-American War, and later, an Army Judge Advocate referred to it as torture, which the United States could not afford to sanction. After World War II certain Japanese military officials on trial for war crimes were charged with using water boarding, and in 1968, a U.S. soldier was court martialed for water boarding a captured Viet Namese soldier.

So it is easy to see why Judge Mukasey evades the question. A positive answer would render liable to international law everyone who has had a role in approving water boarding—including President Bush, as

Commander-in-Chief of the U.S. Armed Force. But to four retired Judge Advocates General—members of the judicial arm of the U.S. military—the answer is clear. In a letter to the Senate Judiciary Committee they wrote that "the relevant rule—the law—has long been clear: Waterboarding ... amounts to illegal torture in all circumstances."

In 2004, Daniel Levin, a senior official in the Justice Department, in evaluating different interrogation techniques, voluntarily underwent waterboarding and, according to ABC's 20/20, he concluded that it could be illegal torture unless carried out in a limited way and with close supervision. That, of course, is not an unqualified identification of the procedure as torture, but it certainly is grounds for caution.

Officials of the Administration now say that waterboarding has been used only three times—the last time in 2003 on Khalid Sheikh Mohammed, who, they say, after one and one-half minutes gave crucial information about terrorist activities. In fact, according to one member of the Administration, the practice has not been used since it was used on Khalid and Michael Hayden, and when Mukasey became CIA Director last year, he completely banned it.

Why, then, such a stonewalling by Judge Mukasey? Could he not say that it was the recognition that waterboarding is torture that led him to abandon it? Does he simply want to protect those who engaged in the practice on the three earlier occasions? Is he holding out for the possibility that it might be used again? Or is the President playing Humpty Dumpty and giving his own definition to "the United States does not use torture," while concealing a continuation of "extraordinary rendition" of prisoners to countries that are friendly to the U.S. and not averse to torture of any kind, waterboarding included?

There is no biblical basis for expecting any government to live by the teachings of either the Old or the New Testament. All human governments—including that of the United States—are secular institutions. Nevertheless, although in both the Old and the New Testaments God accepted warfare as inevitable in a fallen world, God still condemned excessive cruelty even in warfare. In the Old Testament God called prophets such as Amos to proclaim judgment on nations that violated international laws of decency in warfare. And in the New Testament book of Revelation God's destruction of Babylon is a parable of God's judgment on any and all nations that engage in unbridled violence and cruelty.

As heirs of the biblical people of God, the church and synagogue—and the individual members of both—have a responsibility to remind all nations and all government officials that they stand under the judgment of God and that there are limits to what is permissible even in warfare. To reject or ignore this responsibility is to have on our hands the blood of the victims.

November 7, 2007

VIOLENCE AND THE BIBLE, GOD AND US

The biblical narratives in which God calls for Israel to enact upon another nation some form or another of violence are bothersome to many people. And they should be. After all, people who take God seriously likely will try to live according to their understanding of God's will, and God's will is consistent with God's character. If God is understood to be violent, then it will be considered appropriate, when all else fails, to use violence to solve our problems.

Some people mistakenly assume that in the Old Testament God is a God of wrath and vengeance, but that in the New Testament he is a God of love and mercy. But one of the most common characteristics of God in the Old Testament is mercy and in some of Jesus' parables people are threatened with eternal fires of punishment. The fact is that in both Testaments, God is portrayed in terms of both wrath and mercy. The question is how to reconcile these.

The Old Testament begins with a story that seems to have been a deliberate attack on the idea that violence is basic to God's character or to the Creation. Genesis chapter 1 borrows several features from stories among Israel's neighbors telling how the gods created the world, and in all those other stories, the creation takes place through an act of violence. But the author of Genesis, while using that material, has stripped it of its violence and shows God creating simply by speaking, an act without violence. In Genesis 3–11, God acts violently on only one occasion—when he sends the flood—and afterward God says, in effect, "That didn't solve anything."[1]

The stories of the conquest, in which so many of the stories of violence are found, reached their present form before the Book of Genesis reached its present form. Were the transmitters of the conquest stories also bothered by the violence? This was the national history and tradition,

1. Compare Genesis 6:5–7 with Genesis 8:21–22.

and it could not be denied; but the stories could be placed in a redemptive perspective. The Pentateuch emphasizes the mercy of God and insists that despite the violence, Israel was created to serve not as a weapon of violence, but as God's instrument for the blessing of the entire world.

Leviticus insists that Israel is to be holy because God is holy (Lev 19:12), and *holy* means *different, not like other things in the same category*. Just as Israel's God is not like any other gods, Israel is not to be like any of the other nations. God's people are to be like God.

Usually, of course, people make their gods in their own image. So tell me about your God, and I'll tell you about yourself.

June 18, 2006

VIOLENCE, TERRORISM, AND RELIGION

In today's world fear dominates much of the landscape. And probably nothing is more destructive of life as God intended it than fear—fear of the enemy, fear of disease, fear of job loss, fear of the unknown, and even fear of God. Fear has long been used by adults to make children behave and by some Christians to try to scare sinners into repentance and conversion. Some parents or grandparents have told children that if they didn't behave "the old booger man" would get them.

One of the most famous sermons ever preached in this country was Jonathan Edwards' "Sinners in the Hands of an Angry God," preached in July, 1741, in Enfield, Connecticut. To those in the congregation whom he considered unconverted Edwards warned, "The God that holds you over the pit of hell, much as one holds a spider, or some loathsome insect over the fire, abhors you, and is dreadfully provoked: his wrath towards you burns like fire; he looks upon you as worthy of nothing else, but to be cast into the fire; he is of purer eyes than to bear to have you in his sight; you are ten thousand times more abominable in his eyes, than the most hateful venomous serpent is in ours."[2] According to reports, people trembled and wept, some fainted, and five hundred were converted by the sermon.

Some will point out, of course, that the Bible itself tells us that we should fear God. The Book of Proverbs says that fear of the LORD is the beginning of knowledge (Prov 1:7), and Jesus tells his disciples not to fear the one who can hurt them only physically, but to fear the one who has the

---

2. This sermon can be found in numerous places. A convenient internet location is the Christian Classics Ethereal Library, *www.ccel.org/e/edwards/sermons/sinners.html*.

power to destroy both their bodies and their souls (Matt 10:28). On the other hand, in both the Old and the New Testaments, when someone confronted by God responds in fear, God's first words often are, "Fear not."

The confusion comes from the Bible holding at least two different meanings of the word fear. One meaning is that of being terrified. It is the fear of calamity, death, or destruction. The other meaning is to stand in awe and amazement—open-mouthed astonishment—at God's mysterious and astounding work in the world and at the character (or nature) of God revealed by that work. Terror is an inward-looking, negative fear that you will be destroyed. Awe is a positive, outward-looking amazement at God's boundless love for the entire creation. Terror will cause us to attempt to destroy our enemies for the purpose of our own survival. Awe of God will lead us to seek our enemies' well-being, even at the cost of our own survival. It is terror of which the author of the First Epistle of John spoke when he wrote, "Perfect love drives out fear" (1 John 4:18).

In a time of terror, we make decisions that, often as not, come back to haunt us. It is a commonplace of political wisdom that laws made in rush and on the basis of fear usually turn out to be bad laws and lead to even worse conditions than the circumstances they were intended to remedy. Fear easily leads us to see the whole world as the enemy or the helper of the enemy. Put quite simply, living in fear puts us in danger of becoming our own worst enemy.

June 20, 2004

WARS OF RELIGION

As violence continues in the Middle East, the question occasionally arises as to whether the wars are wars of religion. "The terrorists are not concerned with religion," someone will say, "but with power."

But what is religion? In the ancient world, each nation had its own gods, and all of life was considered a concern of those gods. Even the laws of the nation were said to have come, in one way or another, from the gods. All of life—from the way you dealt with each other in the market place to the quality of the meat you sacrificed on the altar—was lived under the watchful eyes of the gods.

When any nation or group attempts to bring the entire world under the sway of its god or its gods, we have a profound expression of religion. If leaders such as Osama bin Laden seek personal power, it frequently is because they see themselves as having been divinely selected to assert that power in the service of their god.

When President Bush says that God called him to run for President of the United States and that his intention is to spread what he considers God's gift of freedom to all the world, we are dealing with religion.

When Jerry Falwell quotes the book of Esther to say that perhaps President Bush has been called to the kingdom for such a time, we are dealing with religion.

Many of this nation's secular and religious leaders support the President's foreign policy precisely because they believe it their religious duty to defend the nation against its enemies.

Of course we are seeing a war of religions.

I simply have a hard time thinking of Jesus dropping bombs that kill children and shooting, or even owning, an AK-47.

October 31, 2004

THE TRIAL OF SADDAM HUSSEIN

The trial of Saddam Hussein finally is underway. He is charged with crimes against humanity—specifically with the deaths of 148 men and teen-age boys in a Shiite town North of Baghdad in 1982. Many other specific charges will be brought in the months to come.

How should Christians react to this trial? How should the church view it? In light of the New Testament view that baptism into Christ should lead, by the transforming work of the Spirit, to a transformed mind (Rom 12:2 among other places), the question is not strange at all. Should Christians join much of the rest of the world in saying that justice finally is being done? Within the New Testament itself there are lines in some of Jesus' parables and in the book of Revelation that speak of the fiery punishment awaiting perpetrators of great wickedness against the poor, the weak, and the defenseless. And both the Old and the New Testaments portray God as the avenger of the victims of the wicked.

Often, what passes for justice is revenge in disguise. Perhaps that is one reason why Jesus—and Paul, referring to Jesus' teachings—warned that followers of Jesus are neither to seek revenge for ourselves nor to take up the role of avenger of others. Vengeance belongs to God alone.

We cannot forgive Saddam Hussein. That ability, too, rests only with God and with the victims. Our responsibility, as Jesus' disciples, is to seek the well-being of the enemy—to love and pray for the enemy. In fact, in the Old Testament, the Hebrew word translated *justice* actually refers to the condition that exists when chaos has been overcome by an order that benefits everyone.

Of course, the trial of Saddam Hussein will go on. He will be convicted and he may be executed. But for the Body of Christ that should be not an occasion for rejoicing, but an occasion for mourning—mourning over the self-destruction of this human being for whom Christ died, over the suffering and deaths of the thousands who died under his rule, and over those who continue to die because of the response of violence that his regime evoked.

Killing Saddam Hussein might bring revenge, but it would not bring justice. It simply would be another example of how a fallen world knows how to respond to death in only one way—with more death.

December 11, 2005

THE ARMENIAN GENOCIDE AND INTERNATIONAL HYPOCRISY

Until a few weeks ago, most people in this country probably had never heard the term "the Armenian genocide". Armenia, located on the northern borders of Turkey and Iran, became a state in the second century BCE In 301of the current era it became the first nation to declare Christianity its official religion. Eventually, it became a part of the (Muslim) Ottoman Empire, which controlled most of the eastern world and parts of Europe from the 1500s until the end of World War I.

Across the centuries, Muslim states have differed in their treatment of their Christian subjects, from toleration and inclusion to discrimination and oppression. The Ottoman Empire was one of the most despotic. In 1895, when major European nations insisted that Turkey change its way of dealing with Armenians, the Sultan responded by enacting pogroms that massacred approximately 200,000 Armenians. Some of the most prominent persons in U.S. cultural life—Mark Twain, Julia Ward Howe, William Lloyd Garrison, and Stephen Crane among them—organized rallies, raised money, and even traveled to Turkey in an effort to help the Armenians.

In 1908 the Sultan of Turkey was overthrown and there was an effort to return to a constitutional monarchy. The secular wing of the revolution accepted Armenians into the party and into government office, but in 1909 the military-oriented wing, supported by those who wanted to return to an Islamic government, seized power. Many of the followers of the military wing were less well off economically than many Armenians, and they also resented the inclusion of Christian Armenians into the government. When the Turkish economy began to falter, the Armenians were natural scapegoats. In the attacks that followed, between 15,000 and 20,000 Armenians were killed.

The major onslaught by the Turkish government came during World War I. Playing upon the established resentments of many Turks and upon Turkish fears of Armenian-Russian collusion, the government murdered approximately one million Armenians. All succeeding Turkish governments have insisted that those actions were protection against an internal threat and, thus, were not acts of genocide.

The word *genocide* was created in 1944 to describe Nazi policies at the heart of the Holocaust. It combines Greek and Latin words that together mean "death of a group". In 1948, the United Nations, in the Convention on the Prevention and Punishment of the Crime of Genocide, used the term as the starting point to declare genocide an international crime.

The Charter's definition, however, is so broad that it makes it difficult to say what would not be genocide. The definition includes not only "acts committed with intent to destroy . . . an entire national, ethnical, or religious group," but acts against even "part of" such a group. Acts so regarded are 1) killing members of the group; 2) causing them serious bodily or mental harm; 3) deliberately inflicting upon them conditions calculated to bring about physical destruction, in whole or in part; 4) imposing measures intended to prevent births within the group; or 5) forcibly transferring children of the group to another group. In terms of this definition, it is difficult to see how events in Rwanda, Bosnia, or Darfur or the Turks' actions against the Armenians could be seen as other than genocide.

When Speaker of the House Nancy Pelosi attempted to have Congress pass a bill declaring the Turkish actions of World War I to have been genocide, she was accused of using the issue to embarrass President Bush. Politics being what it is, the accusations may or may not have been correct. But the genocide issue is important for Armenia as a nation seeking to have its own view of its history vindicated, and Ms. Pelosi has consistently supported Armenian causes since her first year as a member of the House (1986). The Turks, of course, would view such a declaration as a blot on their history and as an admission that until now their government has been lying to the world. It also would open the door for Armenia to demand from Turkey untold reparations.

Ever since the administration of Woodrow Wilson, the United States has curried favor with Turkey, ignoring the plight of the Armenians because Turkey is viewed as crucial to U.S. interests in the East. So, as generally is true in international issues, human dignity takes a back seat to geopolitics. The Old Testament prophets, with their outrage over injustice and human sufferings caused by international power plays, would have a choice word or two to say.

November 26, 2007

3

Economics

ADAM SMITH, JOHN WESLEY, AND TODAY'S ECONOMIC PROBLEMS

IN 1776, THE YEAR in which the Declaration of Independence was written, Adam Smith published the first edition of *An Inquiry into the Nature and Causes of the Wealth of Nations*, the classic book on capitalism. The economies of Europe at the time were based on mercantilism, which assumed that a nation's wealth was measured by the amount of gold and silver it owned. These metals were to be acquired by a nation's exports exceeding its imports. Since a major element of help in acquiring this excess was a tariff on imports, trade increasingly came under government regulation. The desire of all nations to sell more than they bought led inevitably to gridlock.

Beginning in the eighteenth century, the Industrial Revolution made possible a more rapid production of goods. Whereas one might expect this to be of great benefit to a nation, since it would mean more goods to sell on the international market, in England city populations grew faster than jobs could be created, and the result was massive unemployment and poverty.

Bothered deeply by the plight of the poor, Adam Smith proposed what he considered a better system. Believing that much of the problem was excessive government intervention into the workings of the economy, he proposed what he described as a "laissez faire" (let it be) approach. In this approach the economy would be allowed to work itself out, with only occasional government intervention in cases of extreme necessity.

Smith believed that an invisible hand guides the economic life of nations and that individuals align themselves with that invisible hand by living according to self-interest. This view has been echoed in this country in recent weeks by those contending that the current economic situation does not present a crisis and that the government should take no action. The system, according to some, can and will correct itself if the government keeps hands off.

Smith's system is more complex than some of Smith's admirers and some of his critics are aware. For one thing, Smith would never have approved what became exaggerated individualism or corporate greed. And though he was not an enthusiastic supporter of charity, he believed that occasionally, charity could be exercised in such a way that being charitable would make people feel good about themselves, thereby enhancing the self-interest basic to the system.

Self-interest, however, proved to be less benevolent than Smith had assumed. Self-interest became greed, which resulted, within a century, in factories treating workers as expendable objects, producing even greater poverty, and setting the stage for the work of Karl Marx. (Ironically, Marx, too, believed that there is an invisible reality guiding history. He believed that history is guided toward an inevitable golden age by a built-in economic principle. Both Marx and Smith were sheer optimists, though Smith believed that government should keep hands off the movement of history, while Marx believed that those who understand the process have a responsibility to make government the means by which the future unfolds.)

From a theological perspective, the flaw in Smith's system should have been obvious at the outset. The New Testament views self-interest as a basic flaw that corrupts all human actions. The Apostle Paul called it *sarx*, which usually is translated *the flesh*, but which almost always means *self-interest*. As one writer put it, Smith transformed the vice of greed into the virtue of self-interest, the very heart of capitalism.

Also in 1776, John Wesley was at the peak of his vitality, leading the Methodist movement, which eventually produced the Methodist Church. Wesley and Adam Smith both were graduates of Oxford University, but they hardly could have differed more in their economic views. Wesley taught that everything we have, even our very self, belongs to God. We are mere stewards, said Wesley, servants entrusted with someone else's property. Therefore, he said, any money we have beyond what is required for our basic necessities and for the necessities of our families is to be used for the needs of others. God, he said, enabled us to gain the extra money for that very purpose. On the basis of this view, Wesley taught his followers: "Earn all you can, save all you can, give all you can."

Smith would have been in wholehearted agreement with "earn all you can." "Save all you can" would have received, at best, a lukewarm reception. But "give all you can," by completely rejecting self-interest, stabs at the very heart of Smith's approach. Unrestricted charity, according to Smith, gums up the works of the flow of history by opposing the invisible hand. (Smith never identified the invisible hand, but it hardly seems possible that by the term he meant anything other than God, though we can't be certain about much of the nature of God as Smith viewed God.)

Wesley frequently was distraught because so many of his followers were unwilling to follow these instructions. Were the world today to live by them, all traditional economic systems, including capitalism, would collapse from the strain. Even all Methodists, themselves alone, following Wesley's instructions would make a sizeable dent in the current economic condition. But seriously advocating those teachings for anyone would be considered kooky, perhaps even un-American.

October 16, 2008

SPECULATION, USURY, AND THE CURRENT FINANCIAL CRISIS

The language of finance can be as indecipherable as an unfamiliar, foreign language. Little wonder, then, that the financial news of the last couple of weeks has been so difficult to understand. In fact, the entire financial system has become so complex that even some experts do not fully comprehend it. I am no expert in economics, but recent reading in the basics of economics and finance has been enlightening.

Modern finance practices have become a game of chance—spell that *gambling*. To illustrate, suppose a hospital floats a bond issue through a bank for money for new construction. As an incentive for someone to buy the bonds, the hospital will pay interest on the purchase price, and the bank also will receive a percentage for its services.

Then suppose that the bond buyer wants to insure his or her investment in case the hospital defaults on the bonds. The buyer can do so by purchasing what the credit system calls a *credit default swap*, an inflated term that simply is a disguise for a type of insurance. The assumption is that if the hospital defaults on the bonds, those selling the insurance—the *credit default swap*—will be able to pay the bond holder what the hospital would have paid had it not defaulted. As in the case of ordinary insurance, everyone assumes that the total amount of claims the insuring agent might have to face from all its clients will be less than the total amount of money it takes in as premiums plus what it can make by investing those premiums. In fact, it is possible that the insurer will also take out insurance on its ability to pay its claims. Obviously, as lenders become borrowers in a spiraling chain, a vast network of creditors and debtors is created.

All this works out well as long as only a few people, institutions, or corporations default on their loans. But if a catastrophe requires the insurer to pay out more than it possesses, the insurer will have to either borrow money from yet another source or declare bankruptcy. In that case, the larger the institution, the greater the damage to the network if an institution cannot pay up. Moreover many institutions buy debts from other institutions in large bundles rather than as individual debts. Those who bundle the debts do so on the assumption that the ones who owe some of those debts will default on them (in other words, won't be able to pay their debts) and that if those bad debts are included in a bundle with good ones, the good ones will make up for the bad ones. The risk, however, is that the number of bad debts will outnumber the good ones, and if this does happen, those who have purchased the bundles will themselves not be able to pay the "bundler".

One further wrinkle is that not all the gamblers in the game, so to speak, are cool headed people simply trying to act responsibly with investors' money. There is a healthy (actually unhealthy) number who speculate for the purpose of excessive profit for their own benefit and some even who do so because of the psychological "rush" they get just by the stakes and chances of the game. They are, in effect, gambling addicts playing fast and loose with other people's money.

Further adding to the complexity is that borrowing no longer takes place within national borders, but has become international in scope. Many debts of institutions in this country are owned by institutions in Europe, Asia, and Africa, especially by institutions in China.

In vastly simplified terms, what we have seen the last two weeks is the bankruptcy and near bankruptcy of institutions that made loans on which they could not collect and of institutions that could not make good on insurance they had sold.

When the Federal government "bails out" several institutions, it does so on the assumption that the collapse of the system would do greater harm to everyone than will taking on the defaults. The government will itself have to borrow money to cover the institutions' defaults, however, and the only place to go—other than to another country—is to us, the taxpayers, through—you guessed it—taxes.

The government, therefore, also gambles. It gambles that helping the institutions will have a positive effect on the overall economy and that citizens can be taxed without nationwide bankruptcy.

Given the interlocking nature of institutions and the government, some economists are wondering whether some other institutions upon which the society is dependent might be facing financial crises not yet anticipated.

What it all boils down to is that the world's economy and financial institutions today are totally dependent upon *usury*—charging money for the use of money—a practice that in the western Middle Ages was considered a sin. The rationale underlying that designation was that you had a responsibility to help, without thought of gain, anyone in need. Islam today still rejects usury. Perhaps the world today cannot get by without usury. But perhaps also those medieval folk might have seen more clearly than we what money can do to a society when its acquisition becomes society's driving force.

October 23, 2008

BANKRUPTCY AND THE HELPLESS

I wonder how the prophets of ancient Israel would respond to the bankruptcy bill presently under consideration by Congress. The majority of bankruptcy claims in this country are filed not by chiselers trying to evade their debts, but by people trapped by financial difficulties beyond their control—most prominent among them being catastrophic medical bills, job loss because of jobs being moved to other countries, responsibility for ill or disabled family members, and identity theft.

At the time of these comments, amendments that would have exempted from the law persons with such inescapable problems have been rejected. On the other hand, in response to lobbyists for banks and credit card companies, corporations would receive lucrative breaks. Under that proposal individuals could have their assets stripped to the bone. Corporations could set up unlimited trust funds that the courts could not touch. In addition, an individual filing for bankruptcy would have to file in the jurisdiction in which he or she resided and take the luck of the draw as to the judge. Corporations, on the other hand, would be permitted to file in any jurisdiction in the nation and thus be able to search for lenient judges. The bill would place a hedge of restraint around the poor and a hedge of protection around corporations.

The prophet Amos pronounced woe upon such corruption in government and upon those who, in his words, "sell the needy ... for a pair of shoes ... and turn aside the way of the afflicted (Amos 2:6–7). It was no less a patriot than Thomas Jefferson who said that he feared for his nation when he considered that God is just. Sooner or later, a nation that operates on behalf of the rich and against the poor will incur the judgment of God. Who knows but what the problems faced by this nation today might be that judgment already coming to pass?

April 3, 2005

POVERTY AND WORK

Poverty and starvation continue to stalk the world. Children and adults with extended bellies and hollow stares are routine fare on the evening news. In comparison, even the homeless of this nation seem well-off.

It is appropriate to criticize governments and international corporations and institutions for financial arrangements that feather their own nests at the expense of the poor they pretend to help. But even if such collusions did not exist, money alone would not solve the problem of world poverty. Equally important are human hands.

Each year, hundreds of dentists, orthopedic surgeons, optometrists, nurses, and others of all sorts of occupations—as well as some persons with no special skills, but who go along and learn by doing—take time from their daily routines and, at their own expense, travel to places of the most horrendous conditions to bring healing and hope. The rest of the year these volunteers engage in their jobs, laboring for their own needs and luxuries. But during their time of volunteer service they engage in what approaches a biblical description of true work—labor on behalf of other persons. Adam and Eve did not labor in the Garden of Eden in order to have food. They labored to care for the garden because God had placed that responsibility on them. That labor was work as work was intended. They received fruit from the garden as a gift. After they rebelled, their labor was a struggle to get food. In a fallen world, our labor for our own needs and desires is not work, but is our job.

In such a world, those best in a position to work in a biblical sense are retired persons. Why should Christians regard retirement the way the secular world views it—as a time to play golf and take ocean cruises? Why should Christians spend their retirement income on such luxuries when for far less they could finance their expenses to some ailing part of the world as instruments of the mercy of God?

Perhaps such questions are naïve. But I recall that in a parable on one occasion Jesus represented God as saying, "In as much as you have done it unto the least of these my brethren, you have done it unto me" (Matt 25:40, modified from KJV).

March 20, 2005

ILLEGAL IMMIGRANTS THEN AND NOW

Most people in this nation seem to have very little sense of history. The issue of illegal immigrants is a vivid example. An editorial cartoon a couple of years ago portrayed a group of Native Americans watching the arrival of European ships. And one of them said to the others, "Well, there goes the neighborhood."

We either forget or ignore that most of this country once was inhabited by peoples from whom European settlers—ancestors of many of us—stole it, usually at gunpoint. By chicanery, murder, and broken treaties, settlers took the land and proclaimed a bold new experiment. Now, we want laws against people who simply want in on the experiment.

Although the nation's laws usually have been stacked against certain races, in theory the invitation of the nation always has been the words on the base of the Statue of Liberty: "Give me your tired, your poor, your huddled masses yearning to live free . . . . I lift my lamp beside the golden door." Now, some prefer: "Give me your workers with needed skills and abilities . . . . Otherwise, stay away from my door."

In December, 2005, the House passed a bill making illegal immigration a felony and penalizing anyone aiding an illegal alien. Had the Senate passed the bill, churches and individual Christians—to avoid violating the law—would have had to check a person's legal status before giving help. Obeying the biblical mandate of hospitality to the stranger would have required violating the law

Los Angeles Cardinal Roger Mahony, while acknowledging a nation's right to protect its borders, said that if the bill became law, he would instruct his priests to defy it. "Helping people in need," said the Cardinal, "is part of God's mercy."

While the Cardinal's courage is admirable, his acceptance of the belief that a nation has a *natural* right to protect its borders raises serious theological problems. According to the biblical writers, the entire earth belongs to God. Human beings are to be stewards—caretakers—of the earth on God's behalf. The concept of rights as the term is used today is a modern one growing out of the eighteenth century struggles for political liberty from absolute monarchs. The Bible knows nothing of rights, but only of gifts and responsibilities. Being responsible is viewed as carrying a blessing greater than any right ever could achieve. From this perspective, no individual and no nation has a natural right to private or sovereign ownership of one inch of the earth's soil, including the land on which it rests.

As for aliens in the land (the biblical term is *sojourner*), in the Old Testament, or Hebrew Bible, no distinction is made between them and Israelites, into whose hands the land has been entrusted. The protection assured to Israelites was to be assured also to the aliens. Old Testament law provided for the well being of immigrants unable to find work. The corners of the Israelites' fields were not to be harvested, but were to be left for the aliens, as well as for Israelite widows and orphans. Immigrants thus had a divinely ordained claim on a portion of Israelite crops.

Certainly, unlimited immigration can create problems for any nation. In fact, were the economy disrupted, the immigrants themselves would suffer. But the proper question is not how a nation is to exercise ownership of its land, but how it is to exercise stewardship for the poor and the powerless, including the immigrant. A nation is justified in controlling its borders only when open borders inhibit its ability to exercise its stewardship.

Christians and Jews have a biblical mandate, regardless of a nation's laws, to welcome and care for the sojourner—the immigrant, the alien. We also have a long, admirable history of ignoring laws that would thwart our biblical responsibility. It would not be the first time we have ignored what we have considered unjust laws. Martin Luther King, Jr. and the Berrigan brothers are vivid reminders of this responsibility. And although Christians and Jews have no right whatsoever to demand that a nation obey any biblical mandate, we do have a responsibility to remind any nation—this nation—of its own history, its own traditions, and its own ideals.[1] We have a responsibility to warn the nation of the consequences of losing sight of these or of casting them aside. In his address in front of the Lincoln Memorial, Martin Luther King, Jr. made powerful use of biblical imagery, but the heart of the address was not a call for the nation to act in a Christian way. It was a challenge for the nation to live up to its own proclaimed ideals.

Unfortunately, the debate over illegal immigrants seems likely to continue for some time. Crazy Horse, Geronimo, and Sitting Bull must be chuckling in their graves about the old neighborhood

January 24, 2008

---

1. On this see John Howard Yoder, *The Christian Witness to the State* (Scottdale: Herald Press, 2002).

4

Liturgical Seasons

SOME ADVENT REFLECTIONS ON AMOS AND TORTURE

IN THE OLD TESTAMENT, the prophet Amos proclaims God's condemnation of excessive violence in the world. Of course, you may say—as I do—that any violence is excessive, but Amos and the other Old Testament prophets and writers considered warfare and violence inevitable facts of life. Amos lived, as do we, in a fallen world, and in a fallen world violence is inescapable. But rather than ending violence by turning human beings into puppets, thereby robbing us of the responsibility of making decisions, God enters into this history and uses even its violence for God's own purposes of redemption.

There are limits, however, to what God will tolerate. According to Amos, God condemns treating the enemy inhumanely, selling into slavery soldiers captured in battle, using violence for national gain or revenge, ripping fetuses out of pregnant women, and mutilating the bodies of the dead. With regard to Israel itself, Amos speaks God's judgment upon those who achieve financial wealth at the expense of the poor (Amos 1–2).

I've been thinking about Amos a great deal lately—when I see and hear about the terrorists' violence against the citizens of Iraq, when I read about children in Africa being kidnapped and forced to become killers in conflicts they do not even understand, when I see pictures of U.S. military treatment of prisoners, when I hear of military prisoners taken to countries that promise not to use torture while we wink at those promises, when I hear the warped logic used by both civilian and military personnel to defend the use of torture, and when I hear the nation's president (who claims Jesus as the major influence in his life and who is a United

Methodist) say that we do not torture, but then threaten to veto a bill that would prohibit torture.

As we enter this season of Advent, anticipating that time when Jesus Christ will manifest himself as Ruler and the Judge of all the nations, perhaps we should reflect on Amos' prophecies. And perhaps we also should reflect on the prophet Malachi, whose words used to be read on the second Sunday of Advent: "(Oh yes,) the Lord whom you seek will suddenly come ... But who can endure the day of his coming, and who will be able to stand when he appears" (Malachi 3:1–2, author's translation)?

November 27, 2005

HEROD, THE SCIENTISTS, AND THE THEOLOGIANS

Over the centuries, most of us have come to ignore the political dimension of the Bible and to read it solely as a "spiritual" book. This is not to imply that the Bible is primarily a political book and not a spiritual one. But in the first century what we now call "politics" and "religion" were not two separate things. They were two dimensions of a single view of the world. By concentrating only on the "religious" meaning of biblical stories and ignoring their "political" dimension, therefore, we have robbed the scriptures of much of their original power and meaning. The story of the visit of the Wise Men to the recently born Jesus, in the Gospel of Matthew (Matt 2), is a case in point.

In the Greek text of Matthew's Gospel the word for the visitors usually translated *Wise Men* is *magi*, which means *astrologers*. In the ancient world, astrologers were the scientists in the field of astronomy. Until a few centuries ago, there also was no distinction between several fields that we now separate as science and superstition.

When constructing star charts, astrologers today still consider the time of a star's location in a particular part of the sky in order to interpret the star's implications for events on earth. The Greek text of Matthew usually translated, "We have seen his star in the East," more literally is translated, "We have seen his star at its rising (or at its ascending)." It is an astrological statement.

The star, therefore, had not been not an unusually bright one such as traditional descriptions portray, but an ordinary one noticed primarily by astrologers. The magi associated it with the nation of Judah, and something about its position in the sky indicated the birth of a new heir to the throne of Judah. Because the royal palace was the logical place to look for a new born Judean prince, the magi made the long journey across Mesopotamia to Jerusalem. Had they been following a moving star, they would have gone not to Jerusalem, but to Bethlehem.

The earliest readers of Matthew's narrative easily would have understood Herod's uneasiness over the astrologers' words. In his later years, Herod had been the object of several assassination attempts and had become so distrusting that he sentenced at least one of his wives and several of his own sons to death. Since he knew that none of his wives had recently given birth, the magi's declaration could mean only that a usurper to the throne had been born.

Earlier, as a young man destined for the throne, Herod probably had been educated to some degree in all areas of knowledge in order to understand his advisors in various fields, including astrology. He was able, therefore, to ask the magi what seemed a simple astrological question: "When did the star appear?"

What he really wanted to know was how far back he must go in ferreting out suspects.

Herod then asked the priests, in private, a question that would appear to be rooted in piety: "Where do the scriptures say the Messiah is to be born?"

Herod was not a pious man. His ancestors were not Judeans, but Edomites, a nation hated by many Judeans for events far back in Israel's history. Herod's father had been imposed upon Judah by the Romans. The priests might easily have assumed that his question reflected a sudden burst of piety.

"In Bethlehem of Judea," they replied.

The astrologers then set out for Bethlehem, following the information from the king's theologians. The star "went before them" in the sense that it had gone to Bethlehem some time earlier. Unfortunately, the New Revised Standard Version paraphrases this verse to indicate that the star led the magi, thus compounding the mistaken, traditional interpretation of the story.

Some may be bothered by this description of the magi's journey. But it in no way robs the story of miracle. The star still marks the birth of the Messiah and hangs over the house in Bethlehem. The analysis simply shows the role of the star to be different from the role traditionally described.

After separate conversations with the magi and the court theologians, Herod knew both the time frame and the geographic spot for his search. Soon, his military death squads would use this information for the extermination of all male Judean children two years of age and under. It was neither the first time nor the last that a sly head of state would use naïve religious leaders and scientists as his or her instruments for purposes of death

December 27, 2007

MIND YOUR MANNERS!

The debate over whether Christmas is under attack threatens to become as traditional a part of the season as the Super Bowl. Those who believe that it is under attack have been especially upset by the decision of some businesses to have their employees say not "Merry Christmas," but "Happy Holidays." Even President Bush has been criticized for sending cards with generic season greetings rather than Christmas greetings.

One of the claims of those upset by the generic greeting is that this nation began as a Christian nation. It is true, of course, that many of the first settlers were Christians who came for freedom of religion and that most of the colonies had official churches. But many other settlers came to escape poverty and debtors prison. Unfortunately, some of the colonialists who came for freedom of religion were as intolerant of the religious views of others as British officials had been of theirs. Some of the Puritans even made it a crime to celebrate Christmas.

Because of the experience of religious intolerance, both in England and in the colonies, the First Amendment to the Constitution prohibited any religion from defining the nation. Christians, Jews, and Muslims (then referred to as "Turks") were to be on equal footing. Once the Bill of Rights was ratified, it was no longer possible to speak of the republic as a Christian republic or nation.

Nevertheless, until fairly recently the dominant cultural influence in this country was white, Protestant Christianity. Businesses closed on Sunday—not on Saturday; high schools and colleges preceded graduation with religious ceremonies; federal, state, and local laws reflected Protestant ethics; and the Post Office and mail services still reflect this orientation. (The Post Office doesn't close for Passover or Rosh Hashanah.)

Over the last few decades, however, that consensus has begun to dissipate. The prohibition of Congress making any laws regarding religion, which has been interpreted ever more broadly over the years, has now been interpreted as implying that public officials—including school teachers—may not lead or prescribe religious ceremonies in the course of their official duties and that public property may not be used for religious ceremonies or activities as part of official school functions.

In that context, it is true that until recent Supreme Court decisions, there had been an increasingly effective effort to remove Christian symbols from public places. Christian symbols in public places reflect the power that Christianity has exercised over public affairs in a nation that, by the Constitution, is to be neutral in matters of religion. What we have been seeing is an effort not to destroy Christianity but to remove Christianity from illegally exercised positions of power in venues that properly belong to all the people, not primarily to Christians.

Most of the current heat initially was generated by the charge that the substitution of generic holiday greetings for Christmas greetings is part of a culture wide assault on Christianity. A major weapon in the arsenal of those making this charge has been an economic one: "Watch where you shop! Shop only with merchants who use explicitly Christian greetings!" Ironically, this effort embraces and promotes consumerism—a mind-set that not only has robbed Christmas of its true meaning, but has corrupted the very soul of the church itself. Although the words may be "Merry Christmas," the underlying message is "Merry Mammontide!"

As for the proper greeting, most of my Jewish friends are unperturbed by Christmas greetings. But why use their courtesy as an excuse for insensitivity by Christians? Moreover, there also are Muslims and Buddhists among us. Should freedom of religion mean that we are free to insult Muslims by wishing them a merry Christmas? The apostle Paul saw genuine freedom not as the right to do what I want to do, but the responsibility to seek the well-being of others. Self-indulgence is the opposite of freedom.

I grew up in a small southern town in which you were taught and were expected, whatever your age, to exercise good manners. Historically, one of the functions of manners is to be considerate of others. When I was about to go somewhere, my mother frequently would say, "Don't forget to mind your manners." That might not be a bad way this time of year to approach the whole issue of how to greet others. Mind your manners.

December 22, 2007

CHRISTMASTIDE VS. MAMMONTIDE

In the Sermon on the Mount Jesus warned that no one can serve two masters. But each December, we Christians convince ourselves that we really can. We talk and sing about Jesus, but we lay our money on the altar of Mammon.

Of course, many of us complain about the commercialization of Christmas, but similar to those who complain about the weather, few of us do anything about it. The problem is that we simply cannot escape the trap merely as individuals. Celebrating the birth of the Savior of the world is a community celebration, not an individualistic one, and going cold turkey as an individual in the face of the community's corruption of the season risks causing misunderstanding rather than bringing understanding. Abstention from all community celebration also can be rooted as much in self righteousness as in concern for the proper celebration of Jesus' birth.

I wonder what might happen if a congregation, a family, or a group of families were to decide not to jump to Christmas immediately after Halloween, but to concentrate on the two facets of Advent—a time of preparation for an appropriate celebration of the birth of Jesus and a time to reflect on the final triumph of Jesus Christ over all the Dark Forces that corrupt God's world.

I'm not suggesting that we, for example, give up gift giving. After all, giving gifts in celebration of the Gift of Jesus Christ to the world has been around much longer than modern consumerism. But four weeks of reflection during Advent might help us to give more reasonably and more sincerely—not on the basis of the latest fashions and fads, but on the basis of friendship and gratitude. Until we do so, we do not truly celebrate Christmas. We simply pay tribute to Mammon.

November 28, 2004

CHRISTMAS CAROLS: WHO WILL KNOW THEM?

This time of year, I become nostalgic for my childhood. I recall Christmas afternoons when my parents, my sister, and I would join with my father's brothers and sister and their families in my grandparents' parlor to sing Christmas carols. We would sing the ones we knew, and some that we really didn't know all that well, and then we would sing them again.

A number of years later I was shocked to find that the small congregation to which I had been appointed as part-time pastor didn't know any of the great Christmas songs. The thin paperback song book the congregation used for church services held only *Silent Night* and a couple of others. I reflected then, and I reflect now, on how fortunate I was to have grown up in a family and in a couple of congregations that sang the great Christmas songs.

I think about that often these days, when I reflect on the way so many Protestant churches have abandoned the youth and young adults and said them, "Okay, if you don't like traditional worship, go do your own thing. We'll even let you have your own worship service where you can do what you want to do."

We Protestants do a lousy job of bringing up our children and youth in the power and cohesiveness of genuine worship. And I wonder what that bodes for the great carols of Christmas.

Perhaps I exaggerate, but I attribute my own ability—meager as it is—to move through the smog of commercialism that passes for Christmas and keep my mind fixed on the manger, the holy family gathered 'round it, and the angels singing praise from Heaven, specifically to having been rooted in the great songs of Christmas that we used to sing in the church of my childhood and youth and to those Christmas afternoons around the piano in my grandparents' parlor. And I wonder (some, no doubt, would call me a pessimist): Will our grandchildren know the great carols? I don't mean will they hear them on the radio and over the intrusive sound system of the shopping mall and recognize their names. I mean: Will they *know* them?

December 19, 2004

HANUKKAH, VIOLENCE, AND FAITH

Those who reject violence as a means of solving problems will have ambivalent feelings about a holy season—Hanukkah—associated with violence and death, even in the name of political and religious liberty. And one may suspect, as I do, that the author of the Old Testament book of Daniel considered the rebellion that lay behind the origins of Hanukkah a great mistake.

Of course, not everyone—Jewish, Christian, or other—would agree with that interpretation of the book of Daniel or with that assessment of the Maccabean revolt. But even if one does agree, one still can celebrate Hanukkah and respect the courage and self-sacrifice of Mattathias, his sons, and all those who participated in the revolt. In the final analysis, the importance of Hanukkah does not lie in the bravery and sacrifice of the Maccabean warriors, but in its celebration of the faithfulness of God.

Even if it could be shown that Mattathias and his sons erred in their assumption that God wanted them to revolt, that would not undercut the significance of the oil of the rebuilt altar, which, according to the Talmud, although enough for only one day, burned miraculously for eight. The burning oil was a sign of God's presence even in the midst of violence.

When viewed from this perspective, Hanukkah has significance far beyond an eight-day period of gift giving. It has implications, for example, for the existence of the modern state of Israel. It suggests, among other things, that one need not agree with all, or even part, of modern Israel's foreign policy to see the existence of contemporary Israel as an expression of God's faithfulness to his promises. It would not be the first time that God has condescended to the human condition and manifested his faithfulness through people who, in their freedom, do not always do things quite the way God wishes.

December 5, 2004

ASHES OF REPENTANCE

This past Wednesday was Ash Wednesday, the beginning of the season of Lent, a season of self-examination, confession, and repentance. In both the Old and the New Testaments, repentance means turning around and going in a direction different from the one in which you have been traveling, or living. It is a time for prayer, fasting, self-denial, and concentration on the Scriptures. So Lent is a season not only for examining ourselves and confessing our sins to God, but for actually making changes in the way we live.

On Wednesday evening I attended an Ash Wednesday service, and I was struck by the contemporary overtones of the liturgy.

In a world that finds most of us speeding up more each day, a world in which the attention of span of children and youth has been decimated by the blitzkrieg nature of t-v programming, a world that demands instant gratification—we confessed our impatience.

In a world in which obesity is a national health problem and in which our computers and other electronic gadgets are obsolete almost before we take them from their boxes—we confessed our self-indulgent appetites.

In a world in which hundreds of thousands of men, women, and children suffer and die from poverty and its effects—we asked God to accept our repentance for our blindness to human need and suffering.

In a nation whose government has imprisoned, tortured, and in other ways dehumanized who knows how many men and women simply on suspicion of terrorist activity—we asked God to accept our repentance for our indifference to injustice and cruelty.

In a nation whose leaders consistently undercut efforts to protect the environment—we asked God to accept our repentance for our waste and our pollution of God's creation.

In a nation that persists in increasing the financial burden we are leaving our children and grandchildren—we asked God to accept our repentance for our lack of concern for those who come after us.

As we walked from the church, with the sign of the cross made with ashes on our foreheads, I wondered whether our words of confession and repentance would be lived out in efforts to do something about the conditions in the midst of which we prayed—or whether the remembrance of what we had confessed would vanish even before the ashes disappeared from our foreheads.

March 5, 2006

BELLS OF PEACE IN A TIME OF WAR

On Christmas Day in 1864, while the Civil War was ravaging the soul of the nation, Henry Wadsworth Longfellow, one of the nation's most popular poets, was suffering a personal crisis. Three years earlier, Longfellow's wife had died in a fire that also had damaged Longfellow's face so badly that he never again shaved, and in 1863 his oldest son had been badly wounded in battle.

Longfellow's diary entries for Christmas Day in 1861 and 1862 reveal a man of despair. For Christmas Day 1863, there is no entry. Then, on Christmas Day, 1864, Longfellow expressed his despair in a poem titled "Christmas Bells", a poem that was, in effect, a poem of protest, but that ended with a note of confidence that probably enabled him to write it. In 1872 John Baptiste Calkin removed the battle verses, rearranged the remaining ones, and set them to a tune he had composed earlier for a missionary song. Calkin changed the title to "I Heard the Bells on Christmas Day."

People under fifty years of age may be more familiar with the song as Bing Crosby recorded it in 1956, set to a tune by Johnny Marx, who earlier had written "Rudolph the Red Nosed Reindeer."

Here is the original poem, as it came from Longfellow's pen, with all its despair and hope.

> I heard the bells on Christmas day
> Their old familiar carols play,
> And wild and sweet the words repeat
> Of peace on earth, good will to men.
>
> I thought how, as the day had come,
> The belfries of all Christendom
> Had rolled along the unbroken song
> Of peace on earth, good will to men.
>
> Till ringing, singing on its way
> The world revolved from night to day,
> A voice, a chime, a chant sublime
> Of peace on earth, good will to men.
>
> Then from each black, accursed mouth
> The cannon thundered in the South,
> And with the sound the carols drowned
> Of peace on earth, good will to men.
>
> It was as if an earthquake rent
> The hearth-stones of a continent,
> And made forlorn, the households born
> Of peace on earth, good will to men.
>
> And in despair I bowed my head
> "There is no peace on earth," I said,
> "For hate is strong and mocks the song
> Of peace on earth, good will to men."
>
> Then pealed the bells more loud and deep:
> "God is not dead, nor doth He sleep;
> The wrong shall fail, the right prevail
> With peace on earth, good will to men."

December 4, 2005

THE GOSPEL ACCOUNTS OF THE RESURRECTION OF JESUS

The four Gospels, in their stories of the resurrected Jesus, agree on at least one point: the Jesus who confronted the disciples on the first Easter both was and was not the same Jesus they knew before his crucifixion. He was the same Jesus with whom they had walked thru Galilee and Judah, but he also was radically different. They could physically touch him, but he could pass through solid walls. His post-resurrection form was something completely new.

The Apostle Paul understood resurrection in essentially the same way. In a letter to the church at Corinth Paul described resurrection as a transformation of the whole person. Although Paul spoke of the completion of this transformation as something that takes place with the return of Jesus at some point in the future, he did not see it as completely in the future. It begins here and now, when we are bonded with Christ through baptism.[1]

In baptism we are bonded with Christ in his death so that our old self dies. But in baptism we also are joined with those people who make up the Body of Christ—the Assembly of God's People—upon whom God has sent the Holy Spirit as the agent who, at one level, begins our transformation here and now.

Wherever people are transformed by the power of God's Spirit from self-centered, alienated, destructive human beings into persons who give themselves over to reconciliation and peace with friend and enemy alike, there we see the power of resurrection breaking in here and now upon this world.

The resurrection of Jesus Christ took place in a small, obscure town on the fringe of the Roman Empire almost 2,000 years ago. But its effect continues today, and will continue throughout history, anywhere and everywhere that Death gives way to Life and violence and alienation are overcome by reconciliation.

Easter Sunday, 2004

PASSOVER AND EASTER

It may seem strange that a program produced by a Church related University would on Easter Sunday have as guest a rabbi to discuss the Jewish festival of Passover. I decided to do so for several reasons. For

---

1. Two relevant passages are 1 Cor 15 and 2 Cor 5:16–6:1.

one, all around the world this week, Jews are celebrating Passover. But for another, Christians must always be aware of our roots. Jesus was a Jew. The Apostle Paul, who pointed to Jesus as the doorway into Israel for the Gentile world, was a Jew. And in the words of Pope Pius XII, "We are all spiritual Semites."

But with this reminder also come a couple of warnings. In our efforts at ecumenical relationships between Christian and Jews, Christians must never expect Jews to agree with our self-proclaimed relation to ancient Israel. In fact, we should expect some Jews to be amused by or simply tolerant of our claim and others to be understandably affronted by it. But Christians must never pretend that we do not believe that Jesus is who we say we believe him to be, and Jews must never pretend that the belief is simply a curiosity to be ignored.

A second warning is that Christians must completely reject the view that since Jesus is—in our view—the messiah, Christianity has replaced Judaism as the people of God. This idea is called *supersessionism*. It is a pompous, egotistical belief on whose coffin Paul attempted to nail shut the lid in his letter to the church at Rome. But in some circles, unfortunately, it still holds sway. An assertion sometimes heard from supersessionist Christians is that Judaism is an incomplete, or unfinished, religion. But if we take Paul as our guide, Christianity too is incomplete. "Our knowing is imperfect and our prophesying is imperfect," Paul wrote to the church at Corinth, "but when the perfect comes, the imperfect will pass away" (1 Cor 13:9–10). And although someday we will see reality face to face, he wrote, we now see only dimly, as viewing a mere reflection in a mirror.

Easter Sunday speaks to all of this by its identity as the day on which God, by raising Jesus from the realm of the dead, opened a new order of existence for the Creation. Earlier, Passover, by liberating the Hebrews from Egypt, a land fixated on Death, not only liberated the people who eventually would become Israel, but also indicated that the God of Israel is the One who brings Life out of Death for the whole Creation.

April 8, 2007

5

The Church

AS THE CHURCH MOVES SOUTH

A LARGELY OVERLOOKED OCCURRENCE in the life of the Christian church today is the gradual shift of its population in nearly all denominations—Catholic, Protestant, and Free Churches alike—from the northern to the southern hemisphere. There now are more baptisms per year in the Philippines than in France, Spain, Italy and Poland combined. Nigeria now has more practicing Anglicans than any other country, including England, and for some time, Pentecostal churches have been the most rapidly growing churches in South America. By the middle of this century, if this trend continues, two-thirds of all Christians will live in the churches of Africa, Latin America, and Asia.

Although it would be foolhardy to predict precise consequences of this demographic shift, those consequences may be as significant as anything since the Protestant Reformation—or even since the split between the eastern and western churches in the early Middle Ages. For one thing, the churches of the southern hemisphere are generally more conservative than are those of the North. In the debate over the consecration of a gay man as bishop in the Episcopal Church in America, for example, whereas the Anglican churches of the north were sharply divided in their views, African churches were strongly united in their opposition. And the more traditional view on this matter dominates the churches of Asia and Latin America, as well.

Churches in the southern hemisphere also tend to assume a closer relationship between church and state than do most churches in the North. And it is especially important that in some instances, church growth in the southern hemisphere is in places where Islam also has a strong interest.

What are the long-range implications of this shift in church demographics? What are the implications for the future of Christian-Muslim relationships and consequent efforts toward world peace? What are its implications for the church's sense of its own identity? Perhaps the church might regain a sense of itself as a holy community guided and empowered by the Holy Spirit. On the other hand, it easily could repeat the error of the church in the northern hemisphere by becoming so interlocked with secular society that it loses all sense of its identity and calling.

I am willing to assume that the demographic shift might be God's way of purifying the universal church. But even if that be the case, it gives no more immunity to the seduction of secular power than was granted the church in the northern hemisphere.

March 19, 2006

THE CHURCH MOVES SOUTH

In 2004 the Anglican Archbishops of Africa urged the world-wide Anglican Communion to give the Episcopal Church in the United States three months to repent for consecrating as bishop a man living in a same-sex relationship. If the church did not repent, said the Archbishops, it should face disciplinary action.

It would be a mistake to view the Archbishops simply as discontented minor officials in what was once the colonial mission field, for, in fact, they are harbingers of things to come. Many observers predict that by the middle of this century, the majority of Christians in the world will not be in white, western churches in the northern hemisphere, but in the churches of Latin America, Asia and Africa. Philip Jenkins predicts that by the middle of this century only one Christian in five will be a non-Latino white person. Kinshasha, Buenos Aires, Addis Ababa, and Manila, he predicts, will have become the new focal points of the universal church.[1]

From a Catholic perspective, John L. Allen, Jr. has pointed out that in 1990, of the 266 million Catholics in the world, approximately 75% lived in Europe and North America. Now, only about one-third of the one and one-tenth billion Catholics, live on those continents. The rest live in Latin America, Africa, and Asia. On the other hand, as Allen points out, sixty-

---

1. Jenkins deals with this extensively in *The Next Christendom: The Coming of Global Christianity*, Revised edition (New York: Oxford University Press, 2007) and in *The New Faces of Christianity: Believing the Bible in the Global South*, same publisher, 2006.

three percent of the College of Cardinals eligible to vote for pope are from Europe and the United States. In other words, the greatest political power lies in those areas of the world with the smallest number of Catholics.[2]

The issue is not who holds political power in a secular sense, but whether those with authority are sensitive to the perspective, needs, and problems of those who make up the church's body. People's perspectives and attitudes are heavily influenced by their social environment. Those raised in privilege and prosperity experience the world differently from those raised in poverty, in a minority group, or under subjugation. Thus, the concentration of power in the hands of a minority in any group robs that group of much of its vitality—and certainly of justice.

Jenkins describes the churches of the "global South"—those in Latin America, Asia, and Africa—as primarily biblically oriented, but as not necessarily reading the Bible the way Christians in the "global North" (meaning all of us) read it. On the other hand, neither do all southern churches read it the same way. Whereas some southern interpretations of the Bible sound much like the interpretations of Fundamentalists in this country, others have produced movements of political reform and liberation of the poor. Moreover, although many Church leaders in Africa take the side of U.S. churches that reject full inclusion of homosexuals into the life of the church, they nevertheless view the issue as of minor importance in the face of the human suffering from poverty, hunger, and AIDS that plagues their churches. And as for Pentecostals, the fastest growing churches in South America today, it would be a mistake automatically to assume that Pentecostals in South America are carbon copies or clones of Pentecostals in the United States.

One of the strengths of, but also one of the great dangers for, the Christian gospel has been its ability to embody itself in the cultural elements of the societies in which it has found itself. This ability makes it understandable to and relevant for the culture. The danger is that those who proclaim the gospel will conclude that the cultural elements are a part of the gospel itself. Liberal western Christians easily assume that the latest western cultural trends reflect new enlightenment and new insight into the gospel. Conservative Christians just as easily assume that by defending traditional cultural values they are safeguarding the eternal gospel. If and when world Christianity comes to be dominated by the churches of

---

2. In a public lecture in 2006.

the global South, those churches too may come to equate their cultural ways with the gospel. If that happens, then those churches will have made the same mistake the church in the fourth century made when it identified the gospel with the Roman Empire and created the first *Christendom*. If and when that day comes, a line from the opera *Porgy and Bess* might commend itself to liberal and conservative, northern and southern Christians alike; in the words of Sportin' Life: "It Ain't Necessarily So."

October 29, 2007

THE GOSPEL AND SOCIETY

Whenever a Christian denomination takes on social issues, whether the denomination is conservative or liberal, it faces the question of how to deal with issues without falling into the trap of legalism. In other words, how does the church, or a church, proclaim the Christian message in the social and political arena without sounding as though it is trying to force society to live by Christian rules and regulations?

Basically, the question boils down to whether, with regard to society, the Christian message *is* one of rules and regulations. Many Christians, both conservatives and liberals, often seem to assume that the answer is *yes*. Their message often seems to boil down to: "Society shouldn't be this way because this way is unchristian, or at least immoral from a Christian perspective."

The New Testament message begins at a different point. It begins not with demands, but with a proclamation that is, in effect, a promise. It begins with the proclamation that in the death and resurrection of Jesus, God has acted to free the entire Creation from alienation from God, from self-interest, and from self-destructive ways of living. With regard to racism, for example, the message of the New Testament is not that people shouldn't be racist, but that in Jesus Christ God offers liberation from racism. It is as though God were saying to the world: "You don't have to be self-destructive. I am making it possible for you to be set free from your self-destructive ways of living." And that promise is to be proclaimed both to individuals and to institutions.

When a local group of Christian clergy a few years worked on a statement opposing the death penalty, a major question was how to word the statement so it would not sound as though we were saying that the state should not impose capital punishment because it is unchristian to do so. The solution was to proclaim that because of the renewal of the world that comes in the death and resurrection of Jesus Christ, we do not have to kill and to point out that capital punishment does not bring the victims back to life. We closed the statement with the familiar plea: Do not kill in our name.

The catch is that if the church, in the way it lives within and in its relation to the society around it, doesn't manifest this freedom, the promise will be heard as a lie. So we're not just speaking of the church uttering words. To have an authentic message to the world, the church, to borrow an expression, must not just "talk the talk," but must also "walk the walk." The church must show the world by its own day-by-day demeanor what it means to be truly free.

August 8, 2004

FEMINIZING THE CHURCH OR HUMANIZING IT?

Recently, the popular comic strip *Zits* dealt with the determination of Hector, a friend of the main character, Jeremy, to overcome the reputation of being a good boy. When Jeremy told Hector that people saw him as dependable, compassionate, and having high moral standards, Hector complained that he was every girl's mother's dream—to which Jeremy replied that a good reputation is hard to overcome.

The creator of *Zits*, was exploring a theme prominent in some circles for a decade and a half—the theme of men regaining their masculinity. In his book *Wild at Heart*, John Eldredge describes masculinity in terms of the warrior, glorifying the wilderness over against the orderly life of civilization. Just as do Jeremy and Hector in *Zits*, Eldredge sees being a nice guy as not truly masculine. To do things out of a sense of duty, he says, is to be separated from the masculine heart.

"Little boys," writes Eldredge, "yearn to know they are powerful, dangerous, (and) ... someone to be reckoned with...." "Aggression," he writes, "is part of the masculine design; we are hard wired for it." "(If) a mother will not allow her son to become dangerous...." he later writes, "she will emasculate him."

Eldredge is not alone in this view of the male persona. A recent television segment on the feminization of the church featured men in combat fatigues, organized according to military orders, engaging in "exciting" activities in the woods. It is not surprising, therefore, that Eldredge describes Jesus in heroic terms—describing Jesus' driving the money changers from the Temple as a model of Christian masculinity. One trembles to recall that during World War II, this was precisely the description of Jesus emphasized by the Nazi supporting German Christians on the basis of this passage among others.

Several writers who agree with the charge of feminization of the church do not view it as a recent development, but trace it to the early 1800s and the beginning of the industrial revolution. When men had to move away to find jobs, running the church, so the argument goes, was left to women. Others point out that even in the Middle Ages writers complained of the feminization of the church.

Of course, the critics are correct about the male tendency toward aggression and the desire for adventure and danger, but the New Testament views a tendency toward aggression as the condition not only of men, but of women as well because of the fallen condition of the Creation. The church, therefore, must not ignore this condition. But neither should it provide opportunities to express that condition in order to attract or hold members. In other words, the church must not baptize an expression of sin. The church was created to be God's means of grace for the transformation of men and women into human beings who live and die on behalf of others, not to be a community using sin as a sales gimmick.

Life lived sacrificially on behalf of others is likely to be both adventurous and dangerous, but not in the way that Eldredge and those who share his view desire. Among the primary characteristics of the genuine Christian, according to the New Testament, are humility, patience, kindness, gentleness, forgiveness, and love of the enemy.[3] The masculinity movement sees these as feminine qualities that emasculate real men. The New Testament sees them as gifts of the Holy Spirit that make us truly human. Let Christians in the United States begin to love their enemies, especially when those enemies are enemies of the United States, and they will learn just how adventuresome, challenging, and dangerous the Christian life can be.

I would have been much more impressed by those white, middle class men in the television segment had they pooled their adventure money to send one or two from their group to help protect the victims of the camel riding Janjaweed in Darfur, to minister to the thousands of children or-

---

3. I need mention only the Sermon on the Mount and the Letter to the Galatians as sources for this description.

phaned by AIDS—children who are themselves HIV positive—in other parts of Africa, or to minister to children dying of starvation in Africa and Asia or dying from poisonous products dumped there by United States companies. Talk about danger!

As for the story of Jesus in the temple, Eldredge either does not know or ignores that Jesus' actions on this occasion were a prophetic sign. In the Bible, prophetic actions are not repeated by the prophet, are never understood as heroic, and are never intended as models for imitation. They set into motion events that lead to fulfillment of what they prophesy.

With regard to traditional male-female stereotypes, many Christians—and persons other than Christians—frequently are surprised to learn that the Bible actually challenges many of those stereotypes. For example, one of the words most often associated with God in both the Old and the New Testaments—*mercy*—translates a Hebrew word that refers to a woman's womb. As merciful, God treats us as a mother is expected to treat her child. Jesus' words, "Blessed are the merciful," though written in Greek, were spoken in Aramaic (a close cousin language to Hebrew) and indicate that whether we are male or female, we are to deal with others as though we were their mother.

Perhaps those who criticize the church for not offering men opportunities for aggression, challenge, and danger as they define these should take to heart the words of the Apostle Paul: "When I was a child, I spoke like a child, I thought like a child, and I reasoned like a child. When I became a man, I gave up childish ways" (1 Cor 13:11).

May 13, 2007

WORSHIP VS. ENTERTAINMENT

In many churches today, controversies over styles of worship are as heated as debates over homosexuality. It sometimes seems easier to find a church that attempts to entertain than one concerned with worship.

Genuine worship involves drama. In fact, in most ancient cultures worship began as drama. The ceremony acted out—sometimes symbolically, sometimes quite graphically—events central to the culture's relationship to God or to the gods. In genuine worship this still is true, but it is important to be clear as to who is the audience and who are the actors.

The nineteenth century philosopher and theologian Soren Kierkegaard contended that in genuine worship God is the audience, the congregation is the actors, and the minister and choir are the prompters. Many congregations today seem to view themselves as the audience and the clergy and the choir as the actors. With this understanding, worship easily gives way to entertainment. Many churches today seem to think they must entertain in order to attract people, or potential customers.

When entertainment replaces worship, the guiding principles of the congregation become principles of consumerism. The gospel is perceived as a product to be sold. The way in which the message is delivered, rather than the message itself, becomes vital. The elements of the program must be made attractive. The music need not be a means of worship, but may be a means of attracting customers. The sermon must soothe, give practical advice, or motivate. It is not surprising that some of the most popular televangelists today (such as Joel O'Steen, Creflow Dollar, and Joyce Meyer) are essentially motivational speakers. To modify an expression from Marshall McLuhan, the medium has become the message,[4] and, as a result, the gospel message is lost.

A major point of contention in the worship debates is the music. Controversy over music in the church, however, is nothing new. When the organ was introduced in the sixth century to indicate the entrance of the Pope, many objected that it was a secular instrument, since it traditionally was used in the Emperor's court to announce the entrance of some personage of royalty. Only after several centuries did the organ come to be regarded as the basic instrument for worship. Ironically, practitioners of contemporary worship today reject the organ as being too stodgy.

The introduction of the violin into worship in eighteenth century France also was protested because it was a secular instrument used for dancing, and many traditionalists today object to guitars and drums, precisely because they are considered secular instruments.

As for songs, as late as the 1950s some denominations refused to allow anything except Psalms into their hymnals. Some people object to certain songs as too new and call for "the old songs," not realizing that what they call new songs are from the third and fourth centuries and that what they consider old songs are from the 1800s and early 1900s.

---

4. *The Medium is the Massage* was first published in 1967, but is still available from Gingko Press, 5768 Paradise Drive, Suite J, Corte Madera, CA 94925. A more thorough treatment of the subject is in Marshall McLuhan, *Understanding Media: The Extension of Man* (New York: New American Library, 1964).

In the eighteenth century John Wesley set some of his and of his brother Charles's hymns to drinking songs, saying that the Devil shouldn't have all the good tunes. It should be noted, however, that Wesley spoke of *good* tunes and that the tunes were so familiar to the masses that they were excellent means of both worship and instruction. Many church folk in the nineteenth century objected to songs such as "Just as I Am" because they were considered too sentimental.

One of the ironies of the contemporary controversy is that both groups seem basically to want the same thing - music that evokes a feeling. The traditionalists want a feeling of repose, nostalgia, or both, and those espousing "contemporary" music want a feeling either of exuberance or of wistfulness. It is assumed that if the customer doesn't "feel" something, nothing has happened.

I do not mean to imply that feelings should be of no concern in worship. Worship devoid of all feeling would not for long be genuine worship. The question is what kind of feeling is being sought. From a biblical perspective, worship should celebrate the sovereignty of God in Jesus Christ over nations and empires and over the entire Creation. The proper "feelings" for that celebration are awe, wonder, thanksgiving, humility, and devotion.

In the final analysis, however, as important as feelings may be in worship, the real test is not whether members of the congregation always feel something, but whether by the prayers, hymns, and liturgy God is praised and glorified by the congregation as a whole. The music of much so-called contemporary worship (as well as much of the music of traditional revivalism) predominantly uses first person singular pronouns—"I," "me," and "my." Of course, the book of Psalms also contains many psalms that use the first person pronoun. The dominant mood of the Psalter, however, is expressed in plural pronouns—"we," "us," "our," and the first person pronouns were intended for a people conscious of being part of a community, not self-indulgent individuals.

When worship gives way to entertainment, the choir gives way to vocal solos, duets, trios, and ensembles. The music, rather than aiding the congregation's efforts toward adoration and praise of God for what God has done in and for the world, becomes performance to be applauded. Vocalists and instrumentalists stand facing the congregation as performers, and recorded music often replaces live musicians, because the quality of the music must be such as to attract customers.

In the New Testament the Christian gospel (a word that means "good news") attracted people because of its content. The good news was: "The kingdom of God is at hand; repent and believe in the gospel" (Mark 1:15b)! In words of our day that meant: "God is now asserting God's sovereign reign over the Creation! Turn around, believe the news, and embrace God's reign!" The resurrected and transformed Jesus was proclaimed as Lord of the Creation on God's behalf. It was a message more like newspaper headlines announcing the end of World War II than like a phone call from a sweetheart asking for a date. It was not instruction in how to have an experience, but the proclamation that the Creation was being liberated from the self-centeredness, corruption, and death imposed upon it by the heavenly opponents of God. Worship was a weekly gathering of the community that had embraced the message, a gathering to praise and thank God and to celebrate the Lord's Supper.

Kierkegaard was right. Worship is drama, drama enacted by the congregation before God. What often passes for worship today not only is not good worship; it isn't even good theater.

October 18, 2007

ON ATTEMPTING TO LEGISLATE THE SPIRIT

The United Methodist Church continues to be embroiled in a dispute over whether to ordain someone who is what the Book of Discipline calls a "practicing homosexual." At the present time, a homosexual person may be ordained in the United Methodist Church only if that person commits to a life of chastity.

Those who oppose the church's position argue that the position itself is unchristian, that it flies in the face of the church's emphasis on openness and tolerance, and that it should be overturned. In fact, they seem to believe that until the rule is changed, it should be ignored. On the other hand, those who agree with the church's position contend that it is homosexuality, not the church's rule, that is unchristian.

In its debate, perhaps the church should consider two largely overlooked elements in the theology of the Apostle Paul. Paul believed that to enable the church to function effectively, God gives to Christians individual gifts of the Spirit, or individual abilities. One of those abilities, according to Paul, is chastity—the ability to live without the need for a sexual partner. Why God gives some gifts to certain persons and other gifts to other persons is never mentioned, but Paul never indicates that one gift automatically is accompanied by another.

Perhaps we should debate whether a call to ministry automatically carries the gift of chastity. Methodism has never said that it does. And then we might debate whether God ever calls a homosexual person into the ministry of the church. Some, likely, would say *no*, but not all would agree. And if it we allow the possibility that God might call certain homosexual individuals into ministry, does God automatically confer, along with that call, the gift of chastity?

The other element of Paul's theology that we should consider is his insistence that the church is to live not by law, but by the guidance of the Holy Spirit. As Bishop Ken Carder frequently has observed, we get ourselves into some of our dilemmas by attempting to legislate the answers to our questions. In fact, the deeper we dig our hole, the more we try to legislate our way out.

A greater consideration of Paul in these matters would not automatically answer the questions that now plague us, but it certainly would place them in a more biblical context. And the failure to be more thoroughly biblical in our considerations may be the greatest sin of all.

November 20, 2005

OF SLOGANS AND SUBSTANCE

A year or so ago, the Rev. Ed Johnson, a pastor in the Virginia Conference of the United Methodist Church, refused to receive into membership a person who admitted to being actively homosexual. Mr. Johnson assumed that as senior pastor of the congregation, he had the responsibility to determine when a person is ready for membership.

The Virginia Annual Conference said that Mr. Johnson had acted without authority and placed him on one-year involuntary leave. The Judicial Council of the United Methodist Church then ruled in favor of Mr. Johnson and voided the Conference action. Despite appeals by numerous persons and groups, including a number of United Methodist Bishops, who argued that Mr. Johnson had acted without authority, the Council, in April of this year, refused to reconsider its decision.

Far too many of the debates over the issue have been between legalists, on the one hand, and sloganeers, on the other. The legalists have argued over whether certain passages of the church's law book, the *Book of Discipline*—passages that do not mention homosexuality—are to be connected so as to authorize a pastor, rather than the person seeking membership, to determine when a person is ready for membership.

The sloganeers cite as a basis for church membership the words of the church's multimillion dollar advertising campaign, "Open Hearts, Open Doors, Open Minds." That slogan might have been a welcome source of liberation in a time of heartlessly enforced dogma and church rules, but in an age in which "anything goes" it easily can be heard as an affirmation of the old accusation that one advantage to being a Methodist is that you don't have to believe anything.

The problem with legalism is that it usually seems to have no heart, to have a mind unable to comprehend of shades of gray, and not to care that doors too tightly shut are difficult to reopen. The problem with sloganeering is that it equates the heart with sentimentality, open-mindedness with an absence of critical thinking, and closed doors with isolation and insulation from what is outside.

And as the battle goes on, the more difficult approach of consensus, which seeks to place compassion in a context of order and law in a context of mercy, takes a back seat. And the Body of Christ loses its veracity, its viability, and, consequently, its witness.

June 4, 2006

TO OUR SHAME

The war in Iraq continues, with its ever mounting toll of military and civilian casualties; Palestinian factions Hamas and Al-Fata war among themselves; Iran and North Korea seem determined to develop nuclear weapons; and the reduced size of weaponry now makes it possible for an individual to carry an automatic rocket launcher capable of bringing down a plane in flight.

Just under two decades ago, there was hope that the major powers' steps toward nuclear disarmament might lead eventually to a world safe from a nuclear holocaust. What few people anticipated was the spread of nuclear weapons among smaller nations hostile to the west, especially to the United States, and with centuries old hostility among themselves. We may now be at the beginning of an era in which not only small nations, but small groups, will acquire nuclear weapons and that the world will once again be in danger of mass nuclear destruction.

In the midst of such a world the church is called to be salt and light. "Blessed are the peacemakers," said Jesus, "for they shall be called God's children" (Matt 5:9, author's translation). And he told his disciples that to be his followers required loving their enemies.

Some try to get around these instructions by saying that Jesus was speaking of how individuals should relate to each other, not to how the church is expected to act toward enemies of the nation in which it finds itself. But Jesus was addressing the disciples as the beginning of the church, and he made no distinction as to how Christians are to act toward persons inside and persons outside the church.

It is striking that churches are able to organize effectively to fight against abortion or against the acceptance of homosexuals as members of the clergy, but are either unable or unwilling to organize for peace making. Basically, this is because we usually assume that the nation's enemies are the church's enemies and that if a nation's leaders say war is necessary, the church must, in effect, say "Praise the Lord and pass the ammunition." Officials in the United Methodist, Presbyterian, Baptist, Lutheran, and Catholic churches then call into play the just war theory with the disclaimer, "We are not and never have been a *peace church*," which means a church such as the Mennonites and the Quakers that have traditionally refused to participate in war. To which, it seems to me, the most appropriate answer is, "Then shame on us."

July 1, 2007

TROUBLE OF OUR OWN MAKING

For the last year or so, a controversy has been raging over whether U.S. military chaplains are free to use the name of Jesus in their public prayers. Last year, a chaplain at the United States Air Force Academy charged that some Christian chaplains at the Academy had been exerting undue pressure on some cadets, attempting to convert or proselytize them. In response, a set of interim guidelines was released regarding freedom of speech and freedom of religion at the Academy. The guidelines affirm the Constitution's freedom of religion "excepting when military necessity may lead to some constraint on individual rights . . . ."

Some critics of the guidelines charge that they represent a disguised attack on free speech, on Christian chaplains as such, and on the right to pray according to one's faith. If one reads the guidelines carefully, however, those charges fall apart. The guidelines do require that prayers or presentations in official, formal settings be non-sectarian, but outside those settings, restrictions are placed on expressions of specific faith traditions only if those expressions create disunity or otherwise interfere with military purposes.

What should be of great concern to Christians is that the Academy guidelines stipulate that "free exercise of religion and other personal beliefs, as well as freedom of expression (are to) be limited by military necessity." In other words, a military chaplain is faced with two masters—Christ and Caesar. Jesus warned that no one can serve two masters and that any attempt to do so will result only in loving one and hating the other. The only way to avoid that dilemma is to reject one of the masters. As for who would minister to the men and women in military service if there were no chaplains, it should be pointed out that not only did the first century church not have chaplains in the Roman Legions; it did not permit its members to participate in any part of the military. Some groups today—having taken seriously Jesus' words about not being able to serve two masters—follow the same prohibition. Those of us who are aggrieved by the Academy's guidelines created the problem in the first place when we thought that we knew better than Jesus.

January 29, 2006

ON BRINGING THE CHURCH INTO THE MODERN WORLD

In anticipation of the selection of a successor to Pope John Paul II, some said that the church needs someone who will bring it into the modern world. Usually, this meant someone who would approve abortion, artificial birth control, divorce, and the ordination of women.

While each of these issues is a legitimate topic for debate on biblical grounds, in my own view, John Paul II was correct in his position on abortion, he had some sound theological insights that we should not lightly cast aside with regard to birth control and divorce, and in the matter of ordination of women, simply was wrong. But I hold these opinions on the basis of my understanding of the Bible. The assumption that the church should bring its views of right and wrong into harmony with the world has time and again led the church into deep trouble.

The biblical writers viewed the world as a realm of idolatry, darkness, and Death. This does not mean that the church should ignore or reject the world. On the contrary, because God loves the world, fallen as it is, God established the church to be God's instrument for blessing the world, to bear witness to God's redeeming, transforming work in the world, whenever and wherever God gives it the grace to see that work. But a clear perception of God's activity in the world also will give the church sound reasons for opposing certain trends and habits of the world.

When the church opposes the world, it will anger some inside and outside the church. But if the church looks to the world for signals as to what it should be and do, it will find itself irrelevant for the world, for it will have nothing distinctive to say. Consequently, when the world finds itself desperately in need of a word of truth, the church will be of no help whatsoever.

April 24, 2005

THE CHURCHES AND GENOCIDE

The recently ended twentieth century might easily be called the century of unopposed efforts at genocide. In 1915 the Turkish government attempted to eliminate the Armenians, and the world watched. In the 1930s and '40s, World War 2 was not fought to protect Jews and other victims of the Holocaust, even though high government officials in several nations, including the United States, knew of the horrors taking place, but it was fought to help European Gentile nations resist German aggression. In the 1990s Serbians slaughtered Muslim populations in the former Yugoslavia and Hutus attempted to eradicate Tutsis in Rwanda—and for a long time, the world simply watched

And now, in the first decade of the twenty-first century, the specter of genocide casts its shadow over Darfur—and the world watches. To his credit, President Bush some time ago labeled the war against the people of Darfur as genocide. But the United Nations has refused to use that term, and the United States itself seems to have assumed that simply hurling the term at the conflict will somehow make it go away.

Although the New Testament forbids the church to participate in violence, it does give the church the responsibility to remind the institutions of government—the embodiments of the cosmic Powers and Principalities—of their responsibility to maintain order and justice in the world. Thus, the church is called to remind the United Nations, NATO, the Organization of African Unity, and other institutions of their responsibility to protect the victims in Darfur.

This does not mean telling institutions that they must dirty their hands while we sit on ours. We also have a responsibility to work for reconciliation in the midst of the warfare, placing ourselves on the side of the victims—stepping forth into the valley of the shadow of death, at a risk at least as great as that of the representatives of the powers.

The powers crucify Jesus Christ all over again by expelling, maiming, raping, and slaughtering those for whom Jesus Christ died. So when we sing, as we did recently in the season of Lent, "Were You There When They Crucified My Lord?" we might consider that a second question will be, "If not, why not?"

June 11, 2006

PROTESTANTS' STAKE IN THE PAPACY

Though Protestants may think they have no stake in the papacy, nothing could be further from the truth. For much of the world, the Pope is the primary symbol of Christianity. Consequently, Christians everywhere are judged by what the Pope does. He is the only leader of a world Christian body ever invited to address the United Nations. Even in this country, no other religious leader's Christmas service is annually broadcast over national television. Were the President of the World Council of Churches in the physical condition that now hinders the Pope, I doubt that daily reports of his condition would be in the news. Who of us, in fact, would recognize on sight or even be able to name the President of the World Council. History may well record that when the United States opened the war on Iraq, it was Pope John Paul II who, by reaching out to the leaders of Islam, enabled most of them to understand that the attack was not another Christian crusade.

One could argue, of course, that the nature of the Vatican as a state and the Catholic nature of much of central Europe are major reasons for this attention. But even if that be true, it is the fact of his symbolic role, not the reasons for it, that is important.

But the papacy is important for Protestants for an even greater reason. The office reminds us of the tragedy of a divided church. In what has come to be called his high priestly prayer in the Gospel of John (John 17),

Jesus prayed that his followers might be one in order that the world might see and believe. Regardless of who bears fault for the divisions, a fractured church, by its disunity, betrays its responsibility to bear testimony to the unifying grace of God. We need not be prepared to become Catholic for the office of Pope to symbolize the unity we crave or to remind us of how far we have fallen.

February 13, 2005

THE HELPLESS CHURCH

In the face of the violence and death in the Middle East, a Christian might ask, "What can the church do?" And the answer, with regard to the church as an institution, is, "Probably, nothing."

This is not because Christians do not care—not because Christians do not agonize over the children whose corpses are displayed regularly on t-v and in newspapers and magazines. But it is because of the heavy baggage of the church's history.

In most churches, for instance, we do not teach our members about the Crusades in the Middle Ages, and most Christians have only a vague idea as to what the Crusades were. But in the minds of most Muslims the Crusades are as alive as if they had taken place yesterday.

Moreover, because for two centuries the church piggy-backed on colonialism, people of the Middle East make little distinction between western domination and Christian imperialism. And this is not a misperception on their part, but is an accurate perception of what the church in the West assumed on the one hand, but wished to deny on the other. For centuries, the western church and western governments have been so interwoven that the church long ago lost not only its ability to act as a unique body, but even its ability to understand the world biblically.

In fact, the impossibility of even speaking sensibly of the church as a single, unified body means that even if some denomination or another still were able to perceive the world correctly, that discernment could be set forth only in a small voice among hundreds of diverse voices on behalf of other groups, each of which sees itself as the primary, or even sole, bearer of God's word.

To say that the church can do nothing is not to say that God cannot and will not do something with or through the church. I have no doubt that, sooner or later, God will have his way in the Middle East, either by the violence that human beings enact, by some unforeseen miracle of diplomacy, or by a combination of the two. What the church, and we who are members of it, can do is immerse ourselves in the study of the Scriptures, opening ourselves to the possibility that God might speak anew through those Scriptures; participate regularly in the sacraments, trusting that by means of the sacraments God will transform the life of the church and, consequently, our lives into lives of faithfulness and wisdom; and devote ourselves to the life of prayer, prayer for God's intervention sooner rather than later. Some Christians may even be God's instruments of peace—either as government agents or as private interventionists. But the great burden of those of us who agonize over the corpses of the children is our own helplessness, rooted in an apostasy of the church that took place long before we were born, but to which we often have made our own contributions.

August 6, 2006

ON WHOSE AUTHORITY?

When the bishops of the Episcopal Church met in New Orleans with the Archbishop of Canterbury of the Church of England, the task was to see whether some agreement could be worked out to ease the conflict between the Protestant Episcopal Church in the USA and members of national churches from other countries in the Anglican family of churches. The friction began when the General Assembly of the Episcopal Church approved the election by the diocese of New Hampshire of a homosexual priest, Gene Robinson, as bishop. Whether to bless same-sex marriages also is an issue. The churches of other nations that make up the Anglican family passed a resolution asking the U.S. church not to take any other actions that would threaten the unity of the family. The New Orleans meeting ended with a statement that was not satisfactory to some conservatives, and at this writing it is not clear how other Anglican national churches will react.

Those who opposed the approval of Robinson as bishop did so on the grounds that the Bible condemns homosexuality. One priest has said that what really underlies the conflict is the question of the authority of Scripture, moral authority, and sources of revelation. It is not clear whether the speaker meant "Scripture alone," but he seems to echo the words of other Episcopalians who sound as though that is their position. If the speaker did mean "Scripture alone," he is at odds with his own church, for authority in the Anglican churches always has rested on a three-way relationship among the Bible, tradition, and reason.

My own teaching and preaching for approximately a half-century has been rooted in Scripture. I am in complete agreement that the Bible should be the basic authority for the life and work of the church. But the Bible always has to be interpreted. And therein lies the problem. Each person interprets the Bible in his or her own way.

Some will object that there are some things on which the Bible speaks clearly, with no need for interpretation. But actually, that is not so. The languages in which the Bible was written—Hebrew, Greek, and a smattering of Aramaic—require translation. Look up almost any Hebrew, Greek, or Aramaic word in the dictionary, and you will find at least two or more possible English equivalents of that word. The context will tell you which English word works best, but the translator frequently has to determine the context. Anyone who has ever studied a foreign language knows that although there is a difference between translating and paraphrasing, most translations have to maneuver through that twilight area in which the line between the two is seldom absolute.

Although I assume that reason—and even experience—has to be used to interpret the Bible, my own view of authority is closer to that of Scripture alone than to the Anglican balance of Scripture, tradition, and reason or to the Methodist balance of Scripture, tradition, reason, and experience. So I applaud anyone who stands up for the authority of Scripture. But I wonder how far the person who was quoted is willing to go.

For example, Jesus said that when someone strikes us on one cheek, we are to turn our other cheek to that person. He also said that we are to love our enemies. The Apostle Paul said that when our enemy is hungry or thirsty, we are to give food and drink and that we are not to return evil for evil, but to overcome evil with good. Any church that truly follows the Bible on those teachings will refuse to approve its members entering the military, sitting on juries that condemn people to death, or participate in the legal execution of the condemned. Somehow, I doubt that is what those who call for the authority of the Bible have in mind.

Of course, some will say that I'm not "interpreting" those passages correctly. But such a reply will simply prove my point. What we usually mean by the authority of the Bible actually is the authority of our own interpretation. All interpretation is rooted in a complex blend of personal history and other factors of which we are totally unaware. One should never confuse infallibility of the Scriptures with infallibility of one's own perspective. To do so just might be the greatest sin of all.

October 3, 2007

STANDING SILENT IN THE FACE OF TORTURE

There is increasing evidence that the United States government—while proclaiming human rights and the rule of law—has been transferring prisoners in the war against terrorism to nations it knows will use torture to gain information. In good George Orwell fashion, this practice is called *extraordinary rendition*. Although U.S. officials deny the accusations, reports by the International Red Cross and testimonies of various victims are too many and too similar to be complete fabrications.

Some would say, on various grounds, that the church has no business meddling in such issues. And it is true that there is no biblical basis for expecting any government to live by the teachings of either the Old or the New Testament. All human governments—including the United States—are secular institutions, not Christian. In the Old Testament the nations were not expected to live by the instructions God gave to Israel. Nevertheless, God did call prophets such as Amos and Jeremiah to proclaim judgment on those nations for certain actions that violated international laws of decency. Amos denounced all the surrounding nations for cruelty in warfare. Although God accepted warfare as an inevitable reality in a fallen world, some acts were considered excessive even in a fallen world. And God commanded Amos to speak against those excesses.

Similarly, the Church of Jesus Christ has the responsibility to remind the nations that they stand under the judgment of God—to remind them that while God expects them to provide for the protection and well-being of their own citizens, there are limits to what is permissible, even in warfare. If the church and we as individual Christians reject this responsibility, when God sits in judgment on the world, our hands too will be stained with the blood of the victims.

March 6, 2005

THE SACRAMENTS AS POLITICAL ACTS

A friend of mine, who died more than a decade ago, once remarked that baptism is the most political step a person can take. By this he meant that to affirm that Jesus Christ is Lord—an affirmation that we make as part of the baptism ceremony—is to affirm that in Jesus Christ the God who created the universe and everything in it has laid claim to that universe and that we will now live our lives completely in obedience to him.

In baptism, according to the Apostle Paul, we die to what we have been and take on new identities and new allegiances. Consequently, all those relationships by which we usually identify ourselves must take a back seat to our identities as subjects of God in God's kingdom. If we truly understand what we are doing in baptism, the cross of Jesus replaces the national flag as our primary standard, and Pentecost replaces the Fourth of July as our national birthday. According to Jesus, becoming his disciples even places us in a new family (Mark 3:33–35).

But the Lord's Supper also is a political act. To participate in the Lord's Supper is at least to reaffirm our allegiance to the one whose reign is supreme over all human governments. And for those who view the Lord's Supper as a sacrament, the ceremony also nurtures us and strengthens us in our participation in God's New Order.

Although some Christians who oppose the present Administration reacted scornfully when former U.S. Attorney General John Ashcroft asserted at Bob Jones University that Jesus Christ was his king, Mr. Ashcroft was making a basic biblical assertion. He, my late friend, and I would agree completely on the affirmation. The question is whether we assume that as our King, Jesus sits in judgment on our goals, our ambitions, and our views of right and wrong just as he sits in judgment on those of others or whether we assume that we are so in harmony with God's rule that our will is God's will. Nothing in the New Testament assures us of that.

June 26, 2005

6

The Bible

INTERPRETING ANCIENT TEXTS

A MAJOR DISPUTE IN the interpretation of the U.S. Constitution is over whether the Constitution should be interpreted according to the intentions of its authors or according to later knowledge and sensibilities. A similar debate goes on with regard to interpreting the Bible. For example, should the concern be for what the Apostle Paul intended or for the implications of Paul's words in later settings without regard to Paul's intent?

With original intent, we risk imposing what is in effect an ancient relic on situations the writers never envisioned. The authors of the Constitution, for example, accepted slavery and women not having the right to vote, and they never envisioned a nation as multiethnic as this one has become. The Apostle Paul never envisioned the ability to manipulate genes, transplant organs, or travel to outer space. But if we assume at least some authority for the ancient texts, we cannot completely ignore the intent of the authors. Breaking all the threads of history leads to mere subjectivism.

The church across the ages has taught that there is both a fixed tradition and a developing tradition and that within the Bible there are both enduring elements and elements that reflect the society in which they were written. Few today, for example, would call for capital punishment for those who violate the Sabbath or who curse their parents. When God chooses to do so, the church has said, God uses the Holy Spirit to speak a new word through the Bible—a word not tied to the text, but also not inconsistent with the text. Even so, there are debates over whether a new word truly is the word of God or simply human manipulation of the text—the theological equivalent of making law from the bench. The Supreme Court is now made up of justices who disagree among themselves over which approach—the strict or the loose construction approach—is the correct one. Of course, in its deliberations, the Court does not have the promise of the Spirit, but only the wisdom of human beings appointed by other human beings, whatever the intentions of those doing the appointing.

July 17, 2005

WHO OWNS THE TEN COMMANDMENTS?

The Ten Commandments have been in the news quite a bit lately because of the desire on the part of some public officials and some private individuals and groups to place the Commandments in public places.

In the Bible the Commandments are never actually called *commandments*. They are called *words*, or *sayings*. The word *torah*, the word in the Bible usually translated *law*, of which the Ten Commandments are a part, actually means *instruction*. Torah was God's gift of grace to Israel as a guide by which Israel might live an orderly, fruitful life in the midst of a chaotic world. Torah was to be a sign of God's covenant with Israel, God's chosen people. The Ten Words became Commandments only when they were rejected as gift.

Jesus said that all God's instructions are summed up in two: love God and love your neighbor as you love yourself (Matt 19:19). The Apostle Paul said that whoever loves the neighbor has fulfilled torah—that is, has faithfully followed the instructions (Rom 13:8).

As instruction for the People of God, the Ten Commandments were never intended as law for other nations. The book of Deuteronomy does suggest that other nations might be attracted to torah when the nations see it as a wonderful gift to Israel. The prophet Isaiah anticipated a day when all nations would travel to Israel to learn torah, and, as a result, would live in peace (Isa 2). But this presupposed a world in which each nation was made up of a homogenous population, not a world in which individual nations are populated by people from a variety of cultural and religious backgrounds.

Does this mean that a nation made up of people from all sorts of cultural and religious backgrounds, such as is the case in the United States, has no *right* to display the Ten Commandments in public places? The idea of a nation having the right to do anything is a modern idea. In much of the history of the world power has determined what simply *could* be done. Does an individual in the United States, with its emphasis on freedom of religion, have the right to place the Ten Commandments wherever he or she wishes? It frequently is said that no individual has a right to do anything that intrudes on the right of others. This assertion has complicated implications, however, and it is more correct to say that there often are situations in which rights must be balanced. One person's right might have to be curtailed if exercising it would violate the rights of others. Any nation that chose to make the Commandments a part of its law might do so in a manner in keeping with that nation's legal system. Any culturally and religious diverse nation might decide to display the Commandments in public places, but it probably would not be wise to do so. And if a nation disregards that wisdom or an individual ignores that restriction, it or he or she should be prepared to pay the price.

August 14, 2005

JEREMIAH WRIGHT, HIS CRITICS, AND THE BIBLE

Let me say at the outset that I do not write this as an advocate for Barack Obama. (In fact, I would prefer an entirely different roster of contestants for this election.) But I am struck by the apparent biblical illiteracy of the critics of Mr. Obama and of the Rev. Jeremiah Wright. Although I do not agree with all of Mr. Wright's statements in the sound bites constantly paraded before us, his overall approach to domestic and international affairs is consistent with that of the Old Testament prophets. The prophets used scathing language describing Israel's oppression of the poor, national pride, and violence. In fact, Isaiah said that God was so angered by Israel's oppression of the poor that he would not permit Israel to repent, but would use the Assyrians to destroy it (Isa 6:9–13).

In Mark's Gospel, Jesus, seven hundred years later, says that he teaches in parables so the nation might not understand, repent, and be restored (Mark 4:10–12). And in the book of Revelation, when the Roman Empire—represented by Babylon—is destroyed, the angels sing "Hallelujah" (Rev 19:3)!

True, Mr. Wright does ignore the positive things the United States has done. For example, the U.S. has passed civil rights legislation and established economic and education programs for the benefit of poor blacks and poor whites. But there often is a difference between laws and the mechanisms by which those laws are administered. The attitudes of those who enforce the laws and administer the programs frequently are such that clients are treated with contempt. Racism and economic snobbery are alive and "well" in this country. When Mr. Wright refers to the "U.S. of KKK America", then, he is speaking rhetorically of the subtle indignities that most black persons experience every day.

To see the mindset that engenders these indignities, consider the frequency with which white persons report an incident and refer to "a black man (or black woman)", but ignore color reference if the person is white. White persons simply are incapable of comprehending how a black person daily experiences life in this society.

When Mr. Wright describes U.S. society as controlled by rich white people, however, he draws the circle of discrimination and oppression too small. Martin Luther King, Jr., recognized that poor whites also are victims of the nation's political and economic structures, and the genius of his Poor People's Campaign was its vision of uniting poor blacks and poor whites in a single movement. Unfortunately, that vision, like others, became part of the "dream deferred".

As for attacks on Mr. Wright for his relationship with and accolades for Lewis Farakan, I, too, think that Mr. Wright was mistaken, but it is ironic that many participants in Mr. Farikan's Million Man March a few years ago were white, conservative Christians.

Mr. Wright also is correct that U.S. foreign policy was a major factor in the September 11 attacks, but he should have included U.S. based international corporations. As others have pointed out, the targets of the attacks were prominent symbols of western economic and military power, which almost always is wielded to help others in the world only when it also works for U.S. benefit.

For almost half-a-century I have said that the western world is under the judgment of God. In this, I am far from alone. Secular observers speak of it as the decline of western civilization. As I have acknowledged above, at times this nation has engaged in noble, honorable programs. But it also is true that the nation was born in violence; expanded by stealing much of the land from the earlier inhabitants; in some instances, attempted genocide against those inhabitants; built the economy of much of the nation on slave labor; frequently invaded smaller nations to impose the United States's will; became the only nation ever to have dropped nuclear weapons on civilian populations; and bombarded Viet Nam with napalm and other chemical weapons that left thousands of dead and wounded Vietnamese women and children and created health problems for an untold number of the United States' own military. How, in light of all this, is it reasonable to expect the nation to go scott free?

Critics of Mr. Wright, who say he should not preach politics from the pulpit, but stick to the gospel, apparently have never read the prophets, have been highly selective in reading the New Testament—if they have read it at all—or have simply assumed that those scriptures have no relevance for us.

April 2, 2008

100 WASTED MINUTES

Most major news services last week reported the publication of the *100 Minute Bible*.[1] This version of the Bible reduces the near 800 thousand words of most versions to twenty thousand words in just under sixty pages. It is divided into fifty segments, each of which can be read in approximately two minutes, or the entire book can be read in an hour and forty minutes. Thus, the name the *100 Minute Bible*.

Promoters of the new edition say it may attract people who are not now members of the church or those who are not active, and that by giving them smaller pieces, it may attract them to the gospel. The author—or should we say editor—of the book is reported as saying that the book has "majored on Jesus, because he is the central figure in the Bible." The Old Testament, he says, is "summarized in terms of the chronology and prophetic teachings that provided a context for Jesus."[2]

Unfortunately, this description implies that the only parts of the Old Testament worth presenting are those that Christians believe point to Jesus. Such a view of the Old Testament is especially troubling in a world that desperately needs to hear the prophetic denunciation of social injustice, abuse of power by governing officials, neglect of the poor, national arrogance, and the world-wide prevalence of violence. In addition, the passage from the Creation narrative in Genesis 1 omits any reference to humankind created in the image of God—referring to human beings simply as being among the other animals—and says nothing about humankind's responsibility to care for God's world.

---

1. Michael Hinton, *The 100-Minute Bible* (Canterbury: The 100-Minute Press, 2005).
2. Quoted in an article on the BNET website, September 27, 2005.

Len Budd, proprietor of the 100-Minute Press, speaks of the book as one "for adults," one "written in a style to encourage readers to keep turning the pages, but without resorting to any literary gimmicks."[3]

The BBC described the new, reduced size, holy book as a "page-turner for those who do not have the time to read the full version." And perhaps that is the most damning description of all. The *100 Minute Bible* is simply another attempt to make the Bible palatable. No worry, no demands on one's time. Just squeeze God in when you have a spare moment.

I would never contend that God cannot reach human beings through even the crassest of means. But when we water down the biblical witness in order to attract reluctant people, we are attracting them to a false message.

In the final analysis, one hundred minutes with a domesticated Bible is little more than one hundred wasted minutes.

October 2, 2005

---

3. Reported on the BBC Home website, September 21, 2005.

7

Human Identity

Defining Human Identity ... and Other

ONCE AGAIN, THERE IS a request to permit efforts at tampering with the line that separates human beings from other forms of animal life. This time, teams of British scientists have requested of the British government permission to take DNA from patients with diseases for which there presently is no known cure—such as Alzheimer's and Parkinson's diseases—and inject that DNA into cows' eggs from which the original DNA has been removed. The effort would be to develop cow embryos that carry human DNA, rather than bovine DNA. If the embryos developed, after a few days of growth the embryos would be destroyed, their stem cells would be removed, and the stem cells used for experimentation in an effort to find cures for the diseases of the persons whose DNA was used. The logic is that since the original egg was a cow's egg, no human embryos would have been destroyed.

The use of body parts of other animals for the repair of the human body is not new, but criticism of the contemplated new procedures has come both from Roman Catholic theologians and animal rights groups—the latter concerned about the cruelty to animals, the former concerned with the question of human identity. Catholic teaching in general at the moment accepts genetic crossover as long as it does not threaten human identity. But that is just the question. What gives us our identity? And what gives a cow its identity? If our DNA, which supposedly carries all our physical traits, does not play a vital role in our identity, then what does?

In the Creation narratives in the Old Testament God creates the world by bringing order out of chaos and establishing the components of the world, each with its own identity. In the rest of the Old Testament and in the New, there are frequent references to God as the one who brings order out of chaos. It is reasonable to ask, then, how far it is legitimate to go in confusing those things that God has separated. How far is it possible to go in blending before we are undermining God's Creation? How far do we go before we have obliterated not only the identity of the other creatures, but our own human identity, as well? The answers are not easy, but we ignore them at the risk not only of our own identity as human beings, but of creating a future of chaos that will make our own world, troubled as it is, seem a paradise lost.

April 8, 2007

WHO ARE WE?

In December of last year, French physicians made international headlines by successfully transplanting the nose, lips, and chin of one person onto another. Now, Chinese doctors have performed a similar operation. In typical, misleading shorthand, the media reported in each case that there had been a face transplant, and this raised for some the question of how or whether transplanting a face affects a person's identity.

How is my identity related to my body? On the one hand, I do not seem to lose my identity if I lose a tooth or an eye, an arm or a leg, or if I cut my fingernails. But on the other hand, even the simplest changes in my physical makeup can have enormous effect on my self-perception, on my personality, and—consequently—on my identity. I am not a mere machine.

The Bible, of course, was written before anyone imagined the possibilities of even the simplest transplant, such as skin grafting—not to mention gene manipulation and organ transplanting—so we must be wary of dogmatism. On the other hand, grappling with the question of human identity on the basis of the Bible's overall perspective might lead to wisdom not only in the matter of organ and face transplants, but on a myriad of other questions we not only have not yet confronted, but have not yet even imagined.

The Christian's participation in the discussion always must be an exercise in positive testimony to the good news of what God is doing in Jesus Christ and on the compassion of God revealed in Christ, rather than an exercise in mere legalism. Jesus healed not simply to free a person from some physical or mental disorder, but to free that person from the powers of Darkness, which, by that physical condition, affected the person's outlook, attitude, and motives—all of which were elements of the person's identity. Jesus' healings always were performed with the purpose of freeing from their separation from God both the one who was healed and those who saw the healing.

A serious grappling with the overall biblical witness to the nature of human identity might be a means through which God would grant us an alternative to the mechanistic view that we are simply machines, with body parts that can be exchanged as we exchange the wheels or transmission of an automobile, and the opposite view, that human beings are so self-contained that no transplants ever are to be permitted, no matter how horrible a person's condition. One thing is certain: left to our human devices alone, we easily can create a future so horrible that, to quote an earlier writer, the living would envy the dead.

July 16, 2006

PSYCHOLOGY AND BIBLICAL THEOLOGY

The Bible associates different emotions and activities of what sometimes has been called *the mind* with various parts of the physical body. Sorrow, for example, is associated with the kidneys and the bowels. The heart is viewed as the organ that holds the will and the motives. This is what lies behind Jesus' words that where our treasure is, there will our heart be. In other words, what we most highly value will determine our motives and direct our will.

The biblical writers did not view human beings as mere physical objects walking around with a small bundle of mental functions located somewhere in the head, similar to the way an automobile is a machine that carries us around from place to place. They viewed us as unitary, whole beings, each part interacting with every other part.

Modern psychology has long been aware of this complex, intricate relationship. Intense stress has physical consequences. Emotional dysfunctions can cause blindness, paralysis, and sterility. The name sometimes used for problems arising from this interaction combines two Greek words for body and soul—*psyche* and *soma*—giving us the term *psychosomatic*.

This singleness of the human being also is what lies behind the New Testament refusal to divide us, the way the Greeks did, into body and soul. The New Testament writers do not look forward to the immortality of the soul and the decay of the body, but to resurrection—the total transformation of what we now are into an existence we cannot even begin to imagine. Jesus, in his healing miracles, indicated that the healing of the physical body is an expression of God's liberation of this world from the powers of Sin and Death.

This awareness is what lies behind the proper insistence of many churches that the gospel of Jesus Christ is concerned with the well-being of the whole person and of the whole society, with justice and reconciliation in the real, physical society around us, not simply with the eventual saving of an immaterial soul.

January 9, 2005

DNA TRANSPLANTS AND TESTIMONY TO CHAOS

Experimentation in organ transplants across species lines began in 1906, when a French physician transplanted the heart of one dog into another and the kidney of one cat into another, and another physician transplanted pig and goat livers into separate human beings. Since then, experimentation with animal organs for transplant purposes has become routine. And the use of pigs' valves in human heart surgery is so common that few consider it worth even mentioning.

In 1995 the concept was taken a step farther when brain cells from pig fetuses were injected into victims of Parkinson's disease to see if the human brain could be induced to secrete a chemical that would work against the disease.

And now comes word that human DNA has been inserted into the brains of monkeys. We are assured, of course, that there is no danger of producing monkeys whose brains take on human characteristics. And when the entire effort is for the purpose of saving human lives, who can possibly protest?

But certain biblical narratives suggest another perspective. In Genesis 1, God creates the universe and all things in it by bringing order out of chaos. Plants and animals emerge from the chaos as God establishes order. Later, in the flood story, God allows the world to slip back toward chaos, and to fall back into chaos is, in fact, to fall into Death. Later still, Israel, by its way of life, was to bear testimony to God's preservation of order in the midst of chaos—even by means as quaint as not planting two kinds of seed in the same field and not using two kinds of thread in the same garment.

The belief that God has ordered life on this planet by evolution is not incompatible with this overarching perspective of order over against chaos.

The question is not whether by some natural, secular standard it is immoral to transplant organs and cells across species lines. The question is: to what do we bear testimony—to God's order or to chaos and Death? Is there possibly in the biblical testimony a wisdom which to ignore is to become captive to that very power of Death that we seek to avoid? No, it is not so much a matter of morality as it is the danger that by forsaking the testimony to God's gift of order and coherence, we produce a world of horrors that our flawed minds are incapable even of imagining.

July 2, 2006

ON DEATH AND TECHNOLOGY

In the media circus surrounding Terri Schiavo and the two sides of her family, it was largely ignored that the entire situation was a product of technology. Over the last fifty years we have developed technology that can lengthen the lives of the elderly, save the lives of the young and the middle-aged, and enable infants to live at increasingly earlier stages of removal from the womb. By so doing, we have become the arbiters of life and death.

Of course, we always have been arbiters in matters of death—killing the enemy in warfare, executing criminals, and, in an earlier time, burning at the stake persons convicted of heresy or witchcraft. But the increased ability to save lives places us in an almost god-like position. To cope with this, we have developed a new language—using terms such as *quality of life*, that have no concrete meaning, but whose meaning is rooted in all sorts of presuppositions—both conscious and unconscious. Once we have defined the terms, we can justify whatever we want. We have, in brief, become prisoners of our own technology.

Of course, technology has provided all sorts of benefits. The ability to engage in technology is itself a gift of God. But that ability is marred by ambiguity. In a fallen Creation, even our most humanely motivated solutions create new problems. By saving lives we increase the population and reap the consequent problems, and the more premature a birth, the greater the likelihood the infant will have or will develop chronic health problems.

It is an inescapable dilemma. Simply abandoning technology would be abandoning our God-given responsibility to care for God's world and its creatures. But to allow technology to seduce us into thinking that the ability to do something is also a moral basis for doing it is to court the destruction of that same world and those same creatures.

April 10, 2005

PLAYING CHICKEN WITH HUMAN LIVES

The London *Times* reported a couple of weeks ago that in an effort to eliminate the avian flu, scientists in London are experimenting with the genetic alteration of chickens. The scientists are not trying to find a vaccine for each new generation of chickens, but are attempting to modify chickens genetically so that each new generation will be hatched immune to the virus.

One of the obstacles to overcome, said the *Times*, is resistance to genetically modified food. And the *Times*, undoubtedly, is correct. All one need do is look at recent resistance to genetically modified vegetables and milk. But just as there has not been sufficient resistance to eliminate other genetically modified food products, there probably will not be enough to stop the introduction of genetically modified chickens. The introduction of genetically modified corn took place by selective breeding long before we learned how to manipulate genes with a needle and a microscope.

Most of those who do protest will protest out of fear, the fear of problems the genetic modification will create. That is a legitimate concern. How far should we go in making potentially irreversible changes in the environment without sufficient exploration of possible repercussions throughout the environment?

As creatures in the image of God—that is, as human beings created to serve God in caring for the earth—we have a responsibility to use our knowledge to reduce illness and suffering in the world. But we live in a fallen world—from a secular point of view, an imperfect world—in which both our responsibility and nature itself are flawed beyond our ability to repair.

All technologies are, in the final analysis, human efforts to overcome the fall, to overcome the broken condition of the Creation. And because our technologies themselves share the imperfection, each solution to a problem brings its own set of problems.

I am not suggesting that we not use whatever knowledge we may have. But there is a difference between acting in humility before God and acting out of fear of the immediate problem. Humility will enable us to act with patience and with a relatively clearer measure of whether the risks are worth the effort. Fear will drive us to act quickly, likely creating even greater problems than the one at hand. The risks are too great to play chicken with God's world.

November 13, 2005

THE PRICE OF SECURITY IN AN INSECURE WORLD

According to Privacy International's 2007 report, the United States and the United Kingdom have two of the worst records for privacy in the world, falling below Canada and thirty-nine countries in Europe, Asia, and South America. The invasion of privacy comes both from government surveillance and from numerous private (note the irony) and commercial sources. But privacy and freedom go hand in hand. The members of the Jackson-Madison County school board who have voiced concern about increasing the number of police in the public schools are raising an important issue.

But how many of us will be concerned about Privacy International's report? Most of my students show an amazing lack of concern about the kudzoo-like growth of cameras in department stores, businesses, schools, and at traffic intersections.

Several years ago, I went to a local department store to ask about error on my credit card bill. The clerk asked me to move to the left so the security camera could see me clearly. When I asked why they needed my picture, the clerk replied that it was for my own security, an answer that I still find astounding in its logic. I left the store determined never again to shop there because of the security cameras. Today, were I to boycott stores using security cameras, I would not do much shopping.

In his book *Escape From Freedom*[1], psychoanalyst Eric Fromm speculated as to why the people of Germany, other than Jews, supported the Nazi regime. Noting the commonly acknowledged economic, political, and social turmoil into which Germany had fallen in the wake of World War I, Fromm concluded that people preferred security to chaos. The price of that security, of course, was tyranny.

---

1. Eric Fromm, Escape from Freedom (New York: Henry Holt/Owl, 1994).

The preference for security over freedom can be found in both the secular and the religious realms. The Apostle Paul, for example, confronted the issue in the church in Galatia. Christians in Galatia had come into the Jesus movement from the Gentile (non-Jewish) world rather than from Israelite culture. They had accepted Paul's assurance that by their baptism they entered into a totally new existence—a new order of the Creation. In this new Creation, they must look no longer to written documents—including the Ten Commandments—to tell them how to live, but were to allow the Holy Spirit to transform them and to guide them in this new existence. But soon, the Galatian Christians began to worry. If they did not follow torah, the written law given through Moses, would not God exclude them from God's Kingdom.

For Paul, however, the new life in Christ was true freedom—the freedom to become, by the power and guidance of the Spirit, what God originally intended human beings to be. The Galatian Christians, fearing for their security, had returned to a written set of instructions, thus giving up the freedom of the Spirit-empowered life.

The nineteenth century Russian writer Dostoyevsky spoke to the same conflict in *The Grand Inquisitor*, a portion of his novel *The Brothers Karamazov*.[2] "Humankind," said the Inquisitor, "is tormented by no greater anxiety than to find someone quickly to whom it can hand over that gift of freedom with which it was born."

"Today," he said, "people are more persuaded than ever that they have perfect freedom, yet they have brought their freedom to us and laid it humbly at our feet."

According to Dostoyevsky, we are more likely to be happy when we think we are secure than when we think we are free. I suspect that we also probably are relatively happier with security than with privacy.

For some time now, to an ever increasing extent, phone calls by United States citizens have been seigned and logged by Presidential order. Both major political parties in both houses of Congress have supported this intrusion, assuring us that it is for our security—just as are the cameras, the measures in federal and state office buildings, the body checks in airports, and the presence of police in the public schools. For several decades, we have been living in a technological prison camp—all, we are assured, for the sake of our own security.

2. Fyodor Dostoevsky, The Brothers Karamazov, Book 5, pt 5.

Undoubtedly, there will be more controversy over governmental intrusion into our privacy and, thus, into our freedom. Whether there finally is a general public revolt will depend on whether the government is able to convince us that the intrusion is for our own security. My bet is on the government.

January 8, 2008

TIME OUT!

Some friends and I were talking recently about how, as we get older, time seems each day to go faster than the day before. An entire year can seem to pass in a few days. Although in difficult times, seconds and minutes can seem like hours, months or years later the entire difficulty of one of those times can flit through our memory in a second. I think it was Augustine who observed that time does strange things in our mind.

And of course, none of us see time as God sees time. As the author of 2 Peter puts it, "With the Lord one day is as a thousand years, and a thousand years as one day" (2 Pet 3:8). Though we are created in the image of God, Ecclesiastes reminds us that God has so created our minds that we are limited in our ability both to remember the past and to anticipate the future (Eccl 3:11). We simply are unable to control either.

In fact, time usually controls us. Clocks, invented to serve us, become our masters. We get up by the clock in order to get to work on time by the clock, and we go to bed by the clock in order to get up the next morning by the clock.

The monastic orders attempted to deal with time by organizing it according to a daily routine of prayers. The monks went to bed at sunset, closing the day with Vespers and Compline, and rose a few hours before dawn to say Vigils, keeping watch in the night at approximately the time Jesus was believed to have been resurrected. At various times during the day, all tasks were set aside as the monastery engaged in a liturgy made up primarily from the book of Psalms.

I have been wondering recently about whether it might be possible to order the activities of my own life—teaching, grading papers, serving on committees, and fulfilling various social responsibilities—around set times of prayer, rather than by trying to find time for prayer as those activities permit. Not because of some desire for personal piety, but out of the conviction that people of God are called to worship God in formal ways during the course of each day. In other words, is it possible to order one's day around that call rather than around the job and social responsibilities? What a difference it might make in our perceptions, our sensibilities, and even in our character were we to say to God, with the psalmist, "My times are in your hand" (Psalm 31:14-15)!

January 22, 2006

THE GENOME PROJECT

A magazine cartoon in the middle of the last century showed a woman, dressed something like a sorceress, watching an airplane take off. The caption read: "Evil, evil! Man was never meant to fly!"

The cartoon, of course, was poking fun at the idea that human beings, by our use of technology, might ever step over some boundary, whether natural or divine. The woman in the cartoon may not have been correct, but she also may have known something that we don't like to admit about the human use of technology.

Consider three brief passages from the book of Genesis. In Genesis 11, God, watching the builders of the Tower of Babel, says, "Now, nothing will be impossible for them." Discoveries such as those in the genome project make such a line seem near prophetic. They raise the question whether we *should* do all that we *can* do.

The second passage, in Genesis 1, says that the human race was created in the image of God. That is, human beings are to serve as God's representatives in caring for God's Earth. This suggests that we can sin in either of two ways—by assuming too much and wanting to be gods, not merely creatures in the image of God, or by doing too little, refusing to fulfill the responsibility given us. The difficulty is in knowing when we are in danger of one or the other.

In the third passage, Genesis 3, when Adam and Eve are expelled from Eden, they are thereby cut off not only from the Tree of Life, but also from the Tree of the Knowledge of Good and Evil. They are condemned to decide good and evil without any assurance that what they call good and evil will be what God calls good and evil. But, someone will object, we have the Bible and its teachings. Yes, but the existence of hundreds of Christian and Jewish divisions indicates that although we have those teachings, we are hopelessly at odds over what they mean. All of which, it seems to me, calls for a bit of humility in all of us.

December 12, 2004

WHY EDUCATE?

The local school board and the County Court recently were engaged in a tug of war over the education budget. A majority of the Commissioners seemed to think that it was more important to hold the line against taxes than to provide music, art, and counseling services for students.

Some supporters of the Court said that school the way it was a half century ago was good enough for them, so it's good enough for young people today—walking a few miles (or perhaps several) to school or being transported by a parent; one teacher teaching English, history, science, math, geography, art, music, and all the other subjects in the curriculum; and various other characteristics of the so-called good old days. I often wonder, when I hear the "when I was a child" argument, if those who make it would themselves be willing to go back there in their daily life—giving up their electric clothes washers and driers, electric dish washers, t-v sets, air conditioning, modern medicine and medical care, and all those other things that make life today convenient, and sometimes even possible.

Certainly, there are problems with education today. One easily can find poorly prepared and poorly motivated teachers and administrators and point to increasing political intrusion. One even can make the case that education in the United States today is in critical condition and inferior to that in numerous other nations. But the solution to the problems of education is not to hold the line on school budgets because of some ideological repugnance toward taxes. To assume that the problems of education will be solved by withholding proper funding is like trying to cure cancer by starving the patient.

At the same time, the argument that we should fund education because poor schools will keep businesses and industries from moving into the area risks viewing our children as economic pawns. From a biblical perspective, our children and grandchildren are created to be God's representatives in caring for the earth and its creatures. From this perspective, education should not even be aimed primarily at enabling self regard and self-expression, but should be geared toward developing a greater understanding of and sensitivity toward the world and its inhabitants and should strive to produce men and women who live for others rather than for themselves. This cannot and should not be done in the public schools by teaching about the image of God, but it can be done by teaching a belief shared by all the world's religions—the responsibility of all human beings to protect the earth and to treat others in terms of how we would like others to treat us.

I heard very few people in the recent debates making that argument. And that's the real problem with contemporary education.

August 29, 2005

VIDEO GAMES, VALUES, AND DECISION MAKING

In his recent book, *Everything Bad is Good for You*,[3] Steven Johnson argues that video games are good for children because they train children to make quick decisions and to adjust decisions on the basis of feedback. A *USA Today* writer,[4] after reading the book, suggests that parents should tell their children to "put down that stupid Faulkner novel and get back to 'Halo 2' (a currently popular video game)." Such novels, according to one father, are "unrelated to the way (the children) will be living their lives."

Having played video games with my grandchildren, I think that Steven Johnson's book makes a lot of sense. Video games, in reasonable doses, can help children to react quickly and accurately. But the most popular video games are based on one or both of two goals—winning and surviving, and in those games violence is the primary means of survival.

Yes, it is important that children learn to make decisions—sometimes quick decisions—and to adjust to the consequences of those decisions. But decisions are made on the basis of the kind of persons we are. One need not join the outcry against violence in video games to point out that if a child's character is formed by those games, all split-second decisions will be aimed at survival at any cost, and violence will be accepted as an ordinary means. Good literature, however, can help us to understand what it means to be truly human. The New Testament itself recognizes the prevalence of violence in the world, but it portrays being truly human as rejecting violence and even being willing to accept violence upon oneself rather than inflict it upon another.

I would not say the opposite of the *USA Today* columnist ("Throw out the video games and read Faulkner,") but I would say that we need the

---

3. Steven Johnson, Everything Bad is Good for You (New York: Riverhead/Penguin, 2005).

4. Kevin Maney, "Video games not necessarily turning kids' brains to mush," USA Today, July 12, 2005.

Faulkners of the literary world, as well as the Bible, to remind us of who we are and to help us become what God intended us to be.

August 31, 2005

THE WISDOM OF POGO

The price of gasoline continues to climb erratically, three steps backward followed by two steps forward. On every hand we hear reasons, rationalizations, and accusations—the increasing price of petroleum, the cost of research and exploration, large bonuses and severance packages for oil company executives, an insufficient number of refineries, federal and state taxes—on and on the list goes.

No doubt, each of these factors plays a role. Some impressive statistics, however, suggest that in terms of the relative value of the dollar, a gallon of gasoline today costs roughly what it cost in 1940. Since the value of the dollar today is drastically different from what it was even ten years ago, this observation sounds plausible. But for those things we hold most dear and upon which we most strongly depend, most of us don't want the price to change—period! It is easy to talk about the decreased value of the dollar when complaining about the purchasing value of our salaries, but not nearly so easy when considering the cost of living. We would like for gasoline to cost less than one dollar a gallon regardless of the value of the dollar.

The simple fact is that, as a society, we ourselves are a basic component of the problem. We have organized society—both nationally and internationally—in such a manner that it could not continue as it now is without automobiles, trucks, airplanes, and various other instruments and machines that depend upon energy. Many of us live long distances from our jobs. Food, clothing equipment, and all the other necessities of life must be transported over long distances in a short amount of time. Individually, most of us want to be where we want to be, when we want to be there, and we want our own hands on the wheel of our own vehicles to get us there. Who wants to ride a bus forty-five minutes to reach a location we can reach in ten minutes in our own vehicle? And taking two or three days to travel across country by train when we can make the trip in a few hours by plane simply is not considered an option. We tell ourselves that we don't have the time. And of course, as society now operates, we don't. We have structured our society and, consequently, our minds around immediacy. I count myself among the guilty.

We ignore the fact that someday the oil supply will give out. But we are as little concerned with the plight of our great-grandchildren in the matter of oil as we are with our children and grandchildren in the matter of the national debt. We want what we want, and we want it now! No amount of talk about other forms of energy or about hybrid and electric automobiles is going to change that. In fact, some impressive studies show that the use of methane as a substitute for gasoline will decrease the cost of engergy by only twenty percent. We already have seen that the use of corn as a source of energy drives up the cost of food and other products because so many of the things upon which we depend everyday contain corn.

Any solution to the problem of gasoline prices probably will convince us even further that living selfishly carries no consequences. We are living examples of what the Apostle Paul described (in all English translations of the New Testament) as "people of the flesh". He did not mean, as people who use these terms today usually mean, that people are more concerned with physical matters than with spiritual matters. In Paul's vocabulary the Greek word translated *flesh* does mean, on one level, the meaty substance of the human body. But Paul usually uses the word to mean *self-interest*. He believed that from the moment we are born, we are driven by unbridled self-interest. Jesus held the same view. And neither Paul nor Jesus saw that condition changing other than by God's changing the human heart.

For the first Earth Day, in 1970, cartoonist Walt Kelly produced a poster featuring his popular character Pogo Possum. Pogo's words on that poster, which have become a part of the national vocabulary, are just as apt with regard to rising gasoline prices as with regard to the destruction of the environment. "We have met the enemy," said Pogo, "and he is us."

December 10, 2007

HEALTH COSTS AND THE DESIRE FOR IMMORTALITY

As the cost of health care continues to spiral upward, it is common to blame several factors—including doctors' salaries, expanding medical research, the costs levied by pharmaceutical companies, the cost of malpractice insurance, and various other things. Though all these probably play some role, an equally important factor, usually not mentioned, is the desire of many of us to live forever.

I say this not as judgment, but as confession. When I am sick, I, too, want a cure. I am now considerably older than the actual life expectancy of the typical Israelite when the Psalmist referred to the ideal life span as threescore and ten or even fourscore and ten, but I am not at all ready to die. On the other hand, I do not want to live forever with aches, pains, and disabilities. I want the most up-to-date medicine and technology to prevent or relieve those things so I can stretch out my years in a physically able body.

The deaths of five friends and a brother-in-law during the last three months have led me to ponder more than usual my own mortality. A few years ago, two stents were placed in one of my arteries to relieve blockages. A few weeks later, I almost fainted while walking to my office, and as things began to blur, I wondered whether I was dying. The surprising thing, however, was that I was not so much frightened as I was perturbed. There were several things I wanted to do before I died, and none of them had yet been done.

Of course, people have pondered human mortality for at least as long as we have had written documents. In the story of the Garden of Eden (Gen 3), Death enters the world as a result of the disobedience of the first human beings. Whatever else we might deduce from that story, one implication is that human beings cannot blame the reality of Death entirely upon God. Each generation perpetuates the conditions upon which Death depends. (I spell Death with a capital *D* because for the biblical writers, Death is not simply the cessation of the heart beat or of our breathing, but is a transcendent power that entered the world to intimidate us and to seduce us into thinking that by ingenuity and technological skill we can escape or even defeat it.)

The ancient Mesopotamians reflected on Death in a story about a powerful king name Gilgamesh. After watching his best friend die in battle, Gilgamesh was determined to find the Tree of Life, which supposedly had the power to provide eternal rejuvenation. When he found the tree, Gilgamesh cut a branch from it and started home. Then, seeing a stream, he took off his clothes, placed the tree branch on the bank, and went for a swim. While he was swimming, a small snake stole the tree branch and scurried into the forest, shedding its skin as it went. Immortality, the story suggests, is beyond human reach. Gilgamesh's only immortality would be in his reputation after he died.[5] And, the story implies, the same is true for us.

---

5. The Gilgamesh Epic is available in several translations. I recommend *The Epic of Gilgamesh: An English Version with an Introduction*, Revised edition, Trans. N. K. Sandars

An ancient Judaic legend says that when Adam was about to die, Eve and Seth—Adam and Eve's third son—went to the Garden of Eden and pleaded with the cherubim to allow them enter the garden and take a branch from the tree of life in order to save Adam. The cherubim refused and Adam died. Outside of Eden, no one is permitted to live forever. And all of us are outside Eden.

The New Testament teaches that because baptism incorporates us into the death of Jesus Christ, in baptism we die the only death that really matters. Consequently, we need no longer fear that ending of biological existence called death. This is why the early Christian martyrs went fearlessly to their deaths. We should never surrender to Death by assuming that it has ultimate power over us, but baptism leaves us no sound reason for fearing the mere cessation of our breathing or of the beating of our hearts.

Even if one rejects or discounts this New Testament view of Death, death, and baptism, it is difficult to escape the observation that fear of and anxiety about death, held even by many Christians, provide the infrastructure on which all other costs of health care ultimately are built.

May 28, 2008

OPTIMISM, CYNICISM, AND REALISM

Some who teach at the university level say students today are different from students as recently as five years ago. They say that freshmen show more enthusiasm, more optimism, and a strong service orientation. These teachers feel an obligation not to dampen the enthusiasm of the students by their own more jaundiced view. This reminds me of a comment sometimes erroneously attributed to Winston Churchill: Anyone under thirty and not a liberal has no heart; anyone over thirty and not a conservative has no brains.

In the ancient Near East it was assumed that wisdom comes by learning from experience. There was no shame in a child being foolish, for a child lacked experience. For an adult to be considered foolish, however, was shameful. That adult had not reflected on and learned from his or her experience. Experience counts for nothing if a person has not reflected on it and gained wisdom from it.

There are notable examples, however, of persons who, while learning much from experience, have maintained the liberalism and optimism

---

(New York: Penguin Classics, 1960).

of their youth. For example, Hubert Humphrey—Mayor of Minneapolis, Senator from Minnesota, and Vice-President during the administration of Lyndon Johnson—never lost his enthusiasm and optimism. Although he lost in his bid for Majority Leader of the Senate in 1977, his colleagues showed their appreciation for him by creating, especially for him, the post of Deputy President pro tempore of the Senate. When he died, in 1978, Humphrey had gained the respect of even his staunchest opponents—conservative Southern Democrats—and was remembered by supporters and opponents alike as "the happy warrior."

A nation's vitality depends upon reflective conservatives and reflective liberals alike. A nation is in trouble when both these views are not represented or when persons of either position manifest enthusiasm without discernment, exercise power without reflection, and understand their labels as doctrines or ideologies to be adhered to without thought and defended without reason.

There is a difference between a jaundiced eye and clear eyed realism. Hubert Humphrey was an enthusiastic public servant throughout his political career, but he also was a realist. He understood the potentiality for both good and evil in human society, a wisdom he had gained by reflecting on experience.

Faculty concerned lest their jaundiced view dampen their students' enthusiasm and optimism, must distinguish between cynicism and realism. Cynicism denies the possibilities that lie within each personal or national disaster as a seed lying in the ground after a hurricane offers the possibility of new growth. Realism sees the seed and struggles to nurture it into new life.

Institutions of higher education, therefore, are not doing students a disservice when they help them, through the development of critical thinking, to develop a realistic view of the world and to outgrow shallow optimism. But they do them a great disservice when they leave them to flounder unarmed, lacking the critical skills necessary to confront the world as it really is.

Students graduate into a world in which power is misused; in which hostility awaits those who threaten power by their courage, good humor, and clear thinking; and in which death is the ultimate threat against those who refuse to be squeezed into a preconceived mold. Jesus was the consummate realist. "I send you," he said, "as sheep among wolves." And he told them that they must be as wise as serpents and as innocent as doves.

And just as cynicism must not be confused with realism, sound optimism must not be confused with blind optimism. Uncritical optimism says that our hope rests in education and generosity. Society's problems, it says, are caused by those who simply do not know better. Realistic optimism faces the world without blinders, rolls with the punches, returns generosity for hostility, and finds solidarity with the sheep because it refuses to join the wolf pack. It anticipates the impossible because ultimately, its hope lies not in the powers of this world, but in the hands of the God in whose hands are the reins of history.

October 23, 2008

8

Children

SUFFER THE CHILDREN

Most of the world looked on in horror a couple of weeks ago as masked gunmen held over a thousand adults and children hostage at Middle School Number One in the Russian town of Breslan. The horror was even greater when the hostage taking ended in the deaths of several hundred of the children.

But another horror is that hundreds of children around the world die each month not only from violence and warfare, but from child abuse, poverty, malnutrition, and other causes that only occasionally make international headlines. As great a problem as any today is starvation in large parts of Africa. But this does not make headlines, because it has become so ordinary that it is not considered newsworthy. It is only when something spectacular happens that we or the media take time to watch or to listen. And then, even in the worst cases, after a few days, or a couple of weeks at most, the camera blinks and moves on.

Before the flurry of modern translations of the Bible, people sometimes puzzled over the King James Version's translation of the passage in which Jesus said, "Suffer the little children to come unto me (Matt 19:14)." Why, they wondered, did Jesus seem to want little children to suffer? The fact, of course, was that in the 1600s, when the King James Version was translated, the word *suffer* meant *let*. Jesus was saying, "*Let* the little children come unto me." Far from wanting children to suffer, Jesus embraced children as symbols of what we must become in order to participate in the Kingdom of God.

We will never enter God's kingdom if we turn a deaf ear to the cry of starving children while we have a problem of obesity.

September 26, 2004

CHILDREN AND WAR

Jesus saw children as symbolic of life in the kingdom of God. That is, they symbolized one dimension of the life of all humankind under the future sovereign rule of God. In contrast, children today—young males and females under the age of eighteen—are increasingly used as soldiers of war, a fact that has received only spasmodic attention in the news. In his Nobel acceptance speech in 2002, former President Jimmy Carter said, "We will not learn how to live together in peace by killing each other's children." But today, children more and more are becoming the killers. Soldiers returning from Iraq report that one of the most hideous decisions they had to make was whether they were willing to kill children when those children were combatants.

According to Peter Singer, author of *Children at War,* [1]

- There now are more than 800,000 children soldiers in the world, either as impressed fighters or members of armed forces.
- Forty per cent of all the world's military forces now use children, twenty per cent of whom are under the age of twelve.
- Over the last decade more than two million children have died in warfare.

And the world pays little attention.

But there also is what amounts to a war against children in U.S. society today. Children as young as twelve and thirteen occasionally are tried as adults in cases that could result in the death penalty. Even as the slogan "No child left behind" is touted, government programs that have saved thousands of children from poverty, from lives with chronic health problems, and even from death are drastically cut or eliminated altogether, while the national debt is stretched by a war in which an increasing number of the enemy are children. We are like stage magicians, who long ago learned that basic to stage magic is the ability to distract the audience from what you really are doing.

But the God whose love for children was manifested in Jesus of Nazareth is neither distracted nor asleep, and he will not withhold judgment forever.

June 5, 2005

---

1. Peter W. Singer, *Children at War* (Berkeley: University of California Press, 2006).

CHILD ABUSERS ANONYMOUS

For some time, now, some states have had laws requiring convicted child abusers, upon release from prison, to register their living addresses so parents of small children can know of their proximity. Occasionally, there even have been efforts to require the abusers to place signs in their yards—signs that say "convicted child abuser lives here."

I once was having coffee with a friend who said rather heatedly that he certainly would want to know if he and his family were living next door to a child abuser. Half in jest, half in utter seriousness, I asked my friend how he knew he was not living next door to a child abuser.

We often concentrate only on the more dramatic, more vivid expressions of a problem while ignoring expressions that may be even more destructive because they harm entire populations, not just two, three, or a half-dozen.

For example, what about companies that produce chemicals that poison the soil and ground water and wind up in the organs and bones of children who eat the food grown in that soil and who drink from that water—or that wind up in the bodies of parents whose children are born with various physical and mental disabilities? What about those of us who buy and use those chemicals?

What about food companies that target children with advertisements for foods that not only have no nutritional value, but contribute to obesity? What about parents who buy those goodies for their children?

What about the producers of television programs, music videos, video games, and advertising that glamorize violence and unrestrained sex? What about parents who allow their children to watch these programs or buy the videos and video games for them?

What about government officials who cut hundreds of thousands—even millions—of dollars from programs vital to the health, education, and development of children in poverty and spend it on a war that leaves thousands of children in the other nation homeless, wounded, parentless, or dead? What about those of us who elect those officials?

What about a government that, because of its affinity with corporations and with the wealthy, carries out tax programs that tomorrow will burden today's children and grandchildren with a tax debt almost beyond imagination? Again, what about those of us who elect the officials in that government?

Yes, something should be done about child abuse. The problem is that the more far reaching forms of child abuse are so much a part of our daily routine that we fail to recognize our own complicity in them.

September 18, 2005

MODERN VERSIONS OF CHILD SACRIFICE

Archaeologists of the ancient near east long ago discovered at the base of city walls and gates of some of the cities of ancient Israel the remains of children's bodies. Scholars are divided as to whether these remains indicate the sacrifice of children for the protection of the city or whether they are entombed bodies of children from wealthy families who died of natural causes. A chilling line in the Old Testament book 2 Kings says that one of the reasons God used the Assyrians to destroy the northern kingdom of Israel was specifically that Israel had caused its sons and daughters to "pass through the fire" (2 Kgs 17:31, author's translation), an expression that usually refers to human sacrifice. It seems clear, then, that at least at some point in its history, the northern kingdom did engage in child sacrifice.

Of course, any normal person is horrified by such an idea. Who could possibly offer their children as sacrifice?

The purpose of human sacrifice, as was the purpose of most other sacrifice, was to gain favor with the gods. It was, in short, a matter of self-interest—in this case, sacrifice your child to the gods so things might go better, for you.

Put just that way, is it really true that we don't practice child sacrifice? What is it but child sacrifice when we condemn our children and grandchildren to future crippling tax loads because we cannot control our desires today? What is it but child sacrifice to the gods of war when older people send younger people to die or to be wounded in battle for our protection? What is it, if not child sacrifice, when we condemn our children and grandchildren to an environmentally devastated future because we are too morally and politically retarded to take steps today to protect the environment? What is it, if not child sacrifice, when we use abortion as a means of birth control for our own convenience?

And why should we think that although God judged Israel for child sacrifice, God will ignore those forms of child sacrifice in which we moderns—including Christians—engage?

January 21, 2007

9

Theology and Ethics

WHERE THE SPIRIT MOVES

CHRISTIANS SOMETIMES SEEM TO assume that the Holy Spirit works only in the church or through the church. Whether we belong to denominations that view the sacraments as instruments through which the Spirit works upon us or to denominations that emphasize the outpouring of the Spirit in a service of singing and preaching, we probably never talk much about the work of the Spirit "out there in the world."

To affirm that God is the Trinity—Father, Son, and Holy Spirit—and also to assume that the Spirit works only in and through the church is also to imply that the Father and the Son work only in and through the church, for the Trinity cannot be divided in action. To suggest that any member of the Trinity works only within the church is to say that all members work only there. Obviously, this is counter to the biblical view that God works throughout God's creation. If Jesus Christ is Lord of the entire creation, then surely, Father, Son, and Holy Spirit—as one—work, each in his own way, even in the catastrophes of places such as Bosnia, Iraq, the Sudan, Iran, and all sorts of other places, most of which we probably have never even heard. We may not know what God is up to in such places, but we dare not deny that God is there.

The church has been given the Holy Spirit to empower it to be God's people in the world. It is established by the Father, commissioned by the Son, and empowered by the Spirit. Jesus has promised that he will be with us to the end of the Age, that is, to the end of the world as we know it. He has not said that he will be with only us. The church, as the bearer of the Spirit, is called to bear witness to what God is doing even before the church shows up. Perhaps if we acted on this assumption, all of us would be a bit more humble about what sometimes seems to be the assumption that we Christians have a corner on the God market.

May 23, 2004

A SPIRITUALITY OF INVOLVEMENT

It's not unusual to hear someone say, "Well, I'm not really religious, but I am spiritual." I think that when they say this, people mean that while they don't want any part of organized religion, don't want to be a part of any group, and don't subscribe to the teachings of any particular religion, they do believe in some sort of god and like to read and talk about matters of religion in general. This type of spirituality emphasizes how one feels about one's self. It is sort of like enjoying a soft breeze on a summer afternoon, with a nice, cold drink nearby, and thinking soothing, religious thoughts.

When I was growing up, being spiritual had certain moral implications. It meant being unconcerned about material conditions, never getting angry, and, when amused, showing that amusement by a slight smile—never by an outright laugh. In fact, laughing very often or very loudly branded you as being probably not spiritual at all. People who did think of themselves as spiritual to any degree usually were too modest to say so in public.

It's easy to appreciate today's version of spirituality when you consider the bureaucracy, self-aggrandizement, and hypocrisy of much organized religion. No one could have been any harsher on the corruption of religious structures than the Old Testament prophets and Jesus himself. Jesus sometimes was angry and biting in his comments.

The spirituality of the prophets and of Jesus was not a matter of looking inward to a personal, subjective condition, but of looking outward to consider what God's Holy Spirit was up to in the world and of aligning themselves with that work. Being spiritual in a biblical sense is coming under the influence of God's Holy Spirit and being so transformed by that Spirit that we manifest in our lives the characteristics of Jesus himself.

Manifesting this kind of spirituality, we often will find ourselves angry—angry over the violence and duplicity of this world, over the corruption of human governments, and over the church's frequent timidity toward and outright protection of the structures of this world that harm and destroy human beings. True spirituality often leads to aggressive action on behalf of the disadvantaged in this world. This is precisely the spirituality that the sacraments, received by faith, are supposed to nurture and increase. We might think about that, whether we are Methodist, Presbyterian, Baptist, Catholic, or whatever, the next time we receive the sacrament associated with Jesus' Last Supper.

Just as in the early church, so today, true spirituality can be a dangerous thing.

April 30, 2006

VALUES

Historically, the word *values* has referred to the importance a group, a society, or a nation has placed upon a condition, a way of behaving, an activity, or an object. *Values* has referred to whatever was considered—at the risk of using a word to define itself—*valuable*. Plato believed that the search for truth is the most important value. Confucius considered the fine arts so important for the development of a good society that he believed that a society without the fine arts would not long be a healthy one.

In light of the modern assumption that democratic rule is a value that should be imposed upon the world, it is interesting to note that neither Plato, nor Confucius, nor the writers of the Bible considered democracy an important value. In fact, Plato believed that democracy would lead to the downfall of a society and thought that philosophers should rule, Confucius wanted a good emperor, and the biblical writers longed for the rule of a divinely chosen king.

The values—if we can use that word—of the Old Testament prophets, of Jesus, and of the New Testament writers included both what some today consider personal values (sexual morality, for example) and what some consider social values (for example, fighting against poverty and maintaining honesty in national and international politics). They didn't separate the personal from the social, but assumed that these work in tandem with each other.

Obviously, values will differ from one group, nation, or individual to another.

So for one group or one nation to charge another with having *no* values simply because their values and morals differ from each other is to shanghai the language. And that is a dangerous value indeed.

November 21, 2004

SPIRITUALITY AND SOCIAL ACTION

Spirituality and social action frequently are viewed as two separate compartments of Christian life—spirituality viewed as basic to the authentic life, social action as a desirable, but not essential, outcome of that spirituality.

This view also separates evangelism and social action. Those who emphasize spirituality say that a truly spiritual life will result in Christian deeds, while those who emphasize social action will acknowledge that Christian social action must be undergirded by spirituality. In the latter case, spirituality is a tool that produces action. In the former, action is a desirable by-product of spirituality. Unfortunately, separating the two—even if they are seen as mutually necessary—results in the distortion of both.

This distinction is simply another form of the separation between faith and works—a warped distinction that historically has set Protestants against Catholics and most Christians against Jews. But the New Testament Letter of James had it exactly right: "Show me your faith apart from your works, and by my works I will show you my faith" (James 2:18b). Even the Apostle Paul—who usually is cited as the authority for separating faith and works and exalting faith over works—wrote to the Christians in Rome that God will render to every person according to that person's works (Romans 2:6).

A closer reading of the New Testament reveals that such compartmentalizing is a grave error. In the New Testament, evangelism is the proclamation that in Jesus Christ God has begun to reclaim the entire creation. In the resulting new order, the Holy Spirit—as God's agent—is at work to transform human life from a condition of self-interest into one that impels us actively to seek the well-being not only of all God's creatures, but of all God's Creation. In this view, evangelism is not simply words; it is the totality of our lives. In genuine evangelism, words and actions cannot be totally separated. Our words interpret the nature of our actions—or our works. Our faith is manifested in our works.

Of course, it is possible to act and do good works apart from faith, just as it is possible to consider oneself spiritual—that is, is a person "having" faith—while living a totally self-serving life. But neither of these manifests either the faith or the works of the Kingdom of which the New Testament speaks.

Truly gospel rooted social action is not an outcome of evangelism, but is evangelism by deed, showing the truth of what is proclaimed. In truly gospel rooted spirituality our works—our actions—are not simply the result of faith, but are faith made flesh.

May 8, 2005

MISS AMERICA AND THE VIRGIN MARY

When ABC television announced last year that it was dropping the Miss America pageant, for the first time in fifty years the pageant was in danger of not having a t-v home. Now, the country music channel has picked up the pageant.

Ever since the first Miss America Pageant, in 1921, the image of the beauty queen has been a primary influence in defining womanhood in western society, and Christians—like everyone else—have bought into this ideal. Many church-related colleges and universities have held beauty contests, and beauty queens frequently are invited to give their testimony at religious gatherings. I am not questioning the faith of these women when I ask why homely women are never invited. The answer is simple: even churches know that sex sells. Churches seem not to comprehend the contradiction between condemning sexual immorality and using sex as a sales gimmick.

In today's society, sexual beauty often defines womanhood. In effect, as Harvey Cox pointed out years ago,[1] the beauty queen has become an alternative to and an implicit competitor of the original Madonna—Mary, the Mother of Jesus. The demise of beauty pageants on television does not necessarily mean that this competition no longer exists, but simply that given the nudity and sex available on the cable, the pageants simply have become too tame for many viewers.

Over the centuries, the church has developed an image of Mary rooted in character rather than physical beauty. Depictions of Mary in Christian art have emphasized her serenity and faithfulness. In keeping with the book of Proverbs' observation that "charm is deceitful, and beauty is to no avail, but a woman who stands in awe of the LORD is to be praised (Prov 31:30)," Christian tradition has emphasized the beauty of Mary's character—embodying, at the same time, both gentleness and strength, modesty and self-assurance, submissiveness to God and personal initiative.

---

1. Harvey Cox, *The Secular City* (New York: Macmillan, 1965).

From that perspective, Mary is an attractive model not only of authentic womanhood, but of authentic human nature for all of us, men and women alike.

July 11, 2005

SEXUAL STEREOTYPES AND THE BIBLE

Traditional stereotypes dictate that men are supposed to be strong, tough, and assertive and that women are supposed to be tender, compassionate, and submissive. The sexual revolution of the last half-century challenged these stereotypes, but it also had some interesting consequences. Some women, for example, took on some of the harsher characteristics of the male stereotype. On the other hand, some men's groups opposed what they viewed as the feminization of men in western society.

Because some Christian groups insist that the traditional stereotypes are commanded by divine revelation, other Christians—as well as some persons other than Christian—are surprised to learn that numerous passages in the Bible challenge those stereotypes. For example, one of the words most often associated with God in both the Old and the New Testaments is *mercy*. Many in the ancient world considered mercy undesirable on the grounds that it undercut justice. Many today would agree—at least with regard to justice for others, not for themselves.

The Hebrew word translated *mercy* in the Old Testament translates a Hebrew word that refers to a woman's womb. As merciful, God treats us as a mother is expected to treat her child. Such a word play is not clear in the Greek of the New Testament, but Jesus himself spoke Aramaic, a cousin language to Hebrew. It is reasonable to suppose, therefore, that when Jesus said that God blesses the merciful, he had the Old Testament understanding of mercy in mind. If so, he was saying that whether we are male or female, we are to care for others as we would care for them were we their mother.

The Apostle Paul taught his churches that by their baptism they had been incorporated into a community upon which God had bestowed God's Holy Spirit. If they did not hinder the Spirit, the Spirit would transform the life of the community and—consequently—the lives of the individual members of the community. In his letter to the church in Galatia Paul portrayed that transformation by contrasting the life of self-interest, to which he referred as the works of the flesh, with the fruits that the

Spirit produces. Among those fruits, said Paul, are patience, kindness, and gentleness (Gal 5:22-23)—characteristics usually associated in western society with feminine stereotypes.

Not very *macho*, but thoroughly biblical.

June 27, 2004

SPONGEBOB, TOLERANCE, AND LOVE

Last November, when I asked my moderately conservative daughter what one of my grandsons might like for Christmas, she replied, "Something related to SpongeBob SquarePants." This shows my daughter's tolerance in that she doesn't like SpongeBob SquarePants, but thinks he is too silly. And she's right. SpongeBob is the star of one of the silliest kid shows on t-v. But it is that sort of silliness that is so silly that to some of us it is hilarious. So I bought my grandson a DVD of the first season of the SpongeBob series, and he was delighted.

SpongeBob is under attack now by some who interpret his holding hands with his friend Patrick as an effort to promote tolerance and acceptance of homosexuality. Well, one problem with that is that Patrick is not a sponge, but a starfish. *SpongeBob SquarePants* is not about people who are *alike* holding hands, but about people who are *not* alike being able to live with each other in relative peace and harmony by tolerating those who are different.

On the basis of the New Testament, however, I would have to say that SpongeBob simply doesn't go far enough. Jesus did not teach that we are to tolerate the neighbor—or the enemy—but that we are to love them. The word in the New Testament translated *love* means to give complete, total attention not to our own needs, but to the needs of others—even if the other is our enemy and even if the enemy kills us while we are trying to attend to the enemy's needs.

Tolerance says, "I'm right (meaning *better than you*), but I'll allow you to survive." Love says, "Better you survive than I." Tolerance is acceptance in isolation. Love reaches out in humility to bring us together. But in a pluralistic society divided by anger, hostility, and hatred, SpongeBob's tolerance is not a bad start.

February 6, 2005

THE DELUSION OF ATTEMPTING TO INSTILL ETHICS

For a number of years, colleges and universities across the country have introduced courses and segments of courses on ethics. Earlier, this was done in the name of character education. More recently, it has been in response to corporate business scandals. Apparently, the assumption is that people are more likely to behave ethically if they understand the issue at hand. But having information and having a greater understanding of a matter can just as easily facilitate unethical actions. Education—whether defined as information gathering or as critical thinking—cannot transform the human heart. Any parent who has ever attempted to reason with a headstrong child knows that.

Instead of concentrating on ethics and morality, the church and church related institutions should concentrate on their ethos. An ethos is a person, a group, or a nation's basic perspective on and attitude toward the world. Actions arise spontaneously from our ethos and reveal what we truly are. In other words, our ethos is manifested, or embodied, in our actions. We show what we are by what we do.

The Bible itself does not give us an ethic or a set of ethics, but an ethos. What we usually consider rules and regulations are in reality examples of a way of living—an approach to life. We can establish rules of behavior and enforce them by threats of punishment or by positive reinforcement, but in so doing we do not transform character. We merely strengthen fear or self-interest in those under the rules. Genuine Christ-like character is a creation of God. It is established in community through attention to the scripture and participation in the sacraments.

The apostle Paul said that anything that does not grow out of faith is sin (Rom 14:23)—which suggests that even were we to restore official prayer and Bible reading to the classroom and place the Ten Commandments in every school room in the nation, and if every student then obeyed the Commandments simply as rules and regulations, those students still would be engaging in sin.

It is a delusion, then, to imagine that we can instill ethics or morality in persons of any age. Ethics and morality emerge from within. If we concentrate on ethos, ethics and morals will take care of themselves.

May 31, 2005

NO EASY ANSWERS

The murder of students and faculty at Virginia Tech University led, as incidents of great destruction usually do, to calls on every hand for explanation. In the wake of earthquakes and hurricanes, the question of God's role, if any, inevitably is raised. In the event of mass killings, the questions are about social versus individual responsibility and the reality of evil. Those who emphasize society's role speak of the violent nature of today's society and the easy availability of guns, frequently portraying the killer or killers as themselves victims along with those they have murdered.

Those who emphasize personal responsibility say that the killers would have been able to acquire the weapons no matter how many gun control laws were passed, and they point out that everyone is exposed to violence, but that not everyone becomes a killer. And those who speak of the reality of evil in the world usually have little interest in sociological or psychological explanations.

It is commonly assumed that to explain an event by one discipline is automatically to rule out or make irrelevant the explanations of other disciplines. If we can show the scientific explanation for a tsunami, for example, we may assume that no other consideration, including a theological one, is relevant. On the other hand, those who consider a tsunami the judgment of God usually have no interest in physical explanations.

But reality is not nearly as one-dimensional as these positions assume. In fact, most of our problems on such a scale are not rooted soley in mere human, social causes, but also have a cosmic dimension. The New Testament recognizes that this world is constantly under the influence of transcendent Powers that God created to serve God's purposes in the Creation, but that have gone their own way and constantly seek to undermine God's will by provoking chaos and confusion in God's world. In the words of the Letter to the Ephesians, "We struggle not against flesh and blood, but against the principalities . . . against the spiritual hosts of wickedness in the heavenly places" (Eph 6:12). Ephesians is not speaking here of the familiar comic figure with a pitchfork, horns, and pointed tail, but of something far more serious and far more deadly.

Because the Powers, like God, are transcendent we cannot know them in and of themselves—cannot see them face to face—but can see them only as they manifest themselves in various guises in the daily world—in institutions, organizations, movements, and individuals. Murder and violence, for example—whether by an individual or by an institution—are events in which the Powers manifest themselves.

But to see such actions as the result of the work of the Powers does not make irrelevant the analyses of sociology, psychology, and other disciplines. Instead, the Powers use, as instruments for their work, those very events that sociologists and psychologists accurately and helpfully describe in the language of their disciplines. None of the disciplines, theology included, ever will be able to answer all the questions. Why does the violence of society seduce some and make them a part of the violence, but repel others, motivating them to work for solutions? How far should a perpetrator's background and situation be taken into account in determining innocence or guilt and the nature of the sentence? What can society do to reduce the incidence of violence? Neither psychology, sociology, nor theology has a definitive answer to those questions. Psychology can speak of the mental illness of the perpetrators, sociology can speak of the influence of social structures and culture, and theology can remind us that the problem has cosmic dimensions. Each has a role to play in struggling with the problems. But when all has been said and done, the mystery remains.

May 4, 2007

THE NEW AGE AND CAPITAL PUNISHMENT

To develop a perspective on social issues in New Testament terms—issues such as war and capital punishment—we have to understand the New Testament view of the nature of history. The New Testament assumes that the history of the entire Creation is divided into two different eras—the Old Age and the New Age.

To understand this view, imagine two large circles side-by-side on a sheet of paper. One circle contains the history of this world, from the beginning until the time when God acts to change the course of history. This circle is the world as we know it—a world which, though having known some instances of nobility and humane action, is basically characterized by violence and death. In this world, God has given human governments the responsibility of keeping order and justice. Also in this world, God established Israel to be God's instrument for the blessing of the world; and he gave Israel its own law called *torah*. Because of the violent nature of this world, both secular law and torah contain elements—including rules of war and provisions for capital punishment—with the specific purpose of curbing violence. For example, family insults or injuries are not to be repaid with unchecked bloodshed, but retaliation is limited to only an eye for an eye or a tooth for a tooth. The first circle represents the Old Age.

The other circle represents the New Age, the world as God intends it eventually to be—a world of peace and love. Now, imagine the second circle moved to slightly overlap the first. This represents the New Age's invasion of the Old Age.

Jesus proclaimed that God already is beginning to establish the New Age, here in the midst of the Old. The church stands in this overlapping of the Ages. And in this time of overlapping, the church has two responsibilities. One is to live according to the character of the New Age in order to show the kind of life God now makes possible. The second is to remind the human authorities of the Old Age of their responsibility for justice and order in terms of their own values. The church, for example, must warn the state that capital punishment as it is now carried out is unjust. And it must point out that the cost of capital punishment is financially irresponsible.

On the other hand, these factors of the Old Age are irrelevant for the church's own rejection of warfare and capital punishment. Disciples of Jesus are to reject warfare and capital punishment simply because Jesus said that we are to turn the other cheek and that we are to love the enemy. Warfare and capital punishment are instruments of the Old Age, not of the New. They bring death rather than life. And their acceptance is a repudiation of Jesus himself.

August 13, 2006

JUSTICE AND A MORATORIUM ON THE DEATH PENALTY

Although Tennesseans differ greatly on the issue of capital punishment, it does not follow that those who support the death penalty are unconcerned about whether it is administered justly and fairly. Earlier this year the Tennessee Legislature passed a bill calling for the creation of a special committee to study the administration of the death penalty in Tennessee. In the wake of that law, a coalition of diverse organizations, with differences over capital punishment itself but believing that most Tennesseans support justice and fairness, is now seeking a moratorium on the death penalty pending the committee's report. The committee—composed of government leaders, attorneys, and representatives from a variety of groups with varying positions on capital punishment—has one year to complete its study.

In February Governor Bredesen enacted a 90-day moratorium on the death penalty, apparently because of lawsuits based on the bizarre content of some parts of the state's manual for capital punishment. For example, executioners were advised to have fire extinguishers ready, to "engage the automatic rheostat," and to disconnect the electrical cables before allowing a doctor to examine the inmate. One reason for the confusion in the manual was that it mixed instructions for lethal injection with instructions for the electric chair—two quite different methods of execution. In May, the Governor expressed satisfaction with the revised guidelines and allowed the moratorium to "die a natural death," so to speak.

But not everyone is as convinced as the Governor that the guidelines are yet sufficient. In April the American Bar Association released a report that said that of the widely accepted list of ninety-three criteria for a fair, accurate, and constitutional system of capital punishment, "Tennessee meets only seven . . . , partially meets 31 . . . , and fails to comply with 26 . . . ."

The present effort toward a moratorium is not an attempt to eliminate capital punishment, but is an effort to put it on hold pending an adequate study of its administration. Many people on both sides of the issue of capital punishment support such a moratorium. As long ago as March, 2002, the Nashville Metro government passed a resolution calling for a moratorium.

Most of the people whom I hear defend capital punishment do so, to one degree or another, on the basis of justice. Certain crimes, they say, are so heinous that they justify the death penalty. But although present figures do not prove the state's system to be unjust, they certainly are cause for question. One would think, then, that a strong commitment to justice would lead to support for a moratorium until the present system truly can be thoroughly evaluated. If it is not just, how can it be made just?

Although I personally oppose capital punishment, those who support it are quite able to muster scripture for their position. In his letter to the Romans the Apostle Paul speaks of those exercising governmental authority as wielding the sword under the authority of God for the purpose of punishing evildoers (Rom 13:3-4). This usually is interpreted to mean that the state has the authority to preserve a just order. It implies, however, that any exercise of authority unjustly violates that responsibility. When this occurs, the church and individual Christians have a responsibility—as a prophetic community—to recall the state to its proper use of the sword and to demand, in the name of God, that it exercise its authority in a just, fair, and even-handed manner. A study of the present capital punishment system in Tennessee, to determine whether the State of Tennessee truly is just in its administration of that penalty, is long overdue.

While preparing to write this column, I happened upon a website whose owner, calling himself a Christian, wrote: "While some innocent people probably do get caught in the system, the risk is worth the injustice of the guilty living on death row for 20-plus years." He speculated that probably more guilty people are executed than are innocent ones. So I asked myself, if this person were walking the proverbial last mile, but were innocent of the crime for which he was being executed, do think he would he say to the guards, "It's okay, fellahs. I'm happy to do this; it's my contribution to the protection of the system"?

I wouldn't bet on it.

September 12, 2007

A QUESTION OF MIRACLES

Whenever the United States becomes involved in military action, Christians in this nation seem to forget that we have brother and sister Christians in the nation (or nations) with which the U.S. is in conflict. We may forget or ignore them, but they are there, nevertheless. For example, there are approximately one million Christians in Iraq. Under Saddam Hussein, of course, they were at a disadvantage, but they were there.

When the United States becomes involved—or seems about to become involved—in conflict, the churches of the nation usually become either supporters or opponents of the action. In both instances, the churches usually speak as though they think of themselves as American first and Christian second. But the Christian church—fragmented as it is—is a world-wide body with one Lord. When some church leaders were making what were legitimate objections to the build-up for war in Iraq, might it not have been truer to our identity as the Church, in the weeks leading up to the war, for representatives of all churches to have made contacts with Christians in Iraq to discuss what we might do together to work for peace and justice whether or not war came? A few representatives from a few churches did make such a trip, and they were vilified even by many Christians as traitors and busybodies. But what if all Christians in North and South America, Europe, Asia, and Africa had made a unified effort to stave off the conflict? What might have happened if Christian groups from all over the world had joined hands with peace loving Muslims all over the world, not only to avoid conflict, but to work for humane conditions in the entire Middle East? Of course, we didn't.

One reason we did not make that effort is our division into competing and sometimes hostile bodies within the church. But an even more serious reason is that we simply do not believe in miracles. We may say we believe Jesus literally turned water to wine, walked on water, and brought forth Lazarus from the grave, and some of us may be ready to fight anyone who doesn't believe in the virgin birth of Christ and his bodily resurrection. But that God might use the world-wide church for peace in the face of international terrorism? Why you must think we believe in miracles!

June 6, 2004

THE TWO SIDES OF POLYGAMY

Although the Utah trial of Warren Jeffs on charges of accessory to rape was not about polygamy, it did put the spotlight on polygamy as the context of the offense. The woman in the case is a member of the Fundamentalist Church of Jesus Christ of Latter Day Saints (the Fundamentalist LDS church), and perhaps a brief word about that group will be helpful.

Until 1890 the original Church of Jesus Christ of Latter Day Saints (the LDS church) had taught the practice of "plural marriages" on the basis of four religious beliefs. First, according to LDS doctrine, all human souls exist in the heavenly realm before being born into the earthly realm. Second, Mormons were encouraged to have large families to increase the number of preexistent souls born into Mormon families. Third, Joseph Smith had organized the LDS church according to the structure of Israel in the Old Testament, with a strong emphasis on male rule. And fourth, plural marriage was said to be an exalting practice resulting in highest recognition in the next life.

In 1890, however, in order for the state of Utah to be admitted into the United States, William Woodruff, President of the ruling Quorum and Prophet in the Mormon church, issued a Manifesto stating that Mormons would give up plural marriage. Because many Mormons continued to engage in plural marriages, Woodruff issued a second Manifesto in 1904 affirming the first.

Little wonder that those who believed that Joseph Smith's teachings had been inspired by God considered Woodruff an apostate. Some members left the church and started separate movements. One of those movements—the Fundamentalist LDS Church—claims that in 1886, four years before Woodruff's first Manifesto, Mormon official John Taylor (then head of the church) received a secret revelation from God reaffirming plural marriages. The LDS Church has consistently denied that Taylor received such a revelation and has accepted Woodruff's declaration as authoritative.

The last fifty years have seen an increasing tolerance for polygamy in western states by Mormons and non-Mormons alike. This probably has been in reaction to a 1953 raid on a polygamous colony on the Utah-Arizona border and pictures of children in that raid being taken from their parents and placed in foster homes. But most surprising of all, in 1991 the Utah Supreme Court ruled that it is legal for polygamous families to adopt children.

It would be a mistake to believe that all plural marriages are of the same quality. Some women in plural marriages extol their benefits, while others speak of the difficulties and even the slave-like conditions of the arrangement. But many wives in monogamous marriages outside the Mormon Church also endure all sorts of physical and mental abuse. It is doubtful that the quality of a family is determined by the number of spouses in the arrangement.

In the Old Testament, polygamy was a perfectly acceptable arrangement. The patriarchs Abraham and Jacob and the kings David and Solomon, all, had polygamous marriages. As for the New Testament, although some people correctly point out that it contains no examples of plural marriage, one passage suggests that the early church did not prohibit it: "A bishop must be the husband of one wife" (1 Timothy 3:2). Some interpret this to mean that a divorced bishop may not remarry. Others say it means that a widowed bishop may not marry again. More likely, it is an attempt by a later writer to apply to a later situation Paul's words in 1 Corinthians 14. There Paul points out that those who are married have responsibilities toward their spouse. The responsibilities of a bishop are such that no one can handle the responsibilities of that office and also those of a husband of more than one wife.

In the final analysis, polygamy, in and of itself, is a sociological issue, not a theological one. In any nation, should some disaster result in a population composed of two-thirds women and one-third men, polygamy might—for economic and human security purposes—be a reasonable, acceptable solution. The religious issue would be the quality of the relationships within the marriages—faithfulness, justice, and equity.

I am in no way advocating polygamy for today's society. I am simply questioning whether there is any valid religious reason to prohibit it.

A friend of mine, a United Methodist minister, visited a small village in Africa in which most of the people recently had become Christians, specifically Methodists. When the chief of the village introduced my friend to his several wives, my friend wondered what he could say since in the United States the practice seems often to be—even among Christians—what several have called "sequential polygamy".

I think my friend is a very perceptible fellow.

October 11, 2007

FAITH, DOUBT, AND JOB

Many people seem to think of faith as essentially an activity of thought, a mental collection of beliefs and ideas. People who object to infant baptism, for example, frequently do so on the grounds that an infant is not able to think or to understand the importance of the act. In such a view, baptism requires a mind capable of believing and of knowing what it believes. In such a view of faith, the great enemy of faith is doubt.

It has not been unusual across the years to hear a frustrated student say, "I doubt so many things I was taught as a child that now I don't know *what* to believe. I think I am losing my faith." I have heard teen-agers about to enter college warned about teachers who would force them to question their faith and try to destroy it.

The book of Job, however, suggests that faith is not so much a system of belief or thought as it is a relationship, a relationship that exists and endures despite incomplete knowledge and even despite serious doubts about specific doctrines and ideas. At the beginning of the book, Job knows what he believes. His doctrine is all in order; his theology, all worked out. But this means that he assumes that he has God all figured out. He assumes that God is predictable; therefore, he feels comfortable with God. In brief, he has come to worship a domesticated God.

God then allows Satan to rob Job of his children, his crops, his livestock, and his house. Job himself is covered from head to foot with sores. Only Job's wife remains, and she criticizes Job for his continuing faith.

In the rest of the book, however, Job becomes frustrated and angry because he thinks that God is punishing him for some unknown sin. Eventually, unable to understand what has happened to him, Job demands a face-to-face meeting with God. In the Revised Standard Version Job says that he knows that God will kill him, but that at least, it will not be a godless man who comes before God (Job 13:15-16).

At this point, Job not only has had everything he previously believed about God stripped away from him. He no longer knows what *to* believe, but only what he no longer *can* believe. On the other hand, Job knows that only God can enable him to reshape his belief.

Job's faith is his determination to confront the God about whom he no longer knows what to believe. The loss of belief has not meant a loss of relationship, even though the relationship that remains is one of confrontation rather than one of assent. Doubt has not destroyed Job's faith, but has purified it.

Elie Wiesel observed in a television interview a few years ago that you can be a Jew with God and you can be a Jew against God, but you cannot be a Jew without God. Job's faith was a faith expressed against God, a faith purified by Job's doubt and protest and God's response to that protest.

Faith can be compared to the house in which we live; beliefs, to the furniture in that house. In an ordinary house, from time to time, we shift around the furniture and sometimes even replace some of the old furniture with new. It is the same with the house of faith. From study, experience, or both, we sometimes have to rearrange some of the furniture or even replace some older pieces with newer ones. In such cases, doubt hasn't destroyed the house; it simply has let us know that the furniture needed tending.

April 22, 2007

EVOLUTION, INTELLIGENT DESIGN, AND THE GREAT SOMEONE

Although the debate over evolution versus Intelligent Design has never gone away, the movie "Expelled" has brought it once again to the surface. The proponents of Intelligent Design say that because the theory of evolution assumes that all living things, including human beings, developed through accident, chance, or—specifically—random selection, it promotes atheism.

Although at first that seems to hold a certain logic, various stories in the Old Testament suggest another possibility. For example, in the story of the Hebrews crossing the Red Sea (Exod 14), God is said to have caused a great wind to blow all night and part the sea. Then, when the Egyptians followed the Hebrews, the waters returned to their place and the Egyptians were drowned. The narrative says that when the Egyptian soldiers saw that they were stuck in the mud and that the sea was returning, they cried out that the LORD was fighting against Egypt and for the Israelites. Although some readers, believing in the literal nature of every word in the Bible, will insist that this cry by the Egyptians is factual, it is difficult to see how whoever wrote the account knew what the Egyptian soldiers said. I suspect that had some Egyptian soldier escaped the incident and returned to report to Pharaoh, he probably would have attributed the defeat not to the God of the Hebrews, but to a great wind. Had he seen Moses holding up his rod over the waters, he probably would have considered it sheer coincidence.

Ancient writers sometimes used coincidence to show a divine hand working invisibly in history. In the story of Joseph, for example, Joseph's being sold into slavery resulted in a string of coincidences that eventually put Joseph in a position to save both Egypt and his own family from drought. And in the Protestant Bible's version of the book of Esther, God is never mentioned. Events happen as coincidence.

The Bible, then, portrays God frequently acting through what from a human perspective seems coincidence, chance, or accident. Random selection falls into the same category. But terms such as chance and random selection are human terms that indicate our inability to see and measure any connections among or between specific events. To assert that God is at work in coincidence, chance, accident, or random selection is not a scientific assertion, but one of philosophy or religion. To reject the theory of evolution on the grounds that it assumes random selection, therefore, is to overlook that random selection is a term used to describe only our human perspective. With regard to unmeasurable causes, science cannot be either theistic or atheistic and remain science. It can only be agnostic.

A major problem underlying the debate over evolution versus Intelligent Design is the way that many Christians have separated the work of God from the everyday events of nature and history. If something is viewed as having happened naturally or coincidentally or randomly, it is assumed that God had nothing to do with it. This inevitably leads to what Dietrich Bonhoeffer called "the God of the gaps", the God to whom we attribute involvement only in those things we do not (yet) understand. For Bonhoeffer, however, mystery is at the very heart not merely of what we do not understand but of what we do understand, as well.

Actually, the theory of Intelligent Design has a serious problem with its view of the God whose existence it purports to prove. In the 1950's pop song "I Believe" one line was, "I believe that Someone in the great Somewhere hears every word." Such wording seems to assume that it doesn't matter in what god you believe, just as long as you believe in "a god". It is surprising that Intelligent Design is the brain child of certain conservative Christians, because the god of Intelligent Design is precisely a Someone in the Great Somewhere. Those proponents cannot show that the Someone does hear every word or that, if he (it, she) does hear, he (it, she) can do anything about it. Not very comforting to a parent who watches a child die of leukemia, from a drive-by shooting, or from starvation or to a wife or husband who loses a spouse in the dusty streets of Iraq or Afghanistan.

Among the threats to the beliefs of school children is not that evolution is taught as science, but that science classes might teach them that the God who created the universe and all things in it is simply a great Someone in the Great Somewhere. Christians, Jews, and Muslims should be among the first to reject the god of Intelligent Design, for it is not the God of Abraham and Sarah, of Isaac and Rebecca, of Jacob and Rachel and Leah, of Muhammad, or of Jesus. It is, instead, an idol, and as such, is not merely irrelevant for genuine faith, but is, in fact, destructive of it.

April 24, 2008

ON BEING NICE AND BEING CHRISTIAN

There is a widespread notion that if a person—especially a Christian minister—is rude or disruptive, he or she is not behaving in a Christian manner. Many people expect Christians to be *nice*. Well, some Christian writers recently have leveled strong attacks on this idea. There is nothing Christian, they say, about being *nice*.

The word *nice* comes from a Middle English word that meant *simple, foolish,* and even *silly.* The Latin source of the word was *necius,* which meant *ignorant.* The preferred meanings of *nice* in the *Merriam-Webster Dictionary* are *precise, particular,* and *exacting in standards,* as when we say that someone has a nice taste in music or clothes. The words *agreeable, socially acceptable, polite,* and *kind* appear as less preferred meanings.

Actually, the word *nice* never appears in the New Testament. Jesus never said, "Blessed are the nice." The Apostle Paul never included *nice* in his several lists of the fruit or the gifts of the Holy Spirit. In fact, there are instances when Jesus wasn't nice. He drove the money changers from the Temple and accused the officials of having turned the Temple into a den of thieves and robbers (Mark 11:17). He told his opponents that they were the children of the Devil (John 8:44). He even told his followers they would have enemies (John 15:18-19), which suggests that some who heard them would not consider them *nice.*

So I am not really impressed when someone says of a person who has just died, "He (or she) didn't have an enemy in the world." Our faithfulness to Jesus Christ is measured not by whether we are always nice and have no enemies, but by who our enemies are.

There is, however, a danger in the current attack on being *nice.* It can easily be heard by some as permission to be obnoxious, self-righteous, and egotistical. The seduction of power is perhaps the greatest threat a pastor—or any Christian—faces. That as Christians we may sometimes have to be other than *nice* does no mean that we are free to be as insensitive to others as our ego demands. Christians are not called to be either nice or rude, but to love, and—unfortunately—sometimes that can require not being very nice.

November 5, 2006

NO NATION—OR CHURCH—IS AN ISLAND

As a result of modern means of travel and communication, no nation today can be, to borrow a phrase from John Donne, "an island unto itself." "Each," again to borrow Donne's image, "is a part of the main." A virus from a spot on one side of the globe can spark an epidemic on the opposite side in less than a month. Nuclear warheads can be delivered from one hemisphere to the other more quickly and more efficiently than can food and medical aid.

In such a world, starving and diseased people in the so-called "Third World" can be ignored by nations of plenty and nations comfortably situated only at grave risk to the peace and stability and, eventually, to the economic and health security of the entire world. Although there are no biblical grounds for saying that any nation *must* feed the hungry and clothe the naked of another nation, common sense should tell us that simple, enlightened self-interest makes it advantageous to do so.

The Christian church lives in this same world. And unlike the secular nations, the church *does* have a mandate to care for the poor—even at the cost of self-sacrifice. It has the responsibility—when the media, with their short attention span, have moved on to the next circulation or Nielsen boosting problem or incident—to stick around and maintain its focus. While eating dinner, Christians, just as regularly as others, watch t-v footage of starvation and carnage in the world with those images seldom disturbing our appetites. Perhaps some, touched by the images, will ask why the well-off nations of the world do not do more to help the world's poor and starving. For Christians, however, the first question should not be why the United States or the U.N. does not do more to help the poor, but why we and our churches—with our gymnasiums, bowling alleys, and often exorbitant pastors' salaries—do not do more. I suspect we all know the answer to that one.

May 2, 2004

HOMOSEXUALITY AND THE FALLEN CREATION

Sex, as a subject, appears in many places in the Bible. In one—the creation narrative in Genesis 1—sex is viewed as an important part of God's good creation. The human race is created to be God's representative in the earth, caring for the earth and for all living things. That is what it means for humankind to have been created in the image of God. When God commands the humans to "be fruitful and multiply," therefore, God is not providing simply for the propagation of the human race, but for the perpetuation of the image of God. In other words, God created human beings as sexual beings so there might be a continuation of human beings to care for God's world.

In Genesis 3, however, the distortion and corruption of the good Creation sets in. Alienation between humankind and the animals, between humankind and the earth, and between man and woman sets in.

Alienation begins even within the image of God. And God allows this to happen!

Later, in the New Testament letter to the Christians at Rome, the Apostle Paul portrays many of the negative characteristics of human society as primarily expressions of that distorted, corrupted condition of the world. In other words, Paul does not seem to understand sin the way that most of us understand it. Sin is widely perceived as acts by which we evoke and initiate God's anger. Paul views these acts as symptoms of the world's having already fallen under the power of Sin. Just as pain tells us something is wrong with our body, sinful acts—according to Paul—tell us something is wrong with the human race and human society. In Romans 1, for example, Paul speaks of homosexuality first of all not in terms of a freely chosen act performed by an otherwise good individual—an act that evokes God's anger—but as one of the distortions that characterize and manifest the fallen condition of the world.

Paul does not say, as some people today contend, that homosexuality is good because God would not create something bad. Neither does he view it merely as a decision made in a vacuum. Interestingly enough, genetic research today increasingly suggests that genes play an important role in whether a person is born with a homosexual or a heterosexual inclination. As an inclination, homosexuality is a symptom of the world's being out of kilter. So, however, in Romans 1, are gossip, slander, lack of respect for parents, and all sorts of other things that characterize ordinary human society. Of course, how a person born with a homosexual inclination deals with that inclination becomes a matter of personal choice and decision.

To act on the assumption that homosexuality is not simply a human choice but also is a condition into which some human beings are born would by no means answer all the questions associated with the issue. But it should enable us to ask more discerning questions and to be guided toward more humane and more Christ-like answers.

April 18, 2004

THE THEOLOGICAL CHALLENGE
OF SPACE EXPLORATION

On July 20, 1969, Neil Armstrong and Buzz Aldrin planted a United States flag on the surface of the moon. It was an event watched all over the world on television; but its thirty-fifth anniversary a few days ago went relatively unnoticed. Nevertheless, although NASA now receives less than the four cents from each tax dollar it received in the late 1960's, we continue to send unmanned vehicles to the edge of the solar system and to construct a space station from which to push off to Mars.

Space exploration naturally raises the question of the implications for Christian faith and for understanding the Bible were we to find on other planets something at least resembling human life. Given the changes in the world since Orville Wright's twelve second flight on December 17, 1903, and given the difference between the 120 feet Orville's plane flew and the distance ships can travel today, it would be folly to underestimate what may happen by the middle of the present century.

When nineteenth century science showed the physical universe to be different from the way the writers of the Bible understood it, some theologians made the mistake of building their theology on the base of the new understanding of the universe. The result was an optimistic theology that saw the world and human beings becoming increasingly better from one generation to another.

For those holding the new theology, the horrors of two world wars were like a dash of cold water in the face. Evil, which to many nineteenth century theologians had seemed to be essentially a cultural lag, came to be seen as an enduring fact of life.

For many, this was a sobering warning that a theology too dependent on natural science will have to be abandoned when a particular scientific world view is superseded by another view. A sound theology is one able to view new understandings of the universe without having to be totally overhauled by those new understandings. Again and again, across the centuries, theology firmly rooted in the Bible has been found able to incorporate new scientific discoveries into its frame of reference and to share in mutual enrichment with those new discoveries. Only when the Bible has been assumed to hold a literal account of the history of the universe and of the human history has there been conflict.

Religion and theology can never answer the question of whether there is or might be life on other planets. They can and should, however, reflect on the implications of such discoveries should they occur. Science fiction and fantasy literature has long imagined life on other planets. Some, such as Ray Bradbury, have even speculated on the implications of such life for Christian belief. In one story, a team of space travelers—assuming that the messiah must visit every planet on which there is something akin to human life on Earth—chase relentlessly among the planets, hoping to see the messiah when he arrives.

The discovery of life forms on other planets would not render authentic biblical faith obsolete. It simply would require that we expand our understanding of what it means to say that Jesus Christ is Lord of the entire Creation.

July 25, 2004

10

Islam

WORDS AND THE PEOPLE WHO USE THEM

THE WORD *JIHAD* HAS become familiar today because of its association with attacks on the West by certain Muslim groups. But even among Muslims there is disagreement over which of at least two interpretations of the word should be emphasized.

In Arabic, jihad means *striving, exertion,* or *struggle,* but the precise nature of the struggle depends on who is using the word. In its broadest sense, jihad refers to any act or thought the purpose of which is fulfilling the will of Allah. But it is more often used in two specific senses—the *greater jihad* and the *lesser jihad.*

The greater jihad is a spiritual jihad. It is the struggle to bring under control all personal desires and inclinations that frustrate submission to Allah. In the greater jihad, fasting is especially important as a means of bringing physical desire under control. As one of my Muslim friends puts it, if you think of yourself as a musical instrument out of tune, fasting is a way of tuning the instrument. Fasting as part of the greater jihad, then, has much in common with the original purpose of fasting in Christianity and with the goals and purposes of the cloistered Christian monastic orders.

The lesser jihad involves physical combat, but the Quran describes it as a defensive struggle, not an offensive one. It is the use of force for self-defense when attacked and for the defense of other Muslims under attack. In fact, the specific description of the lesser jihad in Islam has requirements similar to those of the just war in Christianity. For example, the outcome of the struggle must be seen as likely to make conditions better rather than worse. The Quran insists that faith cannot be coerced. Muslims who emphasize the spiritual jihad insist that passages that speak of violence must be read in context, just as passages in the New Testament that refer to Jesus bearing a sword must be read in context.

In light of the lesser jihad, the attacks on the West by al Quaidi and others reflect a certain logic, for they believe that the Muslim way of life is under attack by the intrusion of western culture. For those truly submitted to Allah, therefore, it is mandatory to engage in jihad to defend their way of life. This jihad also must be waged against other Muslims who have adopted western culture, for Islam is the way of life commanded by Allah.

The late Ayatollah al Khomeini once said that Iran was misunderstood by the western world. "We want western technology," he said, "not western culture." On this point the Ayatollah was naïve, for western culture today is the product of western technology. As an old southern adage puts it, "The fleas come with the dog." And both the Quran and the Bible hold a negative view of dogs.

Actually, there is a certain irony in that the criticisms of western culture by militant Muslims also are made by conservative Christians and by many liberals and moderates. All condemn the West's hedonism, blatant exploitation of sex, immodesty of dress by both men and women, idolatry of material goods, and extreme individualism.

Ignoring this motivation of those who wage war on the West has led to several disastrous miscalculations. For example, the belief of some that Osama bin Laden and Saddam Hussein were partners in their opposition to the West ignored the fact that Osama bin Laden viewed Saddam Hussein as a traitor to Islam—in effect, as an infidel—because of his adoption of western ways. For the same reason, although some of the terrorists have been from Saudi Arabia, bin Laden also views the Saud family rulers as traitors. Knowing this, the Saud family fears the efforts of Osama bin Laden as much as does anyone in the West.

In and of itself, then, the word *jihad* is not a word to be feared. The danger lies not in the word itself, but in its interpretation and use by those who use it. But then, the same can be said of most words in our western vocabulary.

August 29, 2007

JEFFERSON, THE QURAN, AND THE AMERICAN GOD

When Congressman Keith Ellison, the first Muslim to be elected to Congress, announced that he would be sworn in using Thomas Jefferson's

Koran, one critic charged that the Congressman was breaking a tradition going all the way back to George Washington. The Congressman asserted that Jefferson's owning a Quran "demonstrates that from the very beginning of our country we had people who ... believed that knowledge and wisdom could be gleaned from any number of sources, including the Quran."

Many bloggers responded that Jefferson studied the Quran because merchant ships of the United States were being attacked regularly by pirates (labeled by the bloggers as Muslims) along the Barbary Coast of North Africa, and Jefferson wanted to "know the enemy."

Actually, all these assertions miss the mark. Various Presidents and members of Congress have been sworn in using books other than the Bible or no book at all.

Jefferson bought his copy of the Quran shortly before he finished his law degree, because a major book in his studies had insisted that the Quran held ideas important for a full understanding of law. This was long before Jefferson had to deal with the problem of the Barbary Coast pirates.

Jefferson also was pleased that the Constitution of the State of Virginia protected "the Jew and the Gentile, the Christian and the 'Mahometan', the 'Hindoo', and the infidel of every denomination." But nothing in Jefferson's writings suggests that the Quran actually influenced his thought.

Of course, portions of the Christian Bible, which includes the Jewish Bible, did help to mold some aspects of western society. Names and expressions from the King James Version are woven into the fabric of the nation's discourse and into the names of cities and towns across the nation. The Ten Commandments were the source of blue laws and sex laws across the nation. But from a biblical perspective, the God of the pledge of allegiance and of the nation's coins and currency is not the God of Jews, Christians, Muslims, Hindus, or Buddhists, but is a sort of generic god in general. And for Christians or Jews to honor that god is idolatry, which, as the Apostle Paul and the prophets of the Old Testament point out, inevitably leads to death.

February 4, 2007

FREEDOM AND INDEPENDENCE

The violence following the publication of cartoons of Muhammad in some European newspapers raises in dramatic form the old issue of freedom of the press everywhere.

Apparently, here is what happened. In 2005, the Danish author of a children's book on Muhammad had difficulty finding an illustrator for the book, because artists feared they might offend Muslims. On September 17 the Danish newspaper *Jyllands-Posten* printed an article about the writer's difficulty and called it "untenable for non-Muslims to be bound by Muslim scripture." The paper invited forty members of the Danish editorial cartoonists union to draw Muhammad as they envisioned him. Twelve cartoonists responded. On September 30 the newspaper printed the cartoons as part of an article it says was intended to stimulate a public debate on self-censorship.

Two weeks later, Muslim leaders in Denmark requested a meeting with the Prime Minister to discuss what they perceived as widespread disrespect for Islam, and they referred to the cartoons as the most recent example. They also asked that the Prime Minister take to task, under the provisions of Danish law, all persons responsible for disrespect of Islam. The Prime Minister replied by affirming Denmark's commitment to freedom of the press. He now says that he refused to meet with the Muslims because he thought they were asking for direct action against the newspaper.

The Muslim leaders then sought support from Muslim leaders in other countries in what they explained as an effort to persuade the Danish government that it had a more widespread problem than it realized. They wanted, they said, to avoid precisely the kind of situation that now exists.

It is unclear how many of these explanations are accurate and how many are efforts at face-saving. But it is possible to make a couple of observations about freedom of the press in general. First, the United States' guarantee of freedom of the press is not for the benefit of the press, but for the benefit of the public. The press must be free to publish what the public needs to know in order to act responsibly. Second, in the New Testament, the Apostle Paul makes a sharp distinction between freedom and independence.[1] Independence says, "I will do whatever I wish. I am not subject to anyone else's authority or desire." Freedom, according to Paul, is deliverance from self-absorption. Freedom asks, "What can I do that is helpful to others?" This, it seems to me, is one of those points on which the New Testament and this nation's ideals are in rare harmony.

February 26, 2006

---

1. This is the heart of the issue in 1 Corinthians 8–9.

ENCOUNTERING RELIGIONS AND MEETING PERSONS

A few days ago, a survey was reported that shows that the majority of Protestant ministers in this country know very little, if anything, about other religions. Among the various aspects of the topic the survey indicated that ministers seem to be more informed about Islam than about Hinduism, Buddhism, and a few smaller religions. In light of events of the last few years and the ensuing publication of a flood of books on Islam, it should not be surprising that the ministers at least think they know relatively more about Islam. Had the World Trade Center and the Pentagon been attacked by adherents to some other religion, that religion probably would stand where Islam now stands in the report.

According to the survey, however, Protestant ministers also know more about Roman Catholicism and Judaism than about any religions other than their own, including Islam. My own experience leads me to suspect that most of the ministers surveyed also know very little about Christian groups other than their own and that many Catholic priests and laity know very little about Protestantism.

There would be some value in not only Christians, but also people who profess no religion, learning the basics of all the world's major religions. On the other hand, every person on the face of the earth simply having basic information about every religion on Earth would not prevent one bomb from being exploded, one bullet from being fired, or one knife from being thrust into the body of another human being. Wars are not fought between religions, but between human beings with distorted views not only of the religion of other persons, but of their own, as well. They are the result not of ignorance, but of dehumanization of the supposed enemy.

The primary goal should not be learning the basic elements of other people's religions, but getting to know individuals of other religions as human beings. This, in turn, will lead to understanding those persons' religions, but in the proper order. There is more hope for peace when two people of different beliefs become friends than when either of them—or both—understands perfectly the religious system of the other.

September 12, 2004

11

The Environment

AN AMBIGUOUS WORLD

WE LIVE IN A strange world indeed. The essential life activity of cells, when accelerated beyond normal speed, becomes cancer, which destroys life. Some animal life forms preserve their existence by eating others—human beings eat cows, chickens, sheep, and fish; the wolf eats the lamb and the calf; the bird eats the worm. The mutation of some viral species enables them to survive and to bring death to the very creatures in which they live. The shifting of tectonic plates results in the beauty of the Alps and the Rockies, but also in tsunamis that leave the ugliness of death and destruction.

With our technology we imitate this double face of nature. The airplane that carries a heart from one coast to the other for a life saving transplant leaves in its wake pollution that poisons the atmosphere and results in the death of some who suffer from asthma.

We live, in fact, in a world in which, as William Stringfellow put it, all living things live at the expense of all other living things. That is what it means to say that we live in a fallen world. It is a world in which, according to the Apostle Paul, all of Creation groans in frustration.

Some Buddhist monks wear masks to avoid accidentally killing an insect by inhaling it. They brush the path in front of them as they walk, to sweep aside insects or other tiny creatures that otherwise might be trampled by the monks' feet.

We must always remember that even the microscopic life forms that result in epidemics and pandemics are themselves creatures of God. It even may be that the reappearance of diseases such as polio, long since considered eradicated, is a sign that, for even the deadliest viral life forms, God has purposes that elude human understanding.

Properly understood, medicine enables all living creatures to hold their tenuous balance in the ongoing struggle of life, and since God created human beings to care for God's other creatures, it is appropriate that we seek to identify and control those microscopic life forms that cause suffering and death. But we always must do so in the awareness that even in that necessary task, we are engaging in the violence that is one of the basic problems of God's agonizing Creation.

July 23, 2006

FINDING THE BALANCE

The book of Genesis portrays God creating human beings to act as God's representatives in caring for the earth (Gen 1:28). Other Old Testament books make it clear that this includes caring for our fellow human beings, as well as for the other animals, vegetation, and Earth's various resources.

It is possible, therefore, to sin either by assuming too much or by assuming too little, by pride or by irresponsibility, by action or by inaction. Adam and Eve and the builders of the tower of Babel are striking examples of pride. Those whom the prophets condemned for ignoring the poor and the needy are examples of irresponsibility.

But knowing when our actions are expressions of pride and when our hesitations are expressions of irresponsibility seldom is clear-cut. Technology is not, as we often are told, neutral, depending upon the user and the purpose for its moral character. It is ambiguous. The invention of the airplane, for example, has resulted in as many problems as benefits. A plane flying across country to deliver a heart for a transplant helps save a life, but it also spews pollution into the atmosphere, regardless of the moral character of the pilot.

We are faced with the same dilemma in the debate over whether to use existing embryos to harvest stem cells. Is using stem cells from embryos that already exist and are to be destroyed an act of pride? Or is refusing to use them for efforts to conquer diseases and save lives an act of irresponsibility? The creation of multiple embryos was itself an act shaded with pride—an act that has forced us to make decisions not about what is the greater good, but about what is the lesser evil.

A common charge hurled at people who make daring moves is, "You're playing God!" I myself sometimes have used those words about some decision or another. But it also is possible to say, "You're refusing to be human." And since we are human, not gods, even the most devout among us can never be certain when our actions are one or the other. Our only option is to act according to our best understanding, trusting God to take actions born of both our wisdom and our stupidity and turn them to his own purposes of redemption and renewal.

July 30, 2006

EARTH'S DISAPPEARING CREATURES

The tigers of Asia, the great apes of Africa, and the vultures of India are disappearing. By the end of another generation, they could be extinct.

The tigers are being slaughtered for both medicinal and decorative purposes. Tiger skins are used for rugs and for conspicuous clothing. Tiger bones are crushed to be used in traditional Chinese medicine and as an additive to wine. Some tiger parts are desired because they are said to increase a man's virility.

The great apes have long been food for dwellers in the Central Congo basin, but until the last few decades the size of the dweller population and the relative seclusion of the apes in the forests provided a sustainable balance between apes and humans. Now, increased cutting of trees for lumber and the increasing popularity of "bushmeat" on restaurant menus have led to a reduction of the ape population by an estimated 80 to 90 percent.

As for the vultures, in India and Pakistan—where cows are sacred animals—because of the belief that the spiritual essence of the cows is thereby returned to the Great Source of all things, the carcasses of dead cows are left for the vultures to eat. From a practical standpoint, then, vultures have traditionally played a crucial role in preventing the spread of disease.

Reverence for cows also has led, however, to the development of *diclofenac*, a pain killing drug for sick cows. Although the drug helps the cows, it is toxic for vultures, and the vultures' eating the *diclofenac* saturated carcasses has resulted in their deaths. The rotting cow carcasses then attract rats and wild dogs, the result of which is an increase in rabies.

The demise of the apes and tigers is largely a result of human plunder and greed; that of the vultures, of good intentions gone wrong.

One need not take the Genesis Creation narratives literally to appreciate their view that the human race was created to take charge of the creatures and vegetation of the earth as God's representatives. To take charge as God would take charge, however, implies caring as God would care—not exploiting, plundering, and destroying for our own selfish purposes.

Genesis notes that God created even the great sea monsters (sometimes translated as dragons, whales or sea beasts), which probably is a reference to one or more types of large sea creatures that by their size and appearance had frightened sailors and inspired tales of the dangers of the sea. Genesis thereby contends that nothing in the great web of nature—not even dragons and monsters—is outside the scope of God's creative work. And if even supposed sea monsters are a part of that web, then so too must be rats and wild dogs, tigers and great apes, and even vultures.

Unfortunately, as part of an imperfect, fallen world the web of nature has many weakened and broken strands, and carelessly hacking away at other strands increases the danger to whatever order remains. Even killing disease-causing bacteria—necessary as this is and humane as our intentions are—has inestimable consequences.

I'm not suggesting that endangered species should be preserved at the cost of human life or genuine human need, but comparing the value of human beings with that of other animals easily can become a diversion masking our greed and our desire for pleasure and convenience. Even our tendency automatically to deal with pests such as ants, mice, and snakes by killing them ignores that they too are parts of the web, and that none can be lost without threatening the entire web, including the human race.

The actions leading to the disappearance of the vultures and the consequences of their disappearance show us that we cannot predict the impact or outcome of even our most nobly or innocently motivated actions. But our human identity is inseparable from our responsibility as caretakers, and when we fail to act, guided by our best understanding, we thereby diminish our humanity.

Acting unavoidably disturbs the web of nature. But if, when forced to act, we did so with caution, contemplation of possible consequences, and sensitivity to the point of disturbance, the need to intervene might occur less often.

September 8, 2008

THE IVORY BILLED WOODPECKER

A few weeks ago, there were reports of sightings of an Ivory Billed Woodpecker—a bird long thought to have been extinct. It isn't clear just how many of the birds exist or—other than the general location—just where it is, or they are. Given the predilection of some to commercialize even the water that God lets fall from the sky to quench our thirst, and given the tendency of some to consider killing rare animals to be great sport, it may be just as well if the bird's exact location remains unknown. In moments of whimsy I sometimes suspect that if the Loch Ness monster were discovered actually to exist, it soon would become part of a water show, be captured for some zoo or museum, or fall victim to some hunter wanting it stuffed for his or her private collection.

The endurance of the Ivory Billed Woodpecker may be a sort of double-edged, prophetic word of hope and of warning. The Creation narratives in Genesis tell us that God created the human race to care for the earth and its creatures as God's representatives. Prophets such as Jeremiah and Hosea, on the other hand, warn us that human sin can result in the earth being returned to a condition of Chaos in which all living things are threatened with Death.

Naturalists tell us that the demise of the Ivory Billed Woodpecker was the result of the reckless, erratic, undisciplined cutting of millions of acres of forests in the southeastern United States from the end of the Civil War thru the 1940's. Mysteriously called back from the black hole of extinction—at least for the moment—that beautiful bird can both assure us that God still gives us time to save and renew the earth's environment—and, consequently, the earth itself—but also to warn us that we do not have forever.

June 25, 2005

TAKING A RISK ON ERROR

In February of 2007 the United Nations International Panel on Climate Change said that evidence of a global warming trend is "unequivocal" and that human activity "very likely" has been the driving force behind the change. Since this was a change from an earlier statement in which the panel had said that human activity is "likely" the driving force, the addition of the word "very" is not to be taken lightly.

Increasing evidence of global warming is convincing a growing list of people. One year ago, eleven retired military leaders—including a former Army chief of staff and President Bush's former Middle East peace negotiator—warned that global warming poses a serious threat to national security. They warned of wars over water and of increased hunger, worsening disease, rising sea levels, and population displacement—all of which easily can lead to war—and predicted that the United States will be drawn more frequently into such situations.

"It's not hard," said General Anthony Zinni, President Bush's former Middle East envoy, "to make the connection between climate change and instability or (between) climate change and terrorism."

On another front, during the last two years two influential groups of Evangelical Christians have issued proclamations calling for action in the name of stewardship of the Creation. One group included prominent figures such as Rick Warren, Bryan McLaren, Jim Wallis, and David Gushee. A more recent document was signed by Union University President David Dockery and Frank Page, President of the Southern Convention.

Of course, not everyone is convinced we face such dangers. Some Evangelical and conservative Christians, for example, have refused to sign either of the two proclamations. Neither James Dobson (head of Focus on the Family) nor Richard Land (President of the Southern Baptist Convention's Ethics & Religious Liberty Commission) signed. Mr. Land says that he too believes in stewardship of the Creation, but he does not believe the warnings are accurate. He recently asserted that the earth is experiencing a cold spell sufficient to eliminate the last hundred years of global warming.

"A lot of scientists," he said, "are now saying ... their computer models were wrong...and that the shifting data ... no longer says that we're going to have (a) global warming crisis."

A major point of disagreement among people who do consider global warming a problem for action is the extent to which, if at all, human beings are responsible. Some reports say that although human activity plays a role, it is not the only cause and that it may not even be the primary cause. Moreover, there is a growing consensus that no matter what precautionary measures we take, we cannot stop the warming; we can only slow it down and give ourselves more time to find ways to adjust.

I can understand the uncertainty and even the skepticism of those who see global warning as a theory not yet settled. In the middle of the last century, U.S. soldiers in training were sent into the aftermath of small nuclear explosions with the assurance that there was no danger after the explosions. Those assurances, we now know, were inaccurate. Consider also the frequency with which scientific opinions change with regard to which foods are good for us and which are harmful. So even though I don't share the "I'm from Missouri" view of those who reject the idea of global warming, I can understand it.

According to the book of Genesis, human beings were created to care for the earth as God's representatives. And Jesus' admonition in the New Testament to love our neighbor as we love ourselves has enormous implications for the way we treat the environment, since just our neighbor is affected, as are we, by that environment.

Even if it should be discovered later that we actually have been incorrect about the continuation of global warming and the contribution of human beings to that warming, since the future of all life on the planet has a stake in the matter, it does seem logical that responsibility should lead to caution. When there is even the slightest possibility of irreversible disaster, it is better to risk erring on the side of safety. Caution certainly will not make life worse, and in some ways it might even make it better.

Which would we rather contemplate—future generations, for whom we have a responsibility, looking back and respecting us for our caution or cursing us for our irresponsibility?

April 15, 2008

THE FLOODS OF HAITI

It is not unusual to hear someone connect great devastation with God. A tornado survivor, for example, may attribute his or her survival to the goodness of God. But this raises the disturbing question: Why did God not save those who died?

The question for many, in the wake of great suffering or death, is precisely why God allows such things to happen—a question which raises the larger one of the very nature of God, a question older than the book of Job. Why would a loving God allow hundreds or even thousands of people to suffer, to be tortured, or to be murdered? Where was God when the Nazis carried out the Holocaust? Why would a loving God allow a child to suffer from leukemia or to be born with some debilitating physical deformity?

For some, the flooding in Haiti raises the question anew. Where is God when nature brings such devastation upon so many people? True, the people of some sections of Haiti, by stripping the land of trees and vegetation, have created conditions that result in the wide scope of the death and destruction. But to blame the Haitians for their own suffering is to heartlessly ignore the question of why they have been reduced to such a condition that cutting the trees and the vegetation has seemed their only means of survival. Where is God when power structures are geared against them and their officials ignore and even profit from their own people's poverty?

Placing on God the responsibility for such devastation is a dodge. Events such as the flooding in Haiti raise questions about us, as well. According to the New Testament, the way we treat and relate to other people is the means by which we treat and relate to Jesus. To oppress others is to oppress Jesus. To attempt to ease the plight of the poor and the oppressed is to deal with Jesus. The people and organizations that have rushed to Haiti or who have raised money and goods to aid the victims of the flooding have recognized this. They have not stopped to ask, "Where was God?" or "Where is God?" They simply have decided to help. They have heard God's question to us: "Where are you?"

June 13, 2004

PART TWO

Sermons, Presentations,
and Book Reviews

12

Sermons

SERMON ON MATTHEW 10:16

(On the occasion of my retirement, I was invited to preach the baccalaureate sermon at Lambuth.)

IN THE TENTH CHAPTER of Matthew, as Jesus sends his disciples out in the world as his representatives, he instructs them in rather stark terms: "Behold, I send you out as sheep in the midst of wolves, so be wise as serpents and as innocent as doves."

These words of Jesus summarize the kind of life that faithful disciples of Jesus Christ should expect to have—lives of danger, of conflict, perhaps even of death. Dietrich Bonhoeffer was not exaggerating when he said, "When Jesus calls (us), he bids (us) come and die."

Jesus' words in this discourse cannot be separated from his words in the other discourses in Matthew's Gospel, for each of the discourses presupposes certain elements of the others. In the first discourse, the Sermon on the Mount, Jesus already has told his disciples that they are the light of the world, which means that by their lives they are to show the world what God is like. Disciples are to be trustworthy, for if they are not trustworthy, or dependable, they will be indicating to the world that God is not trustworthy, or dependable.

Faithful disciples of Jesus, according to the Sermon on the Mount, are to be leery of judging others. We are to judge only when we are willing to be judged by the same criteria. We are to be angry only when there is something about which we assume God would be angry—the oppression of the weak by the powerful; the marginalization of people on the basis of race, ethnicity, economic status, or moral character; the duplicity of national and international leaders; the bureaucracy of institutions that act as cannibals and chew up the people for whom they have responsibility. We are to call people fools only when we are convinced that God regards them as fools and when we are prepared to be judged as to our wisdom or foolishness by the same criteria. So there are times when disciples of Jesus would be unfaithful *not* to be angry. There are times when disciples of Jesus would be unfaithful *not* to show up fools for what they are. But we are to judge only when we are ready to be measured by the same criteria!

Jesus warns us that in a world of wolves we are to be as clever, as shrewd, as insightful (for the Greek word means all these) as serpents. In other words, we are to live as realists about the true nature of the world. Jesus himself was not gullible, and there is no beatitude that says, "Blessed are the gullible for that is the way to be a good Christian." When Jesus instructed us that when we are struck on one cheek, we are to turn the other, he knew full well that we probably will wind up with a bloody face.

To put it another way, we must not romanticize the world. We must recognize that there truly are evil forces at work in God's Creation and that these evil forces use human beings and human institutions as their acolytes to do horrible things. The belief that everyone or even most people really are good at heart and that all we have to do to people who act badly is just manipulate them through some process of education or with some socio-psychological technique or some form of rehabilitation simply is at odds with the biblical understanding of the world. The solution to the world's basic death orientation is not education or manipulation, but transformation—a transformation that God alone can work—a transformation that frequently will use education, socialization, and economic rehabilitation, but that can never be simply reduced to either or all of these. Wolves are not easily tamed, and to take one as a pet is to toy with disaster.

This realistic view of the world includes not being naive even about the church and the church's institutions. Churches and church institutions easily can become members of the wolf pack.

Some of you know that for several years I have had three or four quotations on the bulletin board outside my office. They are three quotations that have for several years been basic guides for my approach to the world. One is a quotation from Umberto Eco's novel *The Name of the Rose*.[1] In the midst of bureaucratic oppression during the Inquisition, Brother William says to his young aide: "Don't trust renewals of the human race when curias (that is, church officials) and courts (that is, the secular government courts) speak of them."

Human institutions are among the deadliest of the wolves. Institutions begin as organizations to serve some noble purpose, but by the time that purpose has been accomplished, the organization has become an institution, and then the primary purpose becomes survival. We begin to try to find a new purpose or a new mission. But the goal is survival. And when survival is the goal, those who question authority or question the power of the institution and its authorities become the enemy. It is at this point that the institution should question its own existence. It should question whether it any longer deserves to survive. But institutions never do this. Instead, they become cannibalistic, feeding on the employees and the clients. And churches and church related institutions—precisely because they are institutions—are no more immune to this cannibalism than any other group. This is why faithful disciples of Jesus must be as wise as serpents. We must recognize the death orientation of all institutions, with the great danger that even the institutional church can be among the enemies.

But Jesus also told his disciples that they must be as innocent as doves. Again, to hear the Sermon on the Mount as a context for Jesus' instructions, Jesus tells his disciples that they are to love the enemy. Followers of Jesus are to embody the innocence of doves by active love for God's Creation, including the wolves. The word translated *love* in that passage is a word that means total, complete, unconditional dedication to seeing that the needs of the enemy are met before your own, even if the enemy kills you while you are working toward filling those needs. When Jesus said, "Love your neighbor as you love yourself," he did not say, "unless the neighbor happens to be your enemy." In terms of the text before us, he might easily have said, "You are doves, and you must love the wolf, even as the wolf eats you."

This is why faithful disciples of Jesus will never make good citizens of whatever nation in which we find ourselves. For good citizens—as the world counts citizenship—must count the nation's enemies as their enemies. They must be ready and willing to kill the nation's enemies on

---

1. Umberto Eco, *The Name of the Rose*, Tr. William Weaver, (New York: Harcourt, Brace, Jovanovice, 1983).

behalf of the nation. And if you are not ready to kill your nation's enemies, you will be considered a coward, a traitor, or both.

Somehow, the churches have deluded us into thinking that to be a good Christian means being a good citizen—that the church must support the nation's wars and the nation's economic policies. But that is not the talk of Jesus. That is the talk of Constantine, the talk of Caesar, the talk of every national leadership. And the acceptance of this kind of talk is what has held the church and Christians in captivity for sixteen hundred years. It is not a captivity that comes in a moment of crisis, but one that creeps up on us slowly. Another of the quotations from my bulletin board is one from the late U.S. Supreme Court Justice William O. Douglas:

> As nightfall does not come all at once, neither does oppression. In both instances there is twilight, when everything remains seemingly unchanged. And it is in such twilight that we must be aware of change in the air—however slight—lest we become unwitting victims of the darkness.

It is clear from Jesus' teachings in their full context that he did not speak of merely turning the cheek as a way of loving. We are not merely to turn the other cheek, but are to reach out in reconciliation to the one who has struck us. In a later discourse in Matthew's Gospel, Peter, the leader of the group that had gathered around Jesus, said, "If a person sins against me, how many times do I forgive him—seven times?" And Jesus' famous response, of course, is "Not seven, but seventy times seven" (Matt 18:21-22).

An interesting thing about this passage is that in Luke's version, Jesus does not speak these words in a conversation with Peter, but in a series of instructions. In Luke, Jesus says, "If your brother sins, rebuke him; if he repents, forgive him. If he sins against you seven times in a day and turns to you seven times and says, 'I repent,' forgive him" (Luke 17:3-4). Matthew has told the story in such a way that the emphasis falls not on our response to the other person's repentance, but on our responsibility to reach out before the person repents. The saying comes in the wake of Jesus telling the disciples that when someone in the assembly has created problems, the members of the assembly are to go to that person and try to work things out, not wait for the person to have a change of heart. Therefore, Matthew has left out the question of how many times I am to forgive when someone comes to me, and has placed the ball completely in our court.

Forgiveness is not simply responding to someone's change of heart. It is reaching out even while the enemy still is the enemy. This is why leaders in some denominations frequently are seen going into the camp of this nation's enemies and attempting to work for peace. And look how those leaders are excoriated by the nation's leaders when they do. "You are meddling in international diplomacy" come the cries! "You are giving aid and comfort to the enemy!"

Genuine love in the New Testament sense is not subject to the corrupted reasoning of the fallen world. Jesus knew that loving the enemy easily could lead to ostracism, loneliness, ridicule, misrepresentation, and even death. And to quote Mother Theresa, using the third quotation from my bulletin board, "Love must be as ferocious as evil."

And, just like the rest of the world, the news media simply do not get it. A few years ago, when Pope John Paul II visited Cuba, his critics said that the visit would serve only to boost the sagging Castro regime. But the Pope was not naïve. He knew that even if his visit gave a momentary boost to Castro, he went as the instrument of God's peace—that, in the final analysis, the outcome of the visit would be not what he accomplished or anything for which Castro might use the visit, but what God chose to do with the visit. And that was up to God. But of course, the newspapers do not know how to report that sort of thing.

Church leaders who visit the nation's enemies are not naive. Most of them go into the enemy's camp with the wisdom of the serpent. But they go seeking to be instruments of God in the midst of a situation in which both sides are made up of wolves. They simply refuse to accept the idea that the nation's enemies are necessarily their enemies. They do not see the world the way those caught up in the ethos of the fallen Creation see it. They view the world from a biblical perspective. They view the world not only in terms of its horror, but also in terms of its hope, the hope that it has under the power of Jesus' death and resurrection. We live in a world in which the wolves are not really in control, though both we and they may, for the moment, think they are. In reality, the world is under the constant forward tug of the Kingdom of God—God's sovereign rule—which already has begun in the death and resurrection of Jesus—God's sovereign rule in which God uses both our best and our worst choices to bring about God's purposes for the renewal and transformation of the entire Creation.

We are not so much *commanded* to love as we are *set free* to love. Jesus assured the disciples that when they were forced to speak before those who would judge them, the Holy Spirit would enable them to speak an appropriate word. We do not stand alone, and we have been loved so that we might love. We are *invited* to love, to love even the enemy who threatens us while we love him or her or them. Love for God's entire Creation is first of all a gift—a gift not only to be embraced, but to be embodied with joy. It is that love that identifies us as truly human. It is only when we reject that gift that the gift becomes the command, "You *shall* love your enemy."

In 1844 the great U.S. poet James Russell Lowell wrote a poem titled "The Present Crisis," parts of which have been used to create the hymn "Once to Every Man and Nation." Here are some of the lines.

> Then to side with Truth is noble when we share her wretched crust,
> Ere her cause bring fame and profit, and 'tis prosperous to be just;
> Then it is the brave man chooses, while the coward stands aside,
> Doubting in his abject spirit, till his Lord is crucified,
> And the multitude make virtue of the faith they had denied.
>
> Backward look across the ages and the beacon-moments see
> That, like peaks of some sunk continent, jut through Oblivion's sea;
> Not an ear in court or market for the low foreboding cry
> Of those Crises, God's stern winnowers, from whose feet
>   earth's chaff must fly;
> Never shows the choice momentous till the judgment hath passed by.
>
> Careless seems the great Avenger; history's pages but record
> One death-grapple in the darkness 'twixt old systems and the Word;
> Truth forever on the scaffold, Wrong forever on the throne —
> Yet that scaffold sways the future, and, behind the dim unknown,
> Standeth God within the shadow, keeping watch above his own.

These lines are a fitting challenge for those who go forth into a world of wolves and who are expected to be as wise as serpents, but as innocent as doves.

Amen.

May 10, 2008

HOMILY ON ISAIAH 2:1–5

(In January, 1998, the Council of Catholic Women of the Memphis Diocese held its annual Ecumenical Prayer Breakfast at St. Mary's Catholic Church in Jackson. Primarily on the basis of my remarks at the memorial service for Mother Theresa,[2] I was invited to deliver the homily.)

> The word which Isaiah the son of Amoz saw
> concerning Judah and Jerusalem.
>
> It shall come to pass in the latter days that
> The mountain of the house of the LORD
> shall be established as the highest of the mountains,
> and shall be raised above the hills;
> And all the nations shall flow to it,
> And many peoples shall come, and say:
> "Come, let us go up to the mountain of the LORD,
> to the house of the God of Jacob;
> That he may teach us his ways
> and that we may walk in his paths."
> For out of Zion shall go forth the law,
> and the word of the LORD from Jerusalem.
> He shall judge between the nations,
> and shall decide for many peoples;
> And they shall beat their swords into plowshares,
> and their spears into pruning hooks;
> Nation shall not lift up sword against nation,
> neither shall they learn war any more.
> O house of Jacob, come,
> let us walk in the light of the LORD.

Isaiah does not describe our world. We do not live in a world in which the nations—including this nation—seek the will of God. We do not live in a world in which nations beat their swords into plowshares and their spears into pruning hooks, but a world in which nations devote far more of their annual budgets to instruments of war than to instruments of human well-being. Weaponry takes precedence over medical research. Military extravagance takes precedence over education and health care.

Nations do continue to learn war. Most nations have their war training colleges (or contract with other nations to provide such training), their special forces, and their secret intelligence. They have their cadre of espionage

---

2. See page 173.

experts whose sole responsibility is to spy on friend and enemy alike, and to undermine and disrupt the stability even of its supposed friends if that undermining and disruption are deemed in the national interest.

The goal of all nations—including this nation—is power. And the Church of Jesus Christ, assembly of the Prince of Peace, blesses—through its chaplains—the swords and spears of men and women who march into war. It sponsors high schools, colleges, and universities that provide military training, but provide no courses or programs in peace making.

The Church of Jesus Christ decided in the fourth century that if it was going to continue to grow in numbers and retain the newly gained favor of the secular powers, it would have to establish guidelines to indicate when Christians are justified in denying the teachings of its Lord. And thus was born the theory of the "just war," a theory perpetuated still in most of the church's manifestations, excepting a few groups generally regarded by the others as odd.

The world of Isaiah 2 is not this world! The world in which we live does not live by the Sermon on the Mount. It is a world not of peace and harmony, but of separation, alienation, hostility, violence, and death.

In a later chapter, Isaiah describes a world of even more extravagant harmony. "The wolf shall be a guest of the lamb, and the leopard shall lie down with the kid; the calf and the young lion shall browse together, with a little child to guide them. The cow and the bear shall be neighbors, together their young shall rest; the lion shall eat hay like the ox. The baby shall play by the cobra's den, and the child shall lay his hand on the adder's lair. There shall be no harm or ruin on all my holy mountain; for the earth shall be filled with the knowledge of the LORD, as waters cover the sea" (Isaiah 11:6–9, *The New American Bible*).

But this was not Isaiah's world. Neither was it Jesus' world. And Isaiah and Jesus *knew* that it was not their world. The Apostle Paul describes the world as a world of idolatry and imprisonment—imprisonment by the Dark Forces of the cosmic realm. According to the Apostle Paul, the world as we know it is not in chaos simply because we human beings do not exercise our natural wills, overcome the world's condition, and make the world better. Instead, God—in response to the human race's preoccupation with things that we can see, and touch, and handle, and possess as our own—has abandoned us to our own desires. In response to our abandonment of him, God has allowed us to become the pawns of dark cosmic forces whose one, controlling goal is the undermining of God's merciful, loving rule over his own Creation (Rom 1:18–32).

The writer of Ephesians, bringing the theology of the Apostle Paul to bear a generation later, describes it in this way: "For we are not contending against flesh and blood, but against the principalities, against the powers, against the world rulers of this present darkness . . ." (Eph 6:12).

The horror of the world as it now is, is that it is in thralldom to cosmic powers that are determined to defeat God himself—determined to destroy the world that God created and to construct a new world in their own demonic image. And when we Christians make power, pleasure, and national pride our goals, we show that we are, in fact, merely pretenders, hypocrites, and imposters.

But my subject is not hopelessness, but hope. And hope is the thrust of Isaiah 2. It also is the primary purpose of the writer of Ephesians. Isaiah promises that God has in store for this world an overturning of the present condition. The verbs of Isaiah 2, in the poem about Zion, are not imperatives, but declaratives. Isaiah does not say, "You must force the nations to live by the instruction of the LORD," or "You must force the nations to walk in the light of the LORD." He does not say, "You must force the nations to beat their swords into plowshares and their spears into pruning hooks." Instead, he promises that one day this *will* happen. It will happen not because nations have been *forced* to act as he describes, but because they voluntarily *decide* to do so. The nations will say, of their own volition, "Come let us go up to the LORD's mountain, to the house of the God of Jacob, that he may instruct us in *his* ways and that we may walk in *his* paths."

This is the divine promise. It is not a condition that we are called upon to establish, but one that is our inheritance, one that God promises to create. It is a promise, not a command.

But the passage does contain imperatives. After the description of the promise, after the description of that for which we can hope, there is the exhortation: "Come, O house of Jacob, let *us* walk in the light of the LORD!"

In other words, of course the world is not yet a world of peace and harmony!

Of course the world does not now live according to the will of God!

Of course the world does not now live in accord with the Sermon on the Mount.

But for the people of God, that is irrelevant. Have you not, at one time or another, heard someone say, "You know you can't live by the Sermon on the Mount! The world doesn't live by the Sermon on the Mount"? I repeat: For the people of God, that is irrelevant. The people of God are called to be holy—that is, to be set apart, to be different. In our baptism, we gave up the choice of whether to live according to the values, motives, and drives of the natural world.

In our baptism, we gave up the right to decide whether we will participate in the traditions and customs of a fallen world.

In our baptism, we, or our parents for us, renounced the principalities and powers, renounced the Devil and all his ways.

In our baptism, we claimed the vision of Isaiah as our own.

In our baptism, we claimed the Sermon on the Mount as the model for our life as a community.

In our baptism, we did not make promises of what we would do of our own power. We made promises of what we would allow God to do through us.

In out baptism, we were marked with the sign of the cross and called, thereby, to die and to live.

In our baptism, we became part of the people of hope.

In biblical terms, hope is not some mere psychological, subjective, inner mental condition. It is a way of life. It is an expression of our whole being. Either it is lived hope or it is not hope at all, but mere spiritual wool-gathering.

Isaiah calls us to that life of hope. Isaiah says to us, "I know that the world as I have described it does not yet exist. But when God claimed you, he empowered you, as a community, to live this way so that the world might see and, thus, itself have hope. This is your holiness—to walk in the light of the LORD, even when the world does not!"

Similarly, Jesus, in the Sermon on the Mount, described a world that did not—and does not—yet exist, but one to which his followers were, by the power of God, to bear testimony in the midst of the world as it is. The Sermon on the Mount does not tell us how to be saved, but how to live as a community that already has been saved!

The author of Ephesians, in a masterful piece of irony, turns the language of the world on its head. He writes: "Finally, be strong in the Lord and in the strength of his might. Put on the whole armor of God, that you may be able to stand against the wiles of the devil.... Therefore take the whole armor of God, that you may be able to withstand in the evil day, and having done all, to stand. Stand therefore, having girded your loins with truth, and having put on the breastplate of righteousness, and having shod your feet with the equipment of the gospel of peace; above all, taking the shield of faith, with which you can quench all the flaming darts of the evil one. And take the helmet of salvation, and the sword of the Spirit, which is the word of God. Pray at all times in the Spirit, with all prayer and supplication. To that end keep alert with all perseverance..."(Ephesians 6:10–11, 13–17).

In the Sermon on the Mount Jesus describes the church in terms of Isaiah 2 when he says that a city built on a hill cannot be hid and that lanterns are not put under baskets. The task of the church is to be a light, a beacon of hope, to the nations.

The church, in its better moments, has known that we are called to this life of hope, to this life of vision. The monastic orders, in their better expressions, have pulled away from the world in order to get a clearer perspective so that they might benefit the world. The Anabaptists of the sixteenth century broke with the imperial order because of what they perceived as the apostasy of the church in both its Catholic and its Protestant forms, and for this they were hunted down and slaughtered by Catholics, Lutherans, and Calvinists alike. Some of the Puritans came to this country not to stay, but to work at a grand experiment, with the anticipation, once the experiment bore fruit, of returning to England to be a beacon to the church in the British Isles.

Throughout the life of Israel and the church, God has consistently and persistently raised up men and women to hold high the vision. In our own day, we have beheld the vision held high by Dorothy Day, by Peter Maurin and the Catholic Worker Movement, by the Berrigans, and also, if we look closely, here and there, by priests and laity of the Memphis Diocese—some quietly, some not so quietly. They have made their presence felt. They have kept alive the vision.

But sad to say, not only does the world not live as Isaiah or Jesus envisions it. Neither, in so much of its life, does the Church of Jesus Christ. The simple fact is that the church itself is in need of conversion. Pope John XXII knew this. Pope John Paul II knows this. There is a fine line between the church clothing itself in the culture of the world for purposes of communication and the church embracing the values of the world. Whereas the former is incarnation, the latter is apostasy. And Catholicism, Protestantism, Orthodoxy, the Free Church and the Pentecostals always are in danger of embracing apostasy in the name of incarnation. This is what underlies so many of the current debates within the Catholic Church as well as within the other members of the Body of Christ—the question of when incarnation is betrayed by apostasy. The vision of Isaiah calls us to a new life that is in the midst of the world, but not guided by the world.

A couple of decades ago, many of the critics of the church had a cute little saying. "The church," they said, "is busy answering questions the world isn't asking." Well, as true as this observation at times may be, in an unfortunate way, it is a mistake to assume that the world always knows the right questions. The church, when it is true to its call to live out the vision of hope, will pose questions for the world, questions that the world may ignore or that may so anger the world that the world will attack the church or its leadership. For example, many critics of Pope John Paul's trip to Cuba say that the visit will serve only to boost the sagging Castro regime. But Pope John Paul is not naive. He knows that even if his visit gives a momentary boost to Castro, he goes as the instrument of God's peace—that, in the final analysis, the outcome of the visit will be not what the Pope accomplishes or anything for which Castro might use the visit, but what God chooses to do with the visit. And that is up to God. But of course, the newspapers don't know how to report that sort of thing.

Pope John Paul is the bearer of a vision. To the extent that it is a human vision, Catholics and Protestants alike are free to disagree with elements of the vision. But to the extent that it is rooted in God's call through the Scriptures, Protestants and Catholics alike should affirm and thank God for the one who keeps the vision alive.

Where there is no vision, there is no hope. And where there is no hope, there is no love. The Apostle Paul says that faith, hope and love abide and that the greatest of these is love. But it also is clear from the witness of the Scriptures and the martyrs that love depends on hope for its life, as a flame depends upon fuel for its fire. Without hope the world perishes. But the church that is bereft of hope also perishes. Because of what God has promised, we are set free from nihilism and set free to hope. And the call to live as people of hope is nothing more nor less than a call to remember our baptism—to remember who we are. It is this hope that, in the words of the Apostle Paul, does not disappoint us!

January 22, 1998

HOMILY ON GENESIS 50:15-21 FOR INTERFAITH SERVICE

I appreciate being invited to deliver the sermonette, or homily, this evening, and I am aware that when a word has *ette* on the end, it means *keep it short*.

I will set the background for the scripture text by sketching the story of Joseph up to the point at which the text begins. Joseph is a young man, apparently a teen-ager or even younger, who has dreams at night and excitedly describes them at the breakfast table each morning. He tells of dreams in which all the sheaves in the field bow down to his sheaves and in which the sun, moon, and stars bow down to him. He is something of a braggart, and his older brothers, understandably, soon become tired of hearing about his dreams. The Koran says that Joseph's father, Jacob, warned him that he should keep quiet about his dreams, but that this didn't stop him.

So the brothers at first plan to kill Joseph, but then decide to sell him. And soon Joseph winds up in Egypt as a household slave. He then is accused of attempted rape, goes to prison, and in prison interprets dreams of the Pharaoh's baker and cup bearer, who also are in prison. The butler later introduces Joseph to the Pharaoh, Joseph interprets dreams the Pharaoh has been having, and as a result is made the Pharaoh's right-hand official.

As the person into whose hands the Pharaoh has handed running the economic life of the nation, Joseph saves Egypt during seven years of drought, and this—in turn—enables Egypt to be a haven for Joseph's brothers and father, thereby saving them from the drought. In brief, the brothers, by selling Joseph into slavery, set off a chain of events that eventually work to their own safety.

The only mention of God in the story of Joseph is, for the most part, occasional references to God watching over Joseph and Joseph's own assertion to the Pharaoh that his ability to interpret dreams rests in God's revelation to him.

Years later Jacob, Joseph's father, dies, and it is at this point that our text enters the picture. "As for you, you meant it for evil against me, but God meant it for good . . . that many people should be saved alive . . ." (Gen 50:20).

The story of Joseph is a story of how God works in this world undetected, unrecognized, in disguise—in ways strange and mysterious, which we, in our human blindness, are likely to label as coincidence, chance, luck, and even freak accident. It also is a story that shows how the biblical writers reconciled the perennial question of how God's actions are related to human actions.

God did not work separately from Joseph's brothers. They sold Joseph for their own purposes, driven by their own motives. Potiphar's wife, who falsely accused Joseph of attempted rape, acted entirely on the basis of her own wrath and her displeasure with Joseph. But God also was at work for God's own purposes. God in, divine freedom, used the freedom of human beings—their motives, purposes, and decisions—to accomplish God's own purposes, bringing about consequences quite unexpected by those same human beings. And each had its place in the jigsaw puzzle of Joseph's life.

We find this same perspective in a passage from the book of Proverbs, in a passage I have slightly edited in order to remove what some would view as its chauvinistic wording. "Our mind plans our way, but the LORD directs our steps" (Prov 16:9).

In other words, we are set in a world in which we are expected, to the extent that we are given light to see, to live faithful to and responsible before God, but a world in which God decides what—if anything—to do with our efforts. And much to our chagrin, God may even at times decide to use our stupidity rather than our "smartness"—or perhaps at times to ignore both—in the accomplishing of the divine purpose.

It is not at all clear what God might do with our meager efforts in Jackson toward harmony and understanding—either our successes or our failures. We come together, most of us, as members of one or the other of three faith traditions—Judaism, Christianity, and Islam. The thing that separates us from the other major religions of the world is our common worship of the same God. And the thing that separates us within our unity is the belief of each of us that in one way or another, our own tradition holds the clue to that future toward which God is drawing the entire Creation.

Let me speak very specifically, very personally, and very theologically. I believe that in Jesus Christ's death on the cross God was at work for the reconciliation and transformation of the entire creation. I believe that because Christ died for the entire creation, my baptism into him automatically binds me to the entire human race as a servant of all. I also believe that to be baptized into Christ binds me to Israel as an adopted son among the children of Abraham. When I am accepted into the fellowship of the Jewish community, it is not because that community accepts my claim of identity, and I cannot and do not expect them to do so. When I am accepted in the Jewish community, it is on their terms, not on mine. I have no right to expect my theology to determine their response to me. But in Judaism there is an historic emphasis on welcoming the sojourner—the stranger (and perhaps they simply find me one of the strangest persons they know)—and there is no place in the entire world where I feel more accepted and more at home—more family—than in the synagogue at Sabbath service and at the holy festivals.

When Majidh and other Muslims accept me and welcome me, they do so on their terms, not on mine. Islam teaches that all persons are born Muslim. The problem is that so many slip away. But those who have slipped away are never shut out.

So we meet, we discuss, we laugh, we pray, we eat, because something in the particularistic dimension of each of our faiths, strangely enough, provides a base for a universal welcoming.

In fact, within the faith community of each of us there are differences often as great as those among the faith traditions themselves. There are differences between Fundamentalist and Liberal Christians, between Orthodox and Reform Jews, and between Wahabi, Shiite and Sunni Muslims as great as—perhaps even greater than—those between most of us gathered here tonight. And it is crucial for interfaith relations that we not pretend that those differences do not exist. We must neither make them the center of our attention, assuming that we can have no relationship until we have eliminated them, nor push them to the margins as though they are irrelevant.

But the difference between Islam, Christianity, and Judaism is one thing. The relationship among Muslims, Christians, and Jews is quite another. One is an objective analysis of differences in doctrine, customs, and liturgy. The other is a personal encounter among human beings created and loved by the same God.

Finally, as much as is to be gained and celebrated with regard to discussions and to celebrations of acceptance and friendship such as this one, there also is much to be gained by working together. For the last two weeks, media reports have been filled with pictures of those whose lives have been devastated by the hurricane Katrina. But the hopelessness of the poverty stricken—the forgotten, the abandoned, the destitute—was there before Katrina. Katrina simply pulled back the curtain.

In Jackson, too, there are many living on the margin, in danger of falling over the edge into oblivion. Even the hurricane a couple of years ago did not pull back the curtain behind which they are ignored. What would it mean for them if the same people of faith who gather to share ideas, to reflect on our faith in ceremonies, and to enjoy refreshments afterward were to decide to *work* together—impelled by our faith to care for the least of these—the ones of whom Jesus, Mohammed, the prophets, and Moses spoke? I suspect that—though they would not have agreed with the contextual nature of the New Testament Epistle of John—Moses, the prophets, and Mohammed might have agreed with the implication of Jesus' words: How we can say we love God, whom we have not seen, if we do not love those around us whom we have seen?

Amen.

September 22, 2005

13

Addresses and Presentations

MOTHER THERESA

(I was invited to speak as a Protestant representative at the memorial service for Mother Theresa at St. Mary's Catholic Church in Jackson It was not my first invitation to speak or to lead studies at the church, but it was perhaps the most challenging.)

IN THE DAYS SINCE her death, many quotations have been attributed to Mother Theresa—some ordinary, some profound, some witty. One of the most penetrating was reported by the host of Public Radio's *Week-end Edition*. According to Scott Simon, Mother Theresa once turned sharply on some slacking sisters and snapped, "Love must be as ferocious as evil." Perhaps this is what we see in her—the wonderful, awesome ferocity of genuine love.

I was struck, a few days ago, by the pictures of the Mother as a young woman—unexpected pictures of a physically beautiful young woman. That is not the image that has impressed itself upon the world's media. We have learned to see her as a plain woman, her face lined—despite her smile—with the pain and suffering she seems to have absorbed into her own body from those among whom she has ministered across the decades. Yet, it is possible to detect, I think—even in those early pictures—a certain spirituality and a certain grace that simply needed contact with Death to give them strength and durability.

Mother Theresa has been much criticized by some for refusing to establish foundations that could fund her work. All of which simply says that the natural world still does not understand the gospel of our Lord. My guess is that Mother Theresa simply assumed that even dictators and tyrants are children of God, that God's grace has changed tyrants before

(St. Paul and Flannery O'Connor would have understood her) and that it is better for the devil's money to be put to works of mercy than to works of Death. Certainly, she was wise enough to understand that foundations, no matter what their origin, quickly become the bailiwick of Mammon rather than of Christ.

Mother Theresa is, in fact, a standard by whom most of us who say that we serve the same Christ are judged and found wanting. She forces me to realize my own bondage to Mammon.

The church, properly so, will take whatever time and engage in whatever examinations are necessary to decide whether the late Mother is one of those holy ones who stand in a special relationship to our Lord. Of course, if and when that determination comes, it will be not an installation or a translation, but simply canonical recognition of what most of us know in our hearts she truly was all along.

Thanks be to God for that ferocious love she embodied!

September 12, 1997

IS WORK POSSIBLE IN A FALLEN WORLD?

(In the mid 1980s Lambuth established a Center for Life and Work. One purpose of the Center was to combine the college's historical emphasis on the Liberal Arts with what in the 1970s had become the college's new emphasis on Career Oriented Education. Some of us had warned in the 1970s that a college must concentrate on the Liberal Arts or on career preparation, but that attempting to do both in a full-scale way would succeed in doing neither well. Obviously, we were not heeded. I was invited to be one of four speakers for the initiation of the new Center.)

Is work possible in a fallen world? In simplest terms, from a biblical perspective—and as a biblical theologian, I intend to speak from that perspective—the answer is both *yes* and *no*. It all depends on how one defines work. I want to explore the nature of work first in terms of the biblical narratives about the Creation, then in terms of the biblical perspective on the present condition of the world, and finally from the perspective of the Incarnation and its impact on the world.

According to Genesis 1, God called the Creation into being and created humankind to represent God and the heavenly council in taking care of the animal life that God had created. Interestingly enough, God is not portrayed as giving humankind dominion over vegetation, but only over other living things that move. This is what it means, according to Genesis 1, to be in the image of God—to be God's representatives, caring for living creatures. The Hebrew words in Genesis 1 translated *subdue* and *have dominion over* are terms ordinarily associated with royalty, which suggests that in Genesis 1 the first human beings are the first royal family—and *together*, not *individually*, but *together*—they constitute God's image.

The Creation narrative in Genesis 2 never uses the term *image of God*, but it portrays God giving the human being the task of naming the animals, and when this story was originally told, naming meant taking authority over. In both stories, then, humankind is portrayed as God's representative in caring for the animals. Adding that the first humans were to *serve*, or *service*, the garden and to *keep* it, in the sense of *protecting* or *watching over* it complements and provides clarification for the Genesis 1 narrative. The Hebrew words used in Genesis 2 refer not to a self-serving royal dominion, but to the dominion exercised by a monarch who takes responsibility for his or her people. The *service* of the garden is the kind of service we mean when we speak of taking our automobile to the *service station* or to the dealership to have it *serviced*.

In both chapters, then, humankind is to exercise dominion over the world as the representative of the Creator, and it hardly seems likely that humankind would be either expected or permitted to exercise that dominion in a manner contrary to that of the One on whose behalf it is exercised. Humankind's dominion is to be exercised as a dominion of service and care.

But then, of course, we come to Genesis 3 and we see God's work and intentions short-circuited by human rebellion. Humankind, from God's own instruction, was to know good (that which is in keeping with God's purposes) and evil (that which is in opposition to God's purposes). Before the rebellion, humankind was not, as some romanticists contend, in dreaming innocence. God had told humankind what to do and what not to do—presumably as the way to be good representatives and caretakers. Humankind, however, wanted to *declare* good and evil (which is what it means to know good and evil as the gods know good and evil) without regard to God. (Here, incidentally, although not immediately related to the subject at hand, it should be pointed out that according to the text, Eve was not alone with the serpent. The story does not clearly place the bulk of blame upon her. She gave some of the fruit to her husband *who was with her*. Adam is equally guilty because he did not attempt to stop Eve!)

In response to humankind's stepping over the boundaries God allows Death, in all its guises, to enter the world. Death, as chaos, displaces order. As futility, it displaces purpose. The animals over which humankind was to have exercised authority are now alienated from humankind (and vice versa) in the continuing hostility between the serpent and the ongoing race of humankind, and the ongoing struggle for power between male and female is an internal shattering of the image of God. (The woman's desire for her husband is not sexual, but is the same kind of desire that sin had for Cain—a desire for power. History, of course, registers that men usually have won the struggle in the social realm.) Now, humankind will no longer find it easy to service the ground, but will have to struggle with the ground. Before the rebellion, humankind worked freely. Humankind was not to be the slave of God—as described in many of the stories of Israel's neighbors—but was to be a corporate body of free creatures responding freely to the Creator. Now, freedom gives way to necessity as work itself becomes not free activity, but necessary struggle.

The words in the Bible most commonly translated *work* refer to giving orders, following orders, or accomplishing something with one's hands. Throughout the Bible, after Genesis 2, work is the way we cope with the world. Work is our struggle for survival. Consequently, if when we speak of things such as *meaning* and *purpose*, we are referring to a sense of resolution, wholeness, and well-being, work in the fallen world is incapable of providing them. Indeed, fallen work frustrates our efforts to achieve these goals.

This somber observation is not refuted by people who, like myself, happen to enjoy much of their work. On the contrary, enjoying our fallen work usually is testimony to the flatness of life outside work. The modern quest for enjoyable work is an effort to impose upon the world of Death, by human effort, a Life that cannot be created by human effort. Of course, there are those rare occasions when one does find genuine joy in one's work, but such moments are not created by the work, but are gifts of grace from God, the only true source of Life, Joy, and Meaning.

In none of this am I suggesting either that we should try to avoid work or that we should seek the most unpleasant job available as a reminder of the true nature of our labor. There is nothing Christian about being unhappy in our work. In fact, avoiding work is as deadly as being obsessed with work. Not only *must* we work to survive; we are *required* to work, lest our survival come at the expense of our neighbor, who also struggles to survive. We also are required to work in order to support the survival efforts of those who either are unable to keep up in the struggle or are prohibited from entering the struggle—in biblical terms, the poor, the widow, the orphan, and the alien. This is not volunteerism, but the command of God.

Both the Bible and rabbinic Judaism insist that willingly living off the work of others is robbery. This is why Jesus' call to his disciples to forsake their occupations and their family and follow him was scandalous. It also explains Paul's admonition to the Thessalonians: "Let anyone who does not want to work not eat" (not, "anyone who does not work," as it frequently is misquoted, but "anyone who does not *want* to work"). Willingly living at someone else's expense is robbery.

The necessity of work, however, is not the last word on the subject. On Work, as on all other subjects, the last word (as well as the first word) is Jesus Christ. In the Incarnation, God has entered into this fallen world, taking upon God's self the fallen world's condition. In Jesus Christ, God is at work, and the culmination of Jesus' work—the event that gives meaning to all his other words and actions—is his sacrificial death on the cross. In John's Gospel, Jesus' sacrificial death is his glorification. It is the supreme moment of his work. In the Revelation, the work of the martyrs is their death as faithful witnesses.

It is of utmost importance to notice that from the standpoint of Jesus' own will, Jesus' work does not come from necessity, but is his own freely chosen act. "No one takes my life from me," he says. "I lay it down of my own accord" (John 10:18). Of course, there is a paradox here. As were Adam and Eve, prior to their rebellion, Jesus is freely submissive, freely obedient, to that which is required. But that it is required in no way qualifies the freedom of it. Work that partakes of redemption differs from fallen work precisely in this respect. It is freely done. It is not subject to necessity.

This is not to suggest that when we think we have a choice in jobs, we are in the realm of grace. Necessity demands that we choose. All choices are superficial with regard to the struggle in that they are not choices that lift us from the struggle, but are choices as to how we will engage in the struggle— and many, perhaps most, do not even have that superficial choice.

A logical model for what might approach redeemed work is the Incarnation. The Incarnation points to redeemed work as that which is freely taken up as a means of helping others and the benefits of which for ourselves—if there be any—are nothing more than unpremeditated side-effects. From this standpoint, and relatively speaking, those who are most fully in a position to engage in work as redeemed work are retired persons. (I do not include the independently wealthy. Those who before retirement have resources enough to make work unnecessary are prisoners to another Power—Mammon, that Power that robs the poor of the things the Bible says God expects us to provide for the poor.)

The implications of a biblical perspective on work are indispensable for a Center on Life and Work in an institution that bears the name of Jesus Christ. Some of those implications, in my opinion, are the following:

1) We should accept as a basic premise that fallen work, by its very nature, is an activity in which human beings are alienated from nature and from each other. We should shun all self-deluding language, therefore, that suggests that either by being Christian or by being liberally educated, we can make our jobs ennobling. The terms *Christian businessman* or *Christian businesswoman, Christian lawyer, Christian doctor,* and the like make no more sense and have no more biblical validity than do *Christian truck driver, Christian teacher,* or *Christian prostitute.* There are Christians who do all these things, but their Christianity does not negate by one iota the fallen nature of what they do.

2) We should lay to rest the illusion that liberal education—even Christian (or church related) liberal education—can reverse the Fall. Liberal education, of whatever brand, can make us neither as wise as serpents (which Jesus enjoins disciples to be) nor as innocent as doves (which Jesus also enjoins). Only when God takes our human efforts at education and makes them God's own instrument in granting us wisdom and innocence can that education become anything other than participation in necessity. On the contrary, Christian higher education entered into naively will inevitably delude us into baptizing our fallen character and consider it Christian virtue.

3) We should make an integral part of our concern helping people find and develop skills in areas of service for which they will not be paid—perhaps not even thanked—but which are areas of pressing human need, areas where there are neither people

enough nor money enough to carry out the necessary tasks—areas that will require using our so-called leisure time, because putting bread and butter on the table still will be the purpose of our job time. In other words, a prime responsibility of our Center for Life and Work, if we are biblical in our approach, will be helping students understand the difference between fallen work and redeemed work and inspiring students—and even faculty—to sacrifice themselves in tasks that receive no monetary reward and few headlines.

Mid 1980s

THE DILEMMA OF THE CHURCH-RELATED COLLEGE

(I was invited to speak at convocation and in a class at Union College, Barbourville, Kentucky. Two friends from the Memphis Annual Conference of the United Methodist Church were on the faculty and staff, and a former college friend was President. I was invited to speak on the subject of the Church related college and university.)

The dictionary defines a dilemma as a problem for which there are two mutually unacceptable solutions. The dilemma of the church-related college or university is the same dilemma as that faced by the church that sponsors the college or university—it is called to be in the world, and, at the same time, forbidden to be of the world. Since the church is to be the salt of the earth and the light of the world, it must be in the world. It cannot wrap a cloak around itself and pretend not to be in the world. On the other hand, if it not only lives in the world, but takes on the basic characteristics of the world, then it will be fit for nothing but destruction.

The church-related college or university, by virtue of being a college or university, is in the world of higher education. It must not, however, at the cost of its soul, allow its life to be determined, or even directed by, the values and goals of secular higher education. And, I might add, since most higher education today has adopted the values and presuppositions of corporate business, the church-related college must ever be on its guard not to allow the corporate business mentality to capture the minds of trustees, administrators, or faculty.

I suspect that it is precisely because church-related colleges and universities have abandoned our sense of being called to a unique role, however, that we find ourselves in disarray. We have, by and large, abandoned our identity as a community of Christian men and women pursuing higher learning, or helping young men and women in pursuing higher learning, in order to be better to prepared as servants of Jesus Christ in the world. We have allowed ourselves to be absorbed into the mainstream of higher education in general. Consequently, we have inherited the plight of our secular counterparts—confusion of purpose, intellectual disorder, and an obsession with survival. We have forgotten that to seek to save your life is to lose it, and that the only way to save your life is to lose it for the sake of Jesus Christ.

We have developed the habit of making decisions not on the basis of faithful discipleship to Jesus Christ, but on the basis of necessity. That is, we have the habit of making decisions on the basis of social, political, and legal forces and obligations that sometimes are threatening, sometimes convenient. These decisions are not necessarily always inconsistent with the life of the gospel—in fact, they may even sometimes be what Christian faith would have called forth—but even those that reflect Christian commitment are made and justified on the basis of common educational practice and the institution's desire to meet the expectations of a plethora of constituencies. For example, Methodist Church related colleges and universities became racially integrated in the South, as well as elsewhere, when racial integration was becoming necessary in the larger society.

A few years ago, at the institution where I teach, the academic calendar was changed providing for graduation at the end of April. We then spent a sizeable amount of time discussing whether there should be a May term. The new calendar provided for two four-month semesters, though the faculty was paid for nine months of teaching. The discussion included considerations of student boredom, time for faculty development, the feasibility of learning in a three-week term, the impact on an already meager summer school enrollment, the pointlessness of a building going unused for an entire month, and numerous other concerns of greater or lesser significance.

The concerns, in other words, were primarily the efficiency or inefficiency of the operation of the institution, cost-effectiveness, and faculty and student psychology. Any question of whether our identity as a church-related college might have relevance would have sounded esoteric. But would it really be esoteric to ask how our task of equipping men and women to become disciples of Jesus Christ might guide us in a wise use of time and facilities? Perhaps some of our conclusions would have been precisely those we did reach, but the work would have been carried out with a different mood, a greater sense of unity and purpose, and all the educational benefits those could have produced.

The dilemma of the church-related college or university today is to be seen specifically in the context of what I believe is a new Dark Age for Western society. Of course, biblically speaking, all human history lies under the basic Darkness of the Old Age, but certain eras of history have been Dark Ages in the special sense that, even by the standards of fallen human nobility and decency, institutions have been excessively violent in their domination of those for whom they were said to exist. In such times, justice, order, and beauty—even in their fallen state—give way to oppression, chaos, and banality. In traditional eras of darkness, those seizing power and bringing the existing order to an end usually are called barbarians or some equivalent name. Barbarians secure their power by undermining all diversity among the conquered people, demanding rigorous obedience to those in power, and imposing their language upon the population.

Today's barbarians are those who advocate and cheerfully embrace a technological approach to life. By technological I do not mean the use of machines—not even the use of computers. I mean, rather, the application of supposed natural laws to achieve power through predictability and efficiency. Rather than technology, I prefer the tern technique. And here I must acknowledge my indebtedness to the writings of Jacques Ellul, the French theologian and sociologist whose books on *technique*, usually mistranslated into English as *technology*, have been nothing less than prophetic with regard to western society in the twentieth and twenty-first centuries. The development of an all embracing system of technique is for the purpose of power and efficiency. Whether we seek to apply natural law to the economy, to human relations, to conduct and administration of education, or to preaching the gospel, we are engaged in technique, and a society dominated by technique is a barbarian society—depending on power for order, valuing beauty and education only as they contribute to order and efficiency, and driven by a quest for consensus rather than for truth.

In a technique-driven system, management—one of the major concerns of people at every level of the educational system today, whether public or private—involves viewing human beings as objects to be manipulated in accordance with behaviorally defined goals and criteria for purposes of evaluation. We can no longer allow conflict to arise in the quest for truth. We must have conflict management, which values avoiding rocking the boat rather than finding the truth. We are prisoners of a system that has adopted behavioral psychology and used it as an all-encompassing model in what a friend of mine has called a technological prison camp—I would say a technique oriented prison camp.

It is common now to hear talk of combining, or unifying, technology and liberal education. If that means learning how better to use new machines in helping people to think critically, all is well and good. But when we use the machine not simply as a tool, but as the model for our endeavors, such talk is self-contradictory. I believe that this is where we now have come. Arguments over the topic, however, usually are fruitless because those who argue for the virtues and benefits of technology usually use the term to mean machines, not realizing how far down the road we have gone toward a society viewed by those in power as itself a huge machine. Technology of this sort inevitably uses education (or what passes for education) for its own ends. All education becomes—through increasingly regulated programmed instruction—mechanized and behavioristic, unable to liberate us, but further imprisoning us in the system. Though the individual student is verbally said to be the beneficiary of the system, the individual actually becomes isolated through programs that are foisted off on gullible participants by the use of the most humane of pretensions. One of the basic necessities of a technological education system is to convince the participants—through the use of propaganda—that whatever is good for the system is for the greater benefit of the individual. In fact, however, education in a society of technique is practiced not for the individual, but for the preservation and enhancement of the system.

It is into a society of technique, characterized by predictability, control, and necessity, that the church-related college is called to be an instrument of freedom, spontaneity, and openness. The church-related college must be in the world of technique, but not of the world of technique. It is called, in the technical prison camp we call western society, to prepare Christian men and women for service to Jesus Christ, and to human beings in the name of Jesus Christ.

Invariably, however, to speak of the task of a church-related college as preparing men and women to be servants of Jesus Christ in a society driven by technique, is to be challenged in terms such as "How is what you propose different from what is done at Bob Jones University or at Liberty Bible College?" Although the publicity and the public comments of the officials of such schools suggest that there is a world of difference, the question simply is irrelevant. To seek to be different from any institution because of theological or political differences would be nothing more than an inverted form of the tendencies basic to the present predicament. To draw up a specific model of degrees, curriculum, and administration for imposition or imitation would be to ignore the discipline of the Word of God and guidance of the Holy Spirit.

To speak of living under the discipline of the Word of God and the guidance of the Holy Spirit, of course, risks inviting misunderstanding, ridicule, and accusations of bouncing ideology off the Almighty. It invites the response, "But we do that already." So be it. It would be interesting, nevertheless, to see what might emerge in an institution where the entire community—from chief administrator to lowest ranking janitor—regularly engaged in free, serious worship and engagement with the Bible. I am not speaking of required chapel, which is a perversion of free worship, nor of highly structured study under the guidance of some expert. I am suggesting something that might be as simple as reading or singing the Psalms together and sharing in traditional or spontaneous prayer.

Although to propose a model for an institution would be to take part in the very idolatry I criticize—a subtle form of ideology—it is possible to speak of characteristics which one might expect to be manifested by a faithful institution. I list here not in order of priority, but at random.

Eschatological orientation. The struggles within institutions usually have been between those desiring to restore the spirit, if not always the letter, of classical liberal education and those seeking to make the curriculum receptive to "consumer demands." Recently, the latter have begun to be displaced here and there by those who claim to be "forward looking," using trend analysis to get the jump on next things. All such efforts are flawed by the same erroneous assumption that the church, in any of its ministries, can be faithful to its vocation while being oriented toward any specific temporal era. To be eschatologically oriented, which is another way of saying oriented toward the reign of God, is to be iconoclastic with regard to all temporal models for human life.

Abraham, going out not knowing where he was to go, but trusting God for his future, frequently is cited as the proper model for the faithful church. But precisely because of the institution's identity, Abraham is an equally appropriate model for the church-related college or university.

Realism. Christian higher education in the west usually has assumed that society is essentially friendly to enlightened discipleship. Church-sponsored institutions, for the most part, have considered it their task to prepare graduates to fit into and to improve an already good society. It is common practice, for example, for church related institutions to gear the curricula for the various departments to meet the demands of the business world, the public education system, or various secular accrediting bodies. In its crasser forms, the business department sends out questionnaires to local businesses to see what they want the institution's graduates to be. Of course, once an institution says that one of its goals is to prepare people for a secular job and recruits students on that basis, it would be immoral to violate the promise made in the recruiting. But the consequences are inevitable. The world, not the reign of God, then sets the agenda. In education jargon that is called *acculturation*. In the Bible it is called *apostasy*.

The biblical testimony is unequivocal that the fallen world, though bombarded by the redeeming grace of God, still prefers the Darkness and the domination of Death. No institution of Christian higher education can ignore this and long remain relevant. A church related institution faithful to its vocation is preparing men and women to be misfits in a Death-oriented society.

Servant orientation. History books tell us that the first institutions of higher education in this country were established for the purpose of educating the leaders of society—those entering what were then the only fields considered *professions*: doctors, lawyers, and ministers. Some social critics view the downfall of higher education as its universalizing, which goes hand in hand with the universalizing of leadership.

The ideal of discipleship in the New Testament, however, whether in Jesus' command to his disciples that they are to be different from the Gentiles by being servants to all, or in Paul's exhortation to his readers to count others better than themselves, is one not of leadership, but of servanthood. This does not rule out, in principle, the possibility of a person who is thrust into leadership genuinely viewing the unsought role as an opportunity for service. Such an event, however, is seldom, if ever, born of a system that advertises itself as preparing people to be leaders in a virtuous world.

Freedom. In biblical terms, freedom is release from domination by Death and self-interest, a release established through God's reconciling work. In an education setting, freedom manifests itself as release from ideology, from the motive of survival, and from domination by all those criteria by which institutions usually are evaluated—enrollment, endowment, accreditation, job preparation, pay scales, and so on. None of these need be despised, and none are irrelevant, but the free institution is not dominated by them in its decision making.

The free institution is especially free to be academically responsible. It is afraid neither of questions nor of answers. It is free to employ teachers most qualified in their respective disciplines without the constraints of politics or ideology. Bound only to God, it does not fear to have on its faculty, in its administration, or in its student body persons of any social, economic, or political persuasion who are committed to the vocation of the community. Such an institution is free under God to flourish on its own terms, free to experiment in the most profound manner, free to die.

For those who insist upon seeing how such an institution would be different from certain others, the characteristics just described, while not giving concrete answer, may help to clarify certain dimensions. On a television broadcast a few years ago, the Rev. Jerry Falwell said that Liberals should not come to Liberty Baptist College unless they are willing to be changed. Well, all education involves change, but the clear implication of the Rev. Falwell's remarks was that the college intends to graduate ideologues. Since he is a Fundamentalist, he probably believes that human nature is fallen. His words imply, however, that the more serious fall is that of this country from a supposed Eden of Conservatism. He does not seem to see as the real enemy the demonic that infests all ideologies, all movements, and all institutions; he sees the enemy as Liberalism. Conservatism, thus, is set forth as a redemptive ideology.

You do not have to look far today to find colleges that emphasize training leaders. Even if leadership is described as a means of service, the tone of stridency and the determination to send out men and women who will transform society by getting into places of responsibility in politics, education, and business, belie a "take-over" image that is difficult to reconcile with servanthood.

No college or university of which I am aware actually attempts to recruit students on the basis of preparing them for a biblically based, realistic Christian servanthood. We simply do not see that as our vocation. No doubt, we also assume that such an approach would repel students, leaving the college to fold; and, as is true for all other institutions, so with us, survival is the name of the game. Like all other institutions, we live off the blood of those we embrace. We are carnivorous.

Moreover, the cost of the freedom I have described for any church-related institution might well be its relation to the sponsoring church. In any case, such witness will be made only if the institution truly comprehends the Darkness and casts its future into the hands of the One True Light.

The church related institution of higher education cannot be truly reformed by human manipulation. Manipulations of the curriculum and of graduation requirements are desirable—even mandatory—from the standpoint of how well the institution prepares its students for ministry in a fallen world. As an institution, however, the university or college will resist such efforts, because they threaten the survival of the institution. Conversion is a threat to institutions as much as to individuals, for it means radical change from the way of life to which the institution has become accustomed. Consequently, the appropriate stance for faithful disciples within the church-related institution is that of the remnant, a remnant offering up its witness to God so that God might use or discard that witness as God sees fit, in the divine economy.

March 3, 1992

COWARDICE AND THE CULTURAL WARS

(Each spring, for several years the Chair of the Department of Sociology put together an interdisciplinary public symposium on a topic of current interest. Topics ranged from the Unabomber *to* Sex, Drugs, and Rock and Roll. *In 2005 the topic was the Cultural Wars. I was asked to represent the field of religion. My comments at that symposium is below, followed by my presentation at one earlier symposium.)*

The stated reasons for any war can be misleading. Usually, there are unspoken factors at work, perhaps unknown even to the participants themselves. I think this is true even in what have called the cultural wars, especially with regard to Christians caught up in those wars.

To understand this unspoken factor, we have to go back to the Old and New Testaments and to their call for the People of God to be holy. It isn't very fashionable today to speak of holiness in sophisticated circles. Holiness is a term widely viewed as quaint, outdated, and—if claimed by the person or group so designated—egotistical. Part of the reason for this is that along the way, the church and the synagogue gave the term a new meaning, one quite different from its biblical meaning.

In the Bible, *holy* means *set apart, different.* The people of God were to be holy not in a moralistic way, but set apart unto God to be used by God as an instrument for the blessing of the entire world. As such, they were to reflect in their life as a community the basic characteristics of God—characteristics such as mercy, dependability, truthfulness, and care for society's marginalized people.

The holy community was to be a priestly assembly—appealing to God on behalf of the world and representing God to the world, again, as God's instrument of blessing upon the world. This is represented in Jesus' words in the Sermon on the Mount that his followers are the salt of the earth and the light of the world. With these words Jesus was not pleading or commanding. He was simply declaring. The church *is* the salt of the earth and the light of the world. That is why it is so terrible when the church somehow fails in or gives up on its mission. Salt that loses its saltiness, Jesus warned, is good for nothing and is cast out as refuse.

Then holy came to be understood not as a relationship, but as morality—not necessarily morality in terms of the biblical presentation of the character of God, but in terms of whatever elite society deemed moral. In the West, being moral came to mean espousal of capitalistic values, devotion to national goals and ambitions, and the baptism of whatever polite society, at any given moment, viewed as moral. Not only conservatives made this jump. So did liberals and moderates. Even John Wesley reflected this different view of holiness when he said that God had raised up the Methodists to spread scriptural holiness throughout Britain. Wesley really meant, "to spread proper British morality throughout the land."

As I said, not only the church engaged in redefining holiness. So did the synagogue. An acquaintance of mine who teaches at Hebrew Union College, and who is an internationally recognized scholar in the history of Judaism, traces the shift in Judaism's definition of holiness to the work of Immanuel Kant. In Christianity, however, it goes back further than that.

At any rate, the result of this for our own day is that many Christians do not see the task of the church as living in the world as a community that is different from that world so that it might be the faithful instrument of God's blessing upon the world. Instead, they see the church's task as that of imposing their own specific view of morality upon the world. Rather than giving themselves over to God to be God's instruments for the blessing of a coarsened world, they see their responsibility as that of legislating away the coarseness.

Now, to be fair, I think that to some extent this reflects a lack of understanding. I think that some Christians really believe that God has called the church to force upon society a specific form of morality in the genuine belief that if they can accomplish this, the world will be a better place for all people. Such Christians do not fall into either the conservative or the liberal category alone. Some are found in both groups, and I think those in both camps are completely unaware of how contemporary western society's capitalistic, consumer-oriented society is itself the antithesis of a biblical concept of the good society. They truly do not recognize that the society they value so highly, and that they think is being destroyed, treats human beings as fuel for the machinery that works for the benefit of the rich and the powerful. Their view of morality, however, deals only with surface issues—issues that, to some extent, are created by the very economic, political, and religious views that they mistakenly assume to be rooted in the Bible. They simply do not perceive the degree to which their utopia is a fascist state.

But, I regret to say, I think that something else also is at work—what is essentially a form of cowardice. Most Christians and most Christian groups attempting to impose their own view of morality on society are saying, in effect, that they want to create a society in which they won't have to be different. It is inconvenient, even embarrassing, to attempt to live in ways substantially different from the ways of those around you. It risks being alienated from your friends. It risks alienating your children if you forbid them, because of the values involved, to participate in activities in which their peers participate. So they find a simple solution. If you don't want the burden of being different, then lobby for legislation that will make everyone like yourself. Then you won't have to restrict your children with regard to what they can watch on television or in the movies. You won't have to restrict them as to the music they buy or to which they listen. The state will do it for you. In brief, you won't have to be holy. The state will remove that God-given responsibility from you.

After all, holiness requires courage. Cowardice finds strength in uniformity.

March 28, 2005

RELIGION, SEX, DRUGS, AND ROCK AND ROLL

Actually, there are three quite different ways to approach the topics of sex, drugs and rock and roll with regard to religion, and I have had a difficult time deciding which would be the most profitable for us tonight.

The first approach would be to examine the way that churches and other religious groups speak about the three areas—either condemning them outright or trying under certain conditions to legitimize them. This approach would be to show how the Christian church has, for example, looked upon sex as serving a divine role in the context of Christian marriage, but has looked upon it negatively when it takes place outside marriage.

This first would note the way that the church has approved the use of powerful drugs when they are used by trained physicians and how it even has commissioned medical missionaries to minister to the sick, the maimed, and the mentally ill in various settings all over the world. This approach would note the way that the church has condoned the use of over-the-counter drugs when they are used in ways that medicate rather than disorient or debilitate the user. It also would show the way the church has frowned upon and usually condemned the use of drugs for recreational purposes or in ways that lead to addiction.

With regard to rock music, the first approach would show that this form of music was at first viewed by the mainline liberal churches as benign and just another fad of youth, while it was viewed by more conservative churches, both mainline and other, as the music of the devil—so viewed, to some extent, because of its association in many minds with sex and drugs, but also because some of the more conservative churches and groups were determined to hold onto racial segregation and correctly saw that rock music would be a racially integrating force in the culture.

But this first approach also would show how some of the conservative groups eventually embraced rock music. Rock music is a sub genre of jazz, and if jazz has any one identifying ingredient, it is its free form. The very heart and soul of jazz is the spontaneous improvisation of the performer. Many Pentecostal groups heard rock as music that would allow them to use modern instruments and modern sounds to produce music that was inspired by the Holy Spirit on the spot, so to speak. So it should not be surprising that rock concerts for Jesus have become commonplace in some branches of Pentecostalism.

The second approach to religion in relation to sex, drugs and rock and roll would be a bit more spicy, and I don't mean in the sense of spicy sex. This approach would show how the mind-set of these cultural elements has been used as recruiting tools. Were I to take this approach, I would point out, for instance, how sex has commonly been used as an advertising gimmick—sometimes for evangelism, sometimes for encouragement of a certain type of moral behavior.

One of the things that commercial advertising experts long ago learned is that **sex sells**; and by this I mean that sex sells a lot of things that intrinsically have nothing to do with sex. Have you ever noticed, for example, the use of beautiful girls in TV ads to sell tooth paste and how the goal of the girl in the ad is to get a good looking male? Have brighter teeth so you can attract your man! My guess is that the average church-goer will think nothing at all about the use of the young woman (and notice she must be a *young* woman) to sell the tooth paste because she has all her clothes on and we never see what they do after she gets him. But we know! And the advertisers are counting on the average church-goer knowing, but not letting himself or herself know that he or she knows! And what does that have to do with religion, other than the fact that I have referred to church-goers watching the advertisements? Well, just watch some of your major evangelism "crusades" on television or elsewhere and see how many times a beauty queen and some well known athlete are used as models of Christian life. Then see how many times you see some homely, or even plain, young woman or some fellow crassly referred to as a geek. These folks are advertising the gospel, and they have learned from Madison Avenue that **sex sells**!

As for drugs, this second approach uses the language of drugs, but applies it to Jesus and the Holy Spirit. One of the more frequently used expressions by people trying to get other people off the no-no drugs is, "Don't get high on drugs; get high with Jesus!" All of which assumes that the primary function of Jesus is to make you feel an emotional high, that if you will just give your life to Jesus, you can have everything the drug culture promises but cannot deliver.

The problem is that the New Testament views the Kingdom of God, into which one is adopted in baptism, as a kingdom that raises serious questions about all our goals and desires. There is a great deal of difference between "Get High With Jesus" and "Take Up Your Cross and Follow Me" or "You shall love your neighbor as you love yourself."

As for rock music, in the second approach the same test should be made of rock that should be made of all music used to celebrate worship of God: To what extent does it enable me to concentrate on God, on what God has done for Israel and for the church across the ages, and on what God calls us to do here and now in the midst of a Death-oriented world?

And to what extent does it simply call attention to itself? To what extent does it emphasize the beat rather than the content?

The so-called praise music and praise services that I have had occasion to observe spend a lot of time praising God, but I never get any idea of what they are praising God for. I never hear praise of God for having delivered Israel from Egyptian slavery in the Exodus or delivering Israel from the Babylonian Exile. I never hear praise of God for what God has done throughout the ages in the history of God's people in the world—God's mighty deeds and mighty acts. All I hear is a very personal praise of God for *feelings* and for what God has done *for me*. To what extent does a piece of music enable me to worship God as God wishes to be worshipped and to what extent does it enable me to worship God the way *I* want to worship God? Now, if I were going to take the second approach, those are the kinds of things I would say.

Of course, there is a third approach to talking about religion with regard to sex, drugs, and rock and roll. That approach is to look at how many of the things we do that we do not consider religious are, in fact, religious. To what extent do things that we take for granted as being purely secular actually serve a religious function? I will use only the example of sex. In the ancient world, the goddess was the ideal of womanhood. The Mother Goddess possessed the virtues to which all women were expected to aspire. The goddess blessed the crops and protected the children. As Harvey Cox showed long ago, one of the ways we symbolize female or womanly virtues today is the beauty pageant. For example, Miss Tennessee is chosen because she represents what those who still support beauty pageants assume all young girls in Tennessee should aspire to be. In the words of the Miss America pageant's theme song, "There she goes, Miss America. There she goes, your ideal." Miss Tennessee goes into the schools and urges the children to abstain from drugs. And she goes to civic meetings where she can charm the older men and bless their efforts by her presence and her words of appreciation for them. But her doing this depends on her sex appeal. For some people, the beauty queen is what the Virgin Mary is for Roman Catholics—and I say that not as a criticism of Roman Catholicism or of the Virgin Mary, but with appreciation for the role of Mary.

Lambuth University, a church related institution, each year, almost from its beginning, has had the Miss Lambuth Contest. Miss Lambuth, apparently, will be the ideal symbol of that to which every Lambuth female should aspire. Look back over the years and you will not find a homely,

175 pound Miss Lambuth in the lot. All will have sex appeal. Probably, no judge in Lambuth's history ever said to himself or herself, "Now which one would the boys most likely like to go to bed with?" But probably also, no judge would ever have voted for a candidate with so little sex appeal that none of the boys would have wanted to go to bed with her. And although you probably would not find any of the Miss Lambuths having been in danger of academic probation, neither would you be likely to find a Senior Marshal[1]. Like all other beauty queens, Miss Lambuth is presented each year, along with her court, at an athletic event at Homecoming. She fills the role that patron goddesses used to perform at games in the ancient world. And before the game, we pray to the god that we assume will be watching the proceedings with great anticipation—unless, of course, since he knows all things, he will know the score beforehand.

March 28, 2000

REFLECTIONS ON BEING A CHURCH RELATED UNIVERSITY ON 9/11

(When the Word Trade Center and the Pentagon were attacked in September, 2001, the chapel service at the University where I was teaching was heavily nationalistic in tone. The sidewalk leading to the chapel was lined with small United States flags about a foot apart from each other. The following Saturday, when there was an at-home football game, was declared Red, White, and Blue Day and students were urged to wear those colors to the game. The Associate Chaplain also called upon the campus to observe the day of prayer which President Bush had declared. I wrote an e-mail to all faculty and staff, asking, "What in the name of God has happened to us?" I received several positive and several negative responses, as well as some puzzled ones who did not understand a reference to Caesar in my e-mail.

On September 20, the University held an interdisciplinary panel discussion on the attacks on the Center and the Pentagon. I was asked if I would like to be a part of the discussion, which I assumed meant to be a part of the panel and make a presentation as would the other members. I sat with the panel, which included the Associate Chaplain, but after all the other persons sitting on the panel had

---

1. Senior Marshals at Lambuth, historically, are the two students with the highest grade averages at the end of the junior year. In their senior year they lead the procession at formal convocations, showing participants the proper places to sit.

spoken, the moderator asked for conversation among those who had spoken and with the audience. Later, she explained to me that she had only wanted me to be there in case anything came up in the conversation to which I should respond. Consequently, the comments I had prepared went undelivered. Those comments were as follows.)

My comments in this forum will not be as a teacher of religion, but as a Christian. Not that I view these as mutually incompatible, but neither do I view them as the same thing.

I speak as someone who has died. I don't know the exact date, but I know that it was on a summer evening in 1943, in rural Alabama, that, in any significant sense of the term, I died. That is to say, on a summer evening in 1943, at the age of eight, in a small Methodist church in rural Alabama, I was baptized. I was baptized into the death and resurrection of Jesus Christ. And by being baptized, I died. All of us who were baptized have died, and our life is hid with Christ in God (Col 3:3).

This death in Christ is liberation, a liberation that shall be complete in whatever that event in God's own time is that we call the resurrection and the consummation of history. This liberation means that our relationship to the world in which we go about our daily tasks and pleasures can never be regarded in the same way we would have regarded it outside of Christ. Essentially, this death frees us from any and all obligations that this world might attempt to force upon us.

Let me put it another way before elaborating. In baptism we are incorporated into the Body of Christ. And just as Jesus Christ is treated as a stranger, an alien, by this world, so we—in him—become aliens to this world and in this world. The biblical testimony insists that God's people are, universally, a nation—a separate nation, a priestly nation—and, as such, destined always and in all places in this world to be exiles and aliens with regard to all races, all cultures, all governments that make up this world. One cannot truly be a citizen of any earthly nation, in the full sense of citizenship, and also a citizen of the Kingdom of God—which is simply another way of saying that Jesus reminded us that no one can serve two masters.

The grave problem that the church in the western world has faced ever since the Emperor Constantine in the early 300s is our failure to recognize the essential incompatibility between the kingdom of God and the kingdoms of this world.

But the ironic thing about our baptism into Christ is that while it alienates us from all earthly institutions, at the same time, it binds us to all humankind and, ultimately, to all Creation. That is, since Jesus Christ died for all humankind—and for the entire Creation—by being bonded with him in baptism and becoming participants in his Body, we are bound up in his suffering on the world's behalf. And the key word here is *freedom*. We have been set free *from* all earthly institutions so that we might be bound up *with* all humanity, regardless of nation, language, race, or even religion.

And that leads to some very specific observations about how the Body of Christ should respond to any event in any nation such as the events of September 11 in this country.

> Lambuth University should always ask, not how we should react as citizens of the United States, but how we should react as members of the Body of Christ, which has no nationality.

> The answer should be, "By mourning." And the traditional colors of mourning are not red, white, and blue, but black. The Body of Christ in this nation—as in all nations—is bound up with all humankind, not by a national flag, but in the cross, more precisely in the crucifix of Christ.

> I would have thought that as an expression of the Body of Christ, a church related institution such as Lambuth would have draped its lobbies and buildings with black, not with red, white, and blue—and would have lined its sidewalks with crucifixes, not with flags.

> And as for prayer, the early church had the good sense to avoid the traditional times of prayer practiced by other religions so as not be confused with those religions. I would have thought that we would have gone to prayer not when the head of the secular state called the nation's citizens to prayer, but when God called the Body of Christ to prayer.

September 20, 2001

14

Book Reviews

TUTU'S BIBLICAL MESSAGE IN APARTHEID'S THROES

(In the 1980s the editor of the Jackson Sun *wanted to make the Sunday book review section of the paper a place for intellectual reflection. He said that keeping the Sun's space limitations in mind, he wanted reviews in the style of the articles in the* New York Review of Books. *I was one of those invited to participate and contributed approximately one review per month. This review and the two that follow are examples.)*

Crying in the Wilderness: The Struggle for Justice in South Africa. By Desmond Tutu. William B. Eerdmans Publishing Co.

Hope and Suffering. By Desmond Tutu. William B. Eerdmans Publishing Co.

THE NUMEROUS APOLOGISTS FOR the South African government making the rounds of television talk shows recently have been models of logic, reason, and civilized discourse. Logic, however, is not wed to truth and can be used to show the reasonableness of a lie as easily as to defend the truth. One of the favorite disguises of the devil, according to tradition, is that of an angel of light.

The placid faces and voices of the apologists have no blood, no life. Their erudition and logic have been pressed into service as instruments of Death as they have attempted to convince the world that the shroud that covers South Africa is the christening gown of a better day. Their tragedy is that, apparently, they have come to believe their own propaganda. The spokesmen have been dehumanized even more thoroughly than their opponents.

One of the chief opponents of the South African government's policy of apartheid is Desmond Tutu, Bishop of the Anglican Church in South Africa and General Secretary of the South African Council of Churches. Tutu first received international attention by his comments on the Soweto riots in 1976. At the time, he was the Anglican Dean of Johannesburg. In the years that followed, he gained increasing prominence both as a staunch opponent of apartheid and as an equally strong advocate of non-violence. In 1984 he received the Nobel Peace Prize.

Crying in the Wilderness and *Hope and Suffering* are collections of Tutu's writings from 1976 thru 1981. The latter contains complete texts; the former, only fragments of speeches and essays. Both are concerned with present conditions in South Africa, the responsibility of the church in the midst of oppression, and Tutu's hope for the future of South Africa.

Tutu writes and speaks against a background in which the minority white population still holds supreme power in national affairs. Large numbers of the black population have been forcibly relocated in geographic areas completely unsuited for agriculture. Fathers must be separated from their wives and children for months at a time in order to earn a living. Individuals whom the government considers threats are kept in strict isolation, without trial or possibility of redress. And even children are shot by government forces during demonstrations.

In both these books Tutu proclaims his conviction that the gospel of Jesus Christ is the message of reconciliation for all people and that all human barriers to that unifying work of God are inherently evil and must be opposed.

In *Crying in the Wilderness* the bishop writes, "Jesus Christ has inaugurated the Kingdom of God, which is a Kingdom of Justice, Peace, and Love, or fullness of life ... God is on the side of the oppressed, the marginalized and the exploited.... The Church must be the prophetic church ... speaking up against injustice and exploitation, against all that dehumanizes God's children and makes them less than what God intended them to be."

For Tutu, however, the oppressor, just as the victim, is a child of God. Consequently, their dehumanization—brought about by their acts of oppression—is to be resisted as thoroughly as is the dehumanization of the oppressed. Both cooperation with the government in its inhuman policies and participation in violent reaction to those policies are "a surrender to the inhuman."

Citing one government official's remark that the death of the black activist Stephen Biko left him cold, Tutu observes: "He is most to be pitied. What has happened to him as a human being when the death of a fellow human being can leave him cold?"

This double-edged point of view has resulted not only in his being regarded as an enemy by the government, but also in his influence upon militant blacks being eroded as the government has intensified its determination to keep apartheid. Tutu has continued to warn, nevertheless, that unless South Africa dismantles the machinery of apartheid, the nation is in for a bloodbath that could become the spark for World War III.

In reply to those who contend that he mixes politics and religion, Tutu replies (in *Crying in the Wilderness*) that when Bishop Muzorewa of Zimbabwe—who was popular among South African whites—was positive toward white power, nobody accused him of bringing politics into religion. "I suppose," says Tutu, "that if I were to get up and say . . . 'Apartheid is not so bad; it is a genuine attempt to find a solution to our intractable problem'—I would become the blue-eyed boy of the Establishment, and not a whisper would be heard of my being a political hothead."

Actually, Tutu admits that his message is political. It is not rooted in political ideology, however, but is the inevitable political expression of a genuinely biblical approach to life. One of the longer sections of *Hope and Suffering* concerns Liberation Theology. Liberation, Tutu contends, is a major theme in the Bible. In the exodus God liberated the Hebrew slaves in Egypt. This, says Tutu, "was a thoroughly political act . . . . Nothing can be more political than helping a group of slaves escape from their bondage."

As for liberation under Jesus, in *Hope and Suffering* Tutu writes: "Our God cares that children stare in resettlement camps . . . , that people die mysteriously in detention . . .

"Jesus has liberated us from the realm of darkness, forgiven our sins, given us the liberty of the children of God, and released us from the law of our lower nature. (This) includes being set free from political, social, and economic structures that are oppressive and unjust . . . . In setting us free . . . God wants to enlist us as co-workers with Him in the business of the Kingdom . . . . We are to labour with God to humanize the universe and to help His children become even more fully human . . . ."

Tutu's witness is credible because of his simplicity, candor, and self-effacing good humor. For him, concern with the oppressed and dehumanized is not a passing battle, but is the expression of the eternal Word of God. He and those who struggle alongside him have every right to be skeptical of this month's sympathy from the West. Unfortunately, despite the horror of the reality now in play in South Africa, events there have become, for the moment, a media event. Oppression in South Africa has displaced starvation in Ethiopia as the event of the month. If the present unrest does not at this moment erupt into a continent wide bloodbath, next month we will have a new focus for our short-spanned attention.

If taken seriously, *Hope and Suffering* can help us to see that in South Africa nothing less than the biblical witness of both Christianity and Judaism is at stake, attacked under the guise of Christian reason. Such a struggle will not go away when the cameras have moved on—and it is as real in the United States as in South Africa.

August 18, 1985

YOU CAN'T HAVE IT BOTH WAYS

(In 1982 a summit meeting on the world economy was held by the United States, several European countries, Canada, and Japan. At the end of the conference President Reagan made a report in which he said, "we concentrated on ways and means to strengthen our economic performance individually and collectively. We have agreed to reinforce the international institutions which assure cooperation and coordination." Hardly a statement that Adam Smith would whole heartedly have approved. My review of The Next Economy, *by sheer coincidence, was due at about the time the conference was ending.)*

The Next Economy by Paul Hawken (Holt, Rinehart and Winston) is a naively optimistic book. It begins by asserting that the present economic crisis in American society is simply the painful transition form one economic system to another and closes with a call to remake our world.

Hawken labels the old and new economic systems, respectively, *the mass economy* and *the informative economy*. By informative economy he means an economy in which information on how to provide goods and services that use less energy not merely is passed along, but is used to produce those goods and services. For example, automobile manufacturers must not only know how to make fuel-efficient vehicles, but must use that information to make such vehicles. Otherwise, the information has no effect on the economy.

The mass economy, on the other hand, is an economy based on goods and services valued for something other than their fuel conservation—in fact, upon some element that makes them waste energy.

Hawken's description of the new economy is similar to John Naisbitt's description (in the current best-seller *Megatrends*) of trends that are changing American society. Hawken says the economy is shifting to one with the following characteristics: expensive capital, the replacement of large corporations by smaller and more nimble companies, the contraction of government at all levels, the replacement of mass markets by selective buying, the displacement of most middle retailers by direct sales from manufacturers to customers, a widespread shift from borrowing to saving, and a shift from "mass" to "information" in goods and services.

The Next Economy is not a systematic philosophy of economics describing how we ought to behave in order to change prevailing conditions. In this respect, Hawken is not attempting the sort of thing that we find in books such as George Gilder's *Wealth and Poverty*. Instead, he describes what he sees as actual trends and urges us to affirm and benefit from these trends.

Such a difference is not unusual between philosophically oriented and statistically oriented economists. It is precisely in this purpose of the book, however, that not only its inadequacy, but its outright dangerous nature lies. If, as Hawken thinks, trends are inevitable, how can one seriously speak of making society? Throughout the book, Hawken urges us to adapt lest we perish. He warns us not to try to manipulate the economy as though it were something inanimate. Then he says we have the opportunity to remake society! The contradiction is obvious. To *remake* a society requires goals; deliberate, logical planning and execution of the plans; and formulating and enforcing laws to assure that the goals are achieved. If remaking society is possible, it is not accomplished by adapting to trends, for trends develop quite apart from and frequently by overriding human goals and desires. Making or remaking society, in contrast to watching as society makes or remakes itself, is accomplished, if at all, by getting in the way of trends and redirecting them. Remaking by adapting to trends is a bit like a surfer finding a wave and pretending to be guiding it by riding on or just in front of it.

Hawken overlooks that contemporary society actually does already what he advocates. We are determined to control our destiny. We organize at every level to achieve and maintain a rational, efficient system. So deep is this determination that it is hard to comprehend that it has not always been a dominating drive. Before the Middle Ages, respect for spontaneity played an important role in the corporate social consciousness, but since the breakup of the Middle Ages, we have increasingly assumed the rationality of the universe and have tried to take responsibility for the direction of history.

The goal of all economic theories since Adam Smith has been the efficient direction of the economy through the application of or obedience to natural law. This was the basic approach of the New Deal, the Great Society, and the New Frontier and is assumed in supply side economics. It is the drive behind both the mass economy and the informative economy.

Our drive for efficiency also spawns our development of weapons and the wars in which we use those weapons. It is puzzling that Hawken nowhere mentions the possibility that a nuclear war or some other catastrophe could alter trends dramatically. Numerous aspects of the nuclear threat grow precisely out of information about energy and the application of that information.

Both the actual or implied threat in the possession of weapons and the use of them are simply means by which one nation or group tries to achieve or preserve its own brand of efficiency. The U.S.'s problem is that it not only has developed a weapon capable of imposing its own version of efficiency, but it also is face to face with others who are equally able to wage such a war.

Recognizing this drive for rationality and efficiency might have enabled Hawken to see that government is contracting, if at all, only at those points where contraction is expected to result in greater efficiency. In this respect, the recent economic summit meeting held important lessons for anyone who thinks that President Reagan's approach to government is a liberating one.

That summit meeting clearly indicates the necessity for international agreement on trade, the value of exchange, import and export regulations, and every other factor upon which the economy of the separate countries rests. Developments in international transportation and communication have made the interdependence of the nations a necessity, not an option, if we are to survive. Such agreements by governments will be effective only if they are enforced within each nation, and this will leave no individual untouched in some way or other. Reagan's disclaimers at the close of the summit conference are mere wishful thinking.

The development of a genuinely global system requires centralization, and centralization has been made immensely easier by the development of the computer. To enable the unity required for a global economy, however, the computer must contain sufficient information on every individual to locate, identify and stop anyone who is a serious threat to the system.

At the same time, the systematic use of propaganda is capable of converting even the staunchest opponents of the system. In such a world, though politicians or monarchs might appear still to govern, the ultimate maintenance of the system resides, of necessity, with managers.

Hawken seems to believe and to wish us to believe that we are free and that we are moving toward more freedom. At the highest levels of decision making in every area of society we do precisely what Hawken calls for—note trends and plan accordingly. The contradiction between adapting to trends and remaking society, however, is not a mere dialectic and it cannot be overcome merely by wishing it. What freedom is there in adapting? Freedom is not choice among predetermined options. Adapt or perish has nothing to do with freedom.

Books such as *The Next Economy* and *Megatrends* are highly superficial. Their primary accomplishment is to convince those who are taken in by them that bondage is freedom, a perception which is the ultimate euthanasia.

June 26, 1983

THE EYES OF THE FATHERS

Chief Joseph of the Nez Perce: A Poem by Robert Penn Warren. Random House.

Shortly after President Grant, in 1873, declared the Wallowa Valley of Idaho off-bounds to white settlement, gold was discovered in the nearby mountains. In 1875, Grant reversed his order, and the people there were ordered from the valley. The people thus expelled called themselves the *Nimipu*, "the Real People." The French called them the *Nez Perce*, "those of the pierced nose."

The Nimipu had lived at peace with the white nation for more than 70 years. While American solders were driving them from their land, however, a group of settlers stole some of the Nimipu's cattle. In retaliation, a band of Nimipu attacked the settlers and killed 11 of them. The peace had ended.

When the ensuing four month war ended, only a few hundred Nimipu remained—most of them sick, wounded, or both. Some had managed to escape to Canada. The rest were taken by boxcar to Fort Leavenworth, Kan., where many died. From there, about 150, who were considered too dangerous to leave with the others, were taken, in 1885, to what is now the state of Washington. There, they lived out their days.

Among those relocated in Washington was the last great chief of the Nimipu, Heinmot Tooyalaket. The whites called him Prince Joseph. In what may be one of his finest poems, Robert Penn Warren has made Chief Joseph the window by which to explore the universal question of what it means to be truly human.

With great skill and sensitivity, Warren has drawn together with this question three other topics which, though of great interest and concern, seldom are treated together—the culture of native Americans, the problem of violence, and the quest for personal identity.

Early in the poem, Warren describes salmon swimming upstream in the land of the Nimipu, seeking "in blood compulsion . . . the spawn pool that blood remembers"—just as the Native American's identity lies not simply in isolated individuality, but in intimacy with the land and the fidelity to the ways of the fathers.

The lands where the fathers were buried were sacred, and—in the Nimipu version of immortality—the fathers kept watch over the sons to be certain that truth was spoken and that each son showed himself a man—that is, that each lived up to the name Nimipu, "the Real People." "The Great Spirit made the earth," Joseph's father, Old Joseph, had said.

> "Earth is the Mother and Nurse, and to that spot
> Where he was nursed, (each) must,
> In love cling.
> You must never sell the bones of your fathers,
> For selling that, you sell your Heart-Being."

When war comes with the whites, Joseph is torn by the conflict of two traditional values—the value of the land and the commitment to peace. Joseph reflects on the dilemma:

> "We had long back made the promise of peace. We had sworn no white blood to shed, our tongue was not forked. But now we breathed the stink of the wind of Time."

Throughout the conflict, Joseph is conscious of the eyes of his own father and of the eyes of the fathers.

> "... I prayed that my father, whose eyes see all, and judge, might find some worth in an act of mine, however slight."

> "... and yearn only that he can think me a man worthy the work in dark of his loins."

In the war, the Nimipu fight with restraint and nobility, fighting only to protect the land given by the Great Spirit. The white soldiers are led by generals who seek only personal glory, vindication in the press and triumph over their peers. The generals are portrayed not as evil or wicked, but as petty and "crazed." Occasional references to divine destiny are justification for their own lust.

Even the respect with which Joseph is treated after the war is centered in the white ego. "It came to pass," says Warren, "that to praise the red man was the way best adapted to expunge all ... in the mist of bloodless myth." The hypocrisy of the respect is portrayed in the description of the dedication of Grant's tomb: Joseph rides beside Buffalo Bill Cody. Joseph's people had never taken a scalp, yet warm, such as Cody had sliced from the head of an Indian who had shot at him and missed. Such irony simply heightens the humanity of Joseph, even as it diminishes that of his captors.

Those sensitive to the ambiguity of nature may consider the implications of Warren's poem and of the Native American religion that it portrays too unrealistic to be of help. Isolating ourselves from nature and from the deeper rhythms of the creation—corrupted though they may be—however, can lead only to a denial of our identity as human beings.

This is a warning desperately needed as we move increasingly into the multi-dimensional isolation of a technological society. Such isolation from the creation of which we are naturally a part will lead increasingly deeper into that loss of identity upon which violence thrives.

To read *Chief Joseph of the Nez Perce* is to open oneself to judgment. In the latter part of the poem, Warren imagines viewing Joseph in the silent nobility of his closing years. "Frozen," he says, "you stand in that moment of final assessment." And it slowly dawns upon the readers that it is we who are being assessed.

November 20, 1983

JAMES BOND VS. THE SHADOW

Role of Honor, by John Gardner. G.P. Putnam's

The Shadow and the Golden Master, by Walter B. Gibson (a.k.a. Maxwell Grant). The Mysterious Press

Role of Honor is the kind of book that gives escapist literature a bad name. The plot, in and of itself, might have been developed into a first-rate thriller. A computer genius has developed a super computer that will shut down the weapons systems of the world, thereby destroying the balance-of-power upon which world peace supposedly depends. In the worldwide turmoil that is expected to result, power will be up for grabs.

To foil the plan, James Bond pretends to resign from Her Majesty's Secret Service over an insult to his integrity and infiltrates the enemy camp. Naturally, he saves the world from tyranny.

Unfortunately, the potential of the plot is never achieved. The narrative is wooden and just plain boring. Whereas the James Bond movies began as ingenious adaptations of the original Ian Fleming novels, John Gardner seems to be using the outworn formula created for the movies as the key to more novels. The scenes, however, demand the visual effects of the screen and without those effects, the scenes consistently fall flat.

Ah, but *The Shadow and the Golden Master* is another matter. This is not a new novel, but is a one-volume republication of two stories from the *Shadow Magazine* of 1939. Both tell of encounters between the Shadow and Shiwan Khan, a sinister Chinese villain who desires to rule the world. Printed from copies of the original magazine, the stories contain the familiar illustrations of Edd Cartier.

Like the Bond novels, all the original Shadow stories followed a standard formula. Each opened with some puzzling event—frequently a strange death—soon followed by similar events—and eventually, a pattern was discerned. Some sinister force was at work, seeking national or international power. The stories in the present volume follow the formula.

The thing that distinguishes the plots of the Shadow stories from the plot of the Bond novel is the dependence of the former upon constant suspense and Maxwell Grant's ability to sustain that suspense. There is little suspense in *Role of Honor,* which might be irrelevant were the characters well-drawn or the plot full of twists. The characters, however, are one-dimensional and the plot is completely predictable. We have met the characters before. Only the names have been changed.

Those familiar with the Shadow only from radio may be surprised by some of the differences between the books and the radio program. In the books, for example, the Shadow actually is Kent Allard, an ace flier and spy for the French in World War I, who fakes his death and then takes on numerous disguises to fight crime. He persuades Lamont Cranston to let him use Cranston's identity as his main disguise while Cranston spends time in Europe. Within that simple maneuver lie possibilities for numerous mysteries. Moreover, in the books the Shadow's "invisibility" depends not upon some "power to cloud men's minds so they cannot see him," but upon his ability so thoroughly to blend into the darkness and the shadows that even those who see him do not know they see him.

A major difference between all the Bond novels and the Shadow stories is the stereotypical battle between the forces of justice and the forces of evil in the latter and the ambiguous nature of the battle in the former. In the Bond novels the ultimate value is not justice or freedom, but power. Although the Bond novels—apart from their romanticism—probably are more realistic about international politics, the Shadow stories are mythological expressions of how we traditionally have thought the world ought to be. The shock and disbelief in recent years over disclosures of how the CIA and the FBI operate were because this was not the way we had assumed the United States conducts itself in the world. The chastisement of the CIA and the FBI and the effort to rein them in were expressions of that "ought."

The present danger is that we will develop so "realistic" an outlook that we will acquiesce in the amorality of Bond-like conduct in international affairs and accept the premise that justice and decency are irrelevant. The gradual erosion of the congressional reforms that initially were enacted with regard to the conduct of U.S. Intelligence indicates that we are moving dangerously in that direction. We are never as good as our myths, but we must have myths by which to measure ourselves. Consequently, if our myths are degraded, our conduct will be even more so.

In the words of the famous opening to the Shadow radio program, "Who know what evil lurks in the heart of men? The Shadow knows."

Oh, yes, he does.

April 7, 1985

www.ingramcontent.com/pod-product-compliance
Lightning Source LLC
Chambersburg PA
CBHW060606230426
43670CB00011B/1989